PROBABILITY FOUNDATIONS OF ECONOMIC THEORY

Concepts of probability are an integral component of economic theory. However, there is a wide range of theories of probability and these are manifested in different approaches to economic theory itself. In this book Charles McCann provides a clear and informative survey of the area which serves to standardize terminology and so integrate probability into a discussion of the foundations of economic theory.

Having summarized the three main, competing interpretations of probability, the book outlines why it is of such fundamental importance in economics, illustrating this with a comparison of Knight's and Keynes's very different conceptions.

The third part of the book examines three very different schools of thought: the Austrians, Keynesan and the New Classical/Rational Expectations approach. It is shown that the Austrian theories and those of Keynes are consistent with subjectivism, individualism and with a view of decision-making as a process. This entails a form of *necessarianism* as a method of analysis. Rational Expectations, in contrast, is based on quantitative measurement and a need to reconstruct economic theory on instrumentalist grounds. This requires a frequentist approach to probability.

The result should be of interest to people working on the history of economic thought, the methodology and philosophy of economics, the theory of probability in economics, Austrian economics and Keynesian economics.

Charles McCann is an economist specializing in the history of economic thought and economic methodology, and, specifically, the application of probability to an analysis of economic doctrines.

PROBABILITY FOUNDATIONS OF ECONOMIC THEORY

Charles R. McCann, Jr.

Routledge
Taylor & Francis Group

LONDON AND NEW YORK

First published 1994
by Routledge
2 Park Square, Milton Park, Abingdon, Oxon, OX14 4RN

Simultaneously published in the USA and Canada
by Routledge
605 Third Avenue, New York, NY 10017

*Routledge is an imprint of the Taylor & Francis Group, an
informa business*

© 1994 Charles R. McCann, Jr.

Typeset in Garamond by
Mathematical Composition Setters Ltd, Salisbury, Wiltshire

British Library Cataloguing in Publication Data
A catalogue record for this book is available from the
British Library

Library of Congress Cataloging in Publication Data
McCann, Charles R. (Charles Robert), 1956-
Probability foundations of economic theory/
Charles R. McCann, Jr.
p.   cm.
Includes bibliographical references and index.
ISBN 0-415-10867-5
1. Economics—Methodology.   2. Probabilities.   I. Title.
HB 199.M384 1994   93-43881
                                                     CIP

ISBN 13: 978-0-415-10867-6 (hbk)

To my mother, and the memory of my father

CONTENTS

CONTENTS

FOREWORD

This volume treats of Maynard Keynes from a different vantage point. Many commentators, having been led to Keynes by his writings in Economics, have found in those writings several enigmas. Axel Leijonhufvud and Alan Coddington, amongst others, have shown that the Keynes seen by the 'Keynesians,' and Keynes, the writer from the standpoint of strict *explication de texte* (devoid of the interpretations of his devotees), are clearly different entities.

Controversies about the 'true' meaning of any man's specific ideas, particularly when interpreted from an ambiguous, even contradictory, single text, are legion. Even more, interpretations about what a man probably meant when he admittedly changed his views frequently, and when he wrote for popular, rather than strictly professional consumption, present massive problems – it is the stuff about which religious wars are waged.

Yet, in the course of arraying evidence favoring one side or another there comes an inevitable moment when most interpreters seem to choose either, to deny the significance of a point found in the man's writings (one which contradicts their interpretation of what 'he must have meant'), or, to treat deviant expressions much in the way any empiricist deals with a single or small number of outlying exceptions – their retreat is to either 'a faulty observation' or to 'Homer must have been nodding.'

Those of us who have lectured on the evolution of Maynard Keynes's writings and thinking have a tendency to interpret his earlier works from the standpoint of what we think his later work suggested; depth of insight comes from seeing what the younger may did in terms of what he came to stress. McCann has rejected this approach. He has tried to treat Keynes's later work in the light of his earlier *Treatise on Probability*. And, to my pleasure I find that he has made a real contribution. So much has recently been published about Keynes, the man, it is hardly necessary to speculate what streaks of genius and what idiosyncracies he possessed. More than anything, what stands out about his working habits is that he suffered from a desire to rush into print – and, with his connections, that rush was never countered for long. But, there was one exception in his experience: the resistance to publication of his *Treatise on*

Probability. For, unlike his later works, usually drafted under the pressure of wanting to get into print and to influence social developments, Keynes was forced to polish *Treatise on Probability* carefully, because Alfred North Whitehead refused to accept it in its initial form. Maynard Keynes had submitted it in 1907 in pursuit of a Senior Fellowship at King's College, Cambridge, a prize granted him in 1909 only after he had passed Whitehead's test. Keynes, himself, then delayed publication for another twelve years.

Today we are generally more accustomed to talking about probability analysis than thinking about what is involved conceptually. In the Edwardian era, the reverse was true; those who talked about probability analysis seem to have thought about what they were trying to say before saying it. Similarly, those who wrote about subjectivity in economic decisions were not in the minority – as I would think that those who write on the subject today must be. To my mind one of the few recent writers who 'did it the old-fashioned way,' that is studying both subjective economics and subjective probability analysis, was G.L.S. Shackle, and, it is hardly surprising that McCann came to his topic via the reading-Shackle route.

What McCann's study shows first is the place of Keynes's *Treatise on Probability* in the unfolding of ideas in pre-World War I Cambridge, the world of Ludwig Wittgenstein and Bertrand Russell. Keynes was writing against an incomplete, but nonetheless a real, background of ideas pertaining to subjectivity and probability distributions. Second, McCann leads us through the evolution of Keynes's ideas, including some deviations introduced as a misplaced *de mortuis nil nisi bonum* effort (reconciliation with Ramsey's statement). Third, McCann shows how Keynes's ideas about the subjective nature of probability analysis have withstood later attacks from a variety of quarters. Indeed, one of the provocative results of McCann's investigation is to show how much tampering has occurred in the presentation of Keynes's probability philosophy by those who are considered masters in one area or another of his economics. The range of these critics not only form a massive spectrum, but also a veritable gallery of famous scholarly names. Yet, withal, McCann argues persuasively that Keynes, the Probability Philosopher, emerges as the real master. But, as the real master in terms of probability analysis, and probably, not unambiguously, also the master in terms of a new economics paradigm.

McCann's findings do not put him in the field by himself; he is not alone in the current debate. His views complement much of what Rod O'Donnell and Anna Carabelli, and Tony Lawson and Jochen Runde and the group at Cambridge are arguing. There were different facets to Keynes's greatness. As time goes on and the perspective changes, attention to his writings on economic policy may be receding, but at the same time, the focus has shifted to highlight his work on subjective probability. That it has taken so long – almost 90 years – for this area of Keynes's work to gain recognition is not surprising.

In the course of my reading McCann's meticulously presented study, I found that the distinction between aleatory and systemic probability was initially announced as an aside by that recognized, yet all but totally neglected, economist, Augustin Cournot. This is not intended to report a serendipitous observation merely. Rather, it is significant, because the work being done in the Cournot tradition by such current French scholars as Christian Schmidt, begins to link what went on in Edwardian England (John Venn vs. Maynard Keynes) to the tradition of economic methodology in nineteenth century France.

Mark Perlman
Pittsburgh, Pennsylvania

PREFACE

This is an essay on the foundations of economic theory. As with other attempts at the elaboration of foundations in other areas of study, the presentation is at once highly general, opinionated, and perhaps more than a bit provocative. This is inevitable. Foundational essays are meant to challenge orthodoxy, to drive debate, to provoke a response. One need not always be cognizant of the foundations of a discipline to function within it; in fact, one may reasonably argue that the best work is done by those ignorant of the foundations. However, foundational essays serve a singular purpose: they help illuminate problem areas and identify sources of confusion. In other words, they serve to focus the disciplinary conversation. That is the point of the present effort: to examine from a completely different perspective three principal competing paradigms of economic thought, to wit, the Austrian, Keynes's own, and the Rational Expectations schools, in an effort to discover whether there is, indeed, at the base level, any commonality and, if not, why not.

In undertaking such an effort, I pretend neither to comprehensiveness nor to objectivity, for this is not in the ordinary sense of the term a history of economic thought; nor, were it so, would I be convinced that objectivity is possible let alone valid conceptually. No historian can claim the existence of an objective historical analysis; no matter how diligently we may make the attempt to the contrary, we cannot help but approach historical analyses from a prejudiced stance that for better or worse shapes what we regard as the appropriate 'facts' upon which the analyses are based. To argue otherwise is to practice 'museum history'. All I claim here is an attempt at initiating commentary by developing a taxonomy within which to categorize economic theories.

With this said, the following essay may be construed as a general introduction to a field still very much in its infancy. It is an essay on the foundations of what is becoming an important new area of debate: the importance of the philosophical aspects of probability analysis as a basis for economic theorizing. Some economists will undoubtedly deny its importance to their fields of enquiry; others will find the work interesting as an introduction to the new field. Historians of thought will (it is hoped) discover a new and different context within which to examine economic theories. Econometricians may likewise come away from the essay with a new perspective on the theoretical underpinnings of their models. It is also hoped that philosophers will find in the present work a new and uncharted area into which to extend application of the tools of the philosophy of science. Economists coming fresh to this area of research may find the same material to be illuminating and helpful in setting up the parameters of the discussion and grounding the debate within the economics discipline. At the same time, philosophers approaching economic theory may find the economic discussion of these problems worthwhile.

Foundations are important in and of themselves; methodology matters. Practitioners of a discipline may deny the *need* for an examination of foundations, yet cannot, if only for reasons of intellectual honesty, deny their *importance*. The very frameworks of analysis upon which they rely for the support of their theories and models are built upon something, and this something is as important as, some may contend more so than, the frameworks themselves. So, while they may deny the necessity for continued emphasis on the bases upon which the frameworks are established, frameworks which they themselves employ, these self-same technicians should at the same time not remain ignorant of the fundamental principles upon which the frameworks are based, i.e., the underlying methodologies.

The foundations, if they serve no other useful purpose, can serve to elucidate for those working in a discipline the elements of importance to them. Foundations highlight aspects of the field relevant to, included in, and excluded from the disciplinary dialogue. They shape the conversation, mold the argument. They determine and give validity to the methods employed. They select the acceptable tools for the carrying out of the analysis. They even function to shape the form and scope of the paradigms. All this while being virtually invisible, absent from any explicit and apparently meaningful role in the process.

The literature on the philosophical foundations of economic thought is of a relatively recent vintage. Alexander Rosenberg's 1976 study, although not readily accepted by economists and economic methodologists then or now, was nonetheless a precursor of much of the work in this area. Studies by economists such as Rod O'Donnell, Anna Carabelli, Bradley Bateman, and Robert Skidelsky have examined early philosophical influences on the economic and other writings of John Maynard Keynes. Martin Hollis (alone, and with economist Edward Nell) has written on the general question of rationality in economics from the position of a philosopher, dividing the field into Kantian and Humean positions. Herbert Simon has written extensively on rationality and behavior in economics, including aspects of psychology, expectations-formation, and decision-making under uncertainty. Kenneth Arrow (1951) surveyed the field of choice under uncertainty, concentrating on means of describing and handling uncertainty in a probabilistic framework in an economic context. There have as well been numerous articles and books written on the methodological and philosophical foundations of the Austrian school of economics, written from the standpoint of the general framework of the school itself and in terms of the beliefs and influences of the individual intellectual leaders of the movement, scholars such as Carl Menger and Ludwig von Mises. The works of Erich Streissler, Gerald O'Driscoll and Mario Rizzo, Emil Kauder, and Israel Kirzner come readily to mind.

But there remains a need to go beyond this, and to elucidate not only the foundations of Keynes's economics and the underlying philosophy of the Austrians in a specific context, removed from a discussion of competing views and interpretations, but to extend the argument to an analysis of the methodological foundations of the Rational Expectationists, and, in so doing, effect some form of connection among the three. This is the task of the present effort.

ACKNOWLEDGEMENTS

The present effort began as an attempt to answer a question posed by Professor Mark Perlman of the University of Pittsburgh in a graduate class on the history of economic thought. That question concerned the relation between Knightian, Shackelian, and Keynesian uncertainty, and the connection of these concepts to equilibrium and expectations-formation in economic theory. The attempt at providing an answer to this question resulted in my doctoral dissertation, *Uncertainty, Expectations, and Rationality in Economic Models: An Analysis of the Foundations of Keynesian, Austrian, and Rational Expectations Models*, upon which this work is based.

There are many individuals without whose input this work could never have been possible. First and foremost among these are the members of my dissertation committee. Professors Mark Perlman, Janet Chapman, and Steven Husted of the Department of Economics, and Professor Wesley Salmon of the Department of Philosophy at the University of Pittsburgh all made significant contributions in defining and reorienting the material and the direction of the presentation of the original dissertation. Suggested readings, focal reorientation, persistent challenges during the overview and final defense, and changes in overall attitude were part and parcel of these recommendations. I cannot, however, claim that the final result is acceptable to a single member of the original committee.

Once the decision was made to publish, again at the behest of Professor Perlman, who in a large sense commissioned this work, other views were elicited. Informal discussions were held with Bradley Bateman and Rod O'Donnell at meetings of the History of Economics Society as to the early philosophical position of Keynes and its influence on his later economic writings. More lengthy discussions with Jochen Runde convinced me that I was on the right track (as we seem to be in substantial agreement on a great number of points).

Dr Runde was also extremely helpful in commenting on earlier drafts of the manuscript, and his contribution will be noted throughout. While I did not take heed of all of his suggestions (he may say I did not accept quite a few),

ACKNOWLEDGEMENTS

they were nonetheless greatly appreciated and certainly forced me to tighten the argument in many places and even jettison some long-held notions.

Finally, I wish to thank the numerous anonymous readers whose contributions to this work are beyond measure, and to thank Alan Jarvis of Routledge for the tremendous encouragement he has given me throughout the project of writing this essay.

I

INTRODUCTION

The purpose of this essay is to explore the use of probability as an integral component in the elaboration of economic theory. To do so requires at the outset that the topic of discussion be adequately posed and defined: just what is probability and what is its importance to economics? Why should economists be interested in a topic traditionally confined to philosophical discourses on epistemology and ontology? Have economists ever given more than a passing thought to the idea of a 'probabilistic' approach to their subject anyway?

Before delving into an examination of these questions, however, it is worth some time and effort to introduce the problem, a problem which is not readily acknowledged or even accepted when so recognized. Consequently, this introductory chapter is to serve as a form of taxonomy. Here will be reviewed various approaches to theory, and the concept of probability will be placed in context.

THE MEASUREMENT OF ECONOMIC PHENOMENA

The measurement problem is not unique to economics, but rather is one basic to all sciences. Among the concerns of theorists and practitioners alike are designating a zero point, establishing a parametric scale, and limiting theory building as it relates to empirical testing to strictly quantitative phenomena. Where the science deals with subjects which lend themselves to measurement, to numerical valuation of the principal magnitudes, e.g., force and work in physics, the problem is handled by the use of universally accepted criteria. Those theorists who concentrate in the 'hard,' exact sciences (e.g., physics, chemistry, astronomy, mechanics), can rely on what is essentially off-the-shelf technology applicable throughout the science; they have for all intents and purposes 'solved' the problem of measurement, of the valuation of desirable magnitudes, and so need not concern themselves any further with such an 'irrelevancy'.[1] Where the science is less exact and the variables within its domain are of a more qualitative character, e.g., consumer demand, utility, and expectations in economics, measurement is more problematic. The problems within the domain of the social sciences, especially within the 'soft'

1

social sciences of political science and sociology, but also within the relatively 'hard' social science of economics, are seldom simply enough posed or even adequately defined to allow of unambiguous, unchallenged resolution. Social science variables are essentially qualitative, but range along a measurable–non-measurable (quantitative–qualitative) continuum: the greater the degree of measurability of the variables of interest to the students of a discipline, the more scientific the discipline appears to be. In fact, some may contend that the mark of a science is the degree to which the variables within its domain are quantifiable.

Economists, in their zeal to be regarded as 'real scientists,' have become especially cognizant of this problem. It has become a truism in modern economic discourse that the problems in which the economist is interested are limited to those amenable to quantitative expression. The theories which are put forward tend to reflect this belief. The prevailing methodological orthodoxy of economics, insofar as one exists and is indeed accepted throughout the discipline, is of a type which legitimizes theorizing characterizable as self-limiting, i.e., the theory itself is limited in scope by virtue of the limitations placed on the variables of inclusion. It is almost second-nature for adherents to this orthodoxy to begin their analyses by limiting the area of study to as minute a portion of the problem as possible which, while perhaps of limited validity in actuality, is valid theoretically and conceptually because the problem is then amenable to the techniques of mathematical optimization.

The Cambridge economist A. C. Pigou required as a precondition for measurability that 'the range of our inquiry becomes restricted to that part of social welfare that can be brought directly or indirectly into relation with the measuring-rod of money' (Pigou, 1920, p. 11). Clearly this poses a challenge, since all areas taken to be within the domain of the subject cannot comply with such a stricture. Still, one needs a starting-point, so a measurable partition must suffice. Tractability is the key: the problem becomes viable because mathematical techniques are applicable to its solution, not because it represents a 'true' picture of the economic situation.

Central to this orthodoxy, this belief in the quantitative expression of economic magnitudes, in the economic system as deterministic and readily reducible to a series of equations (i.e., a closed system), is the role of measurement, both in the formation and the subsequent testing of hypotheses. Economics, being the social science most conducive to numerical measure, is, by and large, subject to the usual restrictive caveats, well-suited to mathematization. After all, prices and outputs, money supply and interest rates, are all measurable quantities which are central to the concerns of the economist. Yet it should be remembered that economics is above all a *social* science in which account must be taken of the inherent ambiguities and uncertainties within the domain of the subject. The social aspect requires that one account for the interactions among individuals as well as the rationale behind the undertaking of any action; sociology and psychology are on this account important but neglected

2

areas for economic research. As the econometrician Trygve Haavelmo (1944) declared, descriptions of economic behavior (themselves dependent on non-quantitative factors) which reference 'a limited set of measurable phenomena' are merely discretionary exercises on the part of the analyst. Economic models are nothing more than 'our own artificial inventions in a search for an understanding of real life; they are not hidden truths to be "discovered"' (Haavelmo, 1944, p. 3). For economic 'quantities,' themselves open to multiple interpretation, no universally accepted or unquestionably valid scale of measurement exists; there may be proposed as many measures for quantifying economic magnitudes as there are researchers interested in pursuing the subject.

Probability is one of the areas which is particularly subject to measurement problems, including problems of inclusion and restriction – the designation of the appropriate domain to which a probability measure is applicable (and definable) – and the understanding (and acceptance) of the fact that there are elements beyond the scope of probability, however defined. It is one thing to assert that the occurrence of an event is probable, or that a proposition, based on given evidence, warrants a given degree of belief. It is quite another to gauge accurately the numerical valuation of this probability with any significant degree of exactitude, given that any real-valued probability exists in the first place. There is even argument as to whether one should or could even attempt such an endeavor. Without such a valuation, be it point or functional, it is not possible to account for qualitative factors that are by nature subject to problematic, probabilistic interpretation, i.e., to non-deterministic factors. Likewise it is no small feat to determine the space for which a probability measure is to be restricted. One is faced here with difficulties as to how narrow a measure to use and still allow conceptual validity.

The probability problem as described has another dimension beyond that of measurement. For while acknowledged to be of immense practical and theoretical importance, being as it is at the center of virtually all discussion in economic theory (especially the recent expositions of rational expectations and even Post Keynesian and new Keynesian economics), little beyond a mere acknowledgement is generally afforded. There is, so far as economists are concerned (not excepting for the most part econometricians who, while conversant in probability as providing a statistical foundation for their sub-field, are not presumed here to have a thorough enough knowledge of probability proper), no pressing urgency, no felt requirement, to go beyond mere acknowledgement and hence quickly dispose of the problem. An understanding of the nature of probability and its role in decision processes is irrelevant on these views, since it soon becomes obvious to the reader of these theoretical expositions in their formal mathematical guise that these presentations employ probability as little more than a technical shorthand, not as an integral part of the description of the economic process. The unresolved problem is actually one of defining what is meant by probability and how this apparatus is to be employed. As will be seen, this is itself a problem for which no consensus has been reached.

It is the dual problems of measurement of both quantitative and qualitative phenomena and the use of probability as an instrument to aid analysis that are of the utmost concern in economics and other social sciences; both problems deal with measurement itself, broadly defined. To see the importance of this for economics, one must review the basics of economic analysis, the method of its classifications and the problems which are included in the study of the discipline.

LAWS OF ECONOMICS

Economic theories may best be understood by the manner of their elucidation. Carl Menger (1883) of the Austrian school proposed separating economics into the theoretical and the historico-statistical, which divisions cannot be studied in isolation from one another. Ideal (theoretical, exact) laws are to be elaborated in concert with those derived inductively (by the realistic-empirical method). The ideal laws are formal, rational constructs, dealing with general knowledge;[2] the inductive laws are statistical, empirical constructs, dealing with individual, material knowledge. Ideal laws are non-empirical and atemporal, holdings subject to sufficiently rigorous constraints, as necessary;[3] they are analytic propositions intuitively obvious.[4] The inductive laws hold only contingently, their validity judged reasonable to a degree of probability; they are synthetic propositions valid for the time and place of their elucidation.[5] As the emphasis shifts from the underlying, universally valid laws governing the operation of the idealized economy to contingent laws governing behavior in an empirical system subject to environmental constraints, probability becomes a fundamental consideration.

There is likewise no simple criterion as to the status of laws within the classical tradition.[6] John Neville Keynes (1917), whom many regard as the leading expositor of the methodology of the classical economic tradition, distinguished as did Menger between *a priori* and *a posteriori* methodology, the *a priori* being 'positive, abstract, and deductive,' and the *a posteriori* being 'ethical, realistic, and inductive' (1917, pp. 9–10). Neither methodology could alone be applied to the discipline of economics: if economics were taken to be a strictly inductive endeavor, then its 'laws' would be valid only contingently and so could not be extended; if deductive, its 'laws' would be restricted by the given assumptions. In the language of philosophy (more fully developed in Chapter II), if economics were inductive its statements could be ampliative; if deductive they could not. Therefore, Neville Keynes held that for economics some combination of the two methodologies was desirable (ibid., pp. 5, 172). To this end, the solution for Keynes was for the initial premises to be derived inductively (they must be expressions of empirical conditions), subsequent inferences from these premises to be derived deductively. These inferences were

4

then to be verified by comparison with observation. It is in this context, on the induction side, that probability plays a vital role in the process of theorizing, as the initial premises are contingent and so the process of verification of the deduced inferences can never be complete.

Many classical economic writers[7] believed in the existence of underlying 'historical laws', i.e., statements concerning human behavior based on the historical record which, once derived, are taken as immutable truths. From these truths could be derived the postulates (theorems) of economics, statements holding valid always and everywhere. Thus certainty could potentially be realized. Yet despite this desire to derive from the environment analytic truths, no such certainty was forthcoming; historically determined 'laws,' being contingent, are not reducible to expression in formal, analytical models, since there can be no historically determined causality. What was required in economics was not the enunciation of inviolable truths, but rather evolutionary statements of tendency.

The position of John Stuart Mill as to the status of economic propositions is even more directly related to the theme of the present work. This position he set forth in his 1872 *Logic of the Moral Sciences*. Reliable, unquestionably valid inductive inferences in economics are not possible owing to the contingent nature of the phenomena of interest; the data of the social sciences are empirical observations perceived and collected and analyzed by individuals possessed of subjective temperaments equipped with but imprecise techniques of perception, apprehension, and measurement. Only deductive inferences are objectively valid as leading to certain knowledge in any case, and these perforce cannot be made from empirical observation.

> We can only make our observations in a rough way and *en masse*. . . .
> These conclusions, besides that they are mere approximate generalisations, deserve no reliance, even as such, unless the instances are sufficiently numerous to eliminate not only chance, but every assignable circumstance in which a number of the cases examined may happen to have resembled one another. . . . What is obtained, even after the most extensive and accurate observations, is merely a comparative result. . . . Since, therefore, the comparison is not one of kinds, but of ratios and degrees; and since in proportion as the differences are slight, it requires a greater number of instances to eliminate chance. . . . Accordingly there is hardly one current opinion respecting the characters of nations, classes, or descriptions of persons, which is universally acknowledged as indisputable.
>
> (Mill, 1872, pp. 51–2)

Empirical generalizations are inadequate to serve as a basis for knowledge because they are predicated on synthetic propositions. They are but inductions based on the available information. One can never, in relying on empirical judgments, secure certain knowledge (truth) if for no other reason than chance and resemblance can never be eliminated. A reliance on empirical generalizations as a basis for the establishment of immutable laws of behavior is thus doomed to failure, since no causal relationship is determinable, as noted by David Hume (1740) in his devastating critique of induction (to be discussed in Appendix I to Chapter II). It is only when empirical generalizations can be converted to deterministic, general laws of behavior that one can arrive at a determination of causality.

For any determination of causality to be made, these general laws must be of such a nature as to allow the isolation of a relationship similar to that of 'constant conjunction' advanced in Hume; but, should this relationship be proven in fact to hold, the laws thus ascribed are valid only as statements of closed (experimental) systems. Once causality is established, prediction is possible. Otherwise, in an open system, the influence of a wealth of possible causes neither expressed nor expressible, act to frustrate any determinism; chance enters the scene as an ever-present but grossly misunderstood feature of the series.[8] As determinism is disavowed so is certainty; reliance must then be placed on probability, from which only contingent conclusions may be derived.

At the level of the individual, however, Mill deemed prediction not only possible, but *theoretically* potentially perfect. Given an individual possessed of a *known* constitution, his behavior is completely determinate; it will be predictable by anyone familiar with his background, constitution, and motivations. The more that is known, the more accurate will be any prediction, until we approach, in the limit, the ideal of perfect predictability. It must be evident that such is the case since, according to Mill, human activity falls into the realm of and is representable as a result of strict laws of behavior, discoverable by anyone so inclined to inquire.

That human action is not in *fact* predicted accurately, even though determinate, is explainable in terms of (1) a lack of complete and even sufficient information as to the circumstances affecting an individual's beliefs, understandings, etc.; and (2) an inability to disentangle the effects of circumstances and character. 'The actions of individuals could not be predicted with scientific accuracy, were it only because we cannot foresee the whole of the circumstances in which those individuals will be placed' (ibid., p. 33). Human beings are not after all automatons; perceptual and other inadequacies are endemic, and extraneous influences on behavior abound. Doubts, as to the opportunities open to ourselves and others, as to the complete list of actions open to us, as to the environment within which these actions must be taken, and as to the consequences of the actions, exist because of limited knowledge on the part of those attempting to arrive at a precise prediction. We as individuals function in an environment our apprehension of which is less than perfect.

CLASSIFICATIONS OF ECONOMIC THEORY

Economic theories may be classified in many and varied ways outside of the manner of their construction, but perhaps the most useful classifications for the present are those which categorize theories in terms of their ability to incorporate a time dimension (statics vs. dynamics), and as they reflect the economy in part or as a whole (partial vs. general equilibrium). It is through these classificatory schema that economic models have been in the past portrayed; it is through these classifications that the models are still best understood because the schema by themselves serve to discriminate qualitative from quantitative models.[9]

Equilibrium is a concept in many ways central to much (but not all) of economic theory. It is the device through which rational economic choice may be defined in formal theoretical general equilibrium models, since its postulation makes it possible for the theorist to identify the actor as possessed of complete and perfect knowledge of the acts of others in occurrences coincident with and simultaneous to his own.[10] Friedrich Hayek perhaps expressed it best. He maintained that equilibrium could only have meaning when applied to a single actor following a set plan of action. In this sense, the *actor* is not in equilibrium, rather 'his *actions* stand in equilibrium relationships to each other' (Hayek, 1937, p. 36; emphasis added).

> Actions of a person can be said to be in equilibrium in so far as they can be understood as part of one plan. Only if this is the case, only if all these actions have been decided upon at one and the same moment, and in consideration of the same set of circumstances, have our statements about their interconnections, which we deduce from our assumptions about the knowledge and the preferences of the person, any application.
>
> (ibid., p. 36)

To extend this description of equilibrium to an entire economy, or simply to interactions between two or more actors, requires a commonality of data upon which expectations will be founded, and a compatibility of action plans decided upon prior to the initiation of exchange (much as the preconditions for a Walrasian tatonnement).[11]

In respect to theories of economics for which the concept is applicable, equilibrium is taken as either partial or general. Partial equilibrium, the equilibrium of a fragment of the totality, is useful in describing the mechanics of the economic system at a specific point in time, where interest in focused on the parameter values of specific variables; the remainder of the variables, while perhaps relevant in a temporal environment, are subsumed under the rubric of *ceteris paribus*. Examples include supply analysis under conditions of constant costs, demand analysis under conditions of unchanging tastes and constant income, and money market analysis under conditions of a constant money supply and constant velocity of circulation. Such a system is definitionally *static*, as this refers to the analysis of the values of the specified endogenous variables (the parameters of interest), given that exogenous variables maintain the values previously stipulated. This type of analysis allows for irrelevant or extraneous parameters to be excluded from consideration; they are constrained from so entering, and may in fact be treated as constants. The system can then be reduced to a few parameters of particular interest, simplifying greatly the exposition. This is the analytical framework purportedly preferred by the economists of the classical school.

The general equilibrium approach[12] refers to an analysis of the economic system in its entirety, whereby explicit recognition is given to the interdependencies among the supply and demand relationships for commodities, money, and factor inputs; nothing is irrelevant, everything measurable and non-measurable matters. Such a system is capable of representation both in static and dynamic terms,[13] or in what G. L. S. Shackle (1965) described as self-contained vs. non-self-contained models.[14] *Dynamics* then requires consideration of the time paths of the endogenous variables of the system and the evolution of the general economic and social environment; it is concerned with process. Everything can change in a dynamic general model (with the sole exception of the underlying rationality postulates); in effect everything is endogenous. The static representation is appropriate when there is little need to incorporate the time component and the anticipations (expectations) of individual decision-makers as to the future course of the economy. The temporal dimension and uncertainty as to the expectations of the future are irrelevant as description is more important than understanding or process. This, the static form of general equilibrium, is the framework credited to Leon Walras in his attempt to develop a comprehensive model of interconnected markets abstracted from time. The dynamic general equilibrium model is thought to be of more recent vintage, as it became possible to convey within a mathematical model measures (or representations) of expectations and uncertainty that had long before been assigned a key role in the economic process.

The shift in economic perspective from partial to general equilibrium analysis[15] accompanied the similar shift from statics to dynamics. As the need arose to account for interactions among economic variables, the mode of analysis tended to a formulation capable of handling the interactions and the interrelationships among the variables. Under any static model formulation, be it partial or general, it is evident that among the data which must be included in the *ceteris paribus* constraint are systemic uncertainty (the uncertainty of the environment), epistemic uncertainty (the uncertainty of our *apprehension* of the environment), and the subjective motivations behind the decision-making process (the means by which economic agents develop anticipations of future events, of the future time path of the economy). These are fundamentally qualitative expressions; they are the quintessential non-measurables. Given fixed parameter values, at a fixed point in time, in the face of external shocks, static models can perforce only incorporate uncertainty and expectations as data

exogenously given. Uncertainty and the expectations we form in order to coun-
teract its effects are temporal, so the static model, insofar as it abstracts from
time, has little to offer under these conditions; in fact, the static model can only
characterize a situation of perfect foresight. In the static model, expectations
and our perception and apprehension of conditions and circumstances serve the
role of shift parameters only, being as they are point values, and not distributional. The static models are thus closed and strictly deterministic.

To allow for the incorporation within economic theory of temporality, uncertainty, and expectations, it must be possible to express the model (or some such
similar construct) in an open, dynamic format, i.e., a general equilibrium
dynamic format, so that *all* variable elements in the economy *can* be accounted
for within the artificiality of the economists' model. This is especially so with
respect to expectations and uncertainty, as they reflect subjective, qualitative
parameters which feed back to and so influence each and every other parameter. It is not enough to state categorically that expectations and uncertainty
are given, and then ignore their influence; to do so is at best an expedient for
pedagogic purposes. Understanding requires sterner stuff. As Paul Sweezy
stated the position:

> For some problems it may be legitimate and necessary to regard them
> [expectations] as largely given, though so long as we are analysing a
> process in time they can never be wholly given. On the other hand, there
> are problems for which we must extend the scope of our inquiry so much
> as to include nearly all of expectations and uncertainty among the
> variables.
>
> (Sweezy, 1937–8, pp. 236–7)

Each and every parameter must be assumed variable, since the parameters are,
after all, behaviorally determined. They cannot be viewed as constants, since
in being so constrained no allowance can be made for shifts in tastes and other
exogenous influences which may feed back into the endogenous parameters.

ENTER PROBABILITY

Granted that dynamic general equilibrium is the proper theoretical basis upon
which economic analysis should be founded, the next consideration must be
in the handling of economic magnitudes. It is in this venue that a general equilibrium model meets the same criticism as does the partial equilibrium model,
viz., it fails to explain sufficiently well the workings of the economy. There are
two major problems which confront the general equilibrium framework.
Firstly, there is no reason to assume that action-plans will ever coincide (either
between individuals or over time), or that the data set of each actor is in any
way compatible with any other actor, as Hayek has pointed out. Secondly, in
order to be viable, as a necessary condition, it must be possible to state the
'model' (economic construct) in probabilistic, and not simply stochastic, terms,

to account for incompatibilities of action-plans, for systemic uncertainties, and for the subjective apprehensions of environmental signals.

At this point a terminological detail must be clarified. Here, as elsewhere throughout this work, the term 'probabilistic'[16] will reference incommensurable, qualitative variables, and those magnitudes of measure zero – magnitudes not readily susceptible to quantitative, statistical treatment, but perhaps representable as an ordered series –, while the term 'stochastic' references measurable, random components representable by a given distribution function.[17] The importance of this concept cannot be overemphasized. A stochastic model is one which is also determinate, since randomness implies the existence of an underlying pattern. Without the probabilistic element, the model retains its determinism and so ignores expectations formation: it is, in a word, static.

Herbert Simon observed that economic theory which asserts at the outset the postulate of perfect competition (market clearing) with 'rational' agents acting in an environment of perfect certainty (perfect foresight), or one in which uncertainty in perception and apprehension has been so reduced as to be of no consequence, is 'deductive theory' (Simon, 1982, p. 321). Once the primary axioms have been established, all that remains is to deduce mechanically the conclusions (outcomes, ramifications) of the model. Deductive theory is tautological since, e.g., profit may be redefined to refer not to the residual of revenue over cost, but to that 'which entrepreneurs maximize' and utility in similar fashion becomes 'that which consumers maximize' (ibid., p. 319); the denial of any of these propositions results in a contradiction, given the acceptance of the initial postulates of the model.

Classical economic theory has been viewed as an exemplar of deductive theory (perhaps because of the influence of David Ricardo and Nassau Senior, heralding the rise of scientific economics) because of its emphasis on analytic postulates presumed to be descriptive of empirical phenomena. Chief among the axioms of classical theory is the concept of equilibrium, be it in a barter or a monetary economy. As exchange in a barter economy requires a coincidence of wants, equilibrium in a monetary economy can obtain only if there is a coincidence of expectations. But should wants and expectations in fact be coincident, i.e., should equilibrium obtain, any adjustments to external events would be immediate and complete.[18] There would be no role for adjustment or facilitating *mechanisms* since adjustment is assured by virtue of the axioms of the theory. The economy of equilibrium is but a rational analytic construct: from the primary axioms follow the conclusions.

These orthodox 'classical' constructions, allowing actors perfect and complete access to all available information covering every conceivable facet of economic activity for which they ultimately rely in the formation of action-plans, are not, according to conventional wisdom, amenable to probabilistic interpretation. The choice process is one whereby utility (or profits or any number of other appropriately defined choice functions) is maximized subject to a given set of constraints; this orthodox view is of a closed, purely mechanical and

10

deterministic universe. There is no allowance for uncertainty; a unique optimum exists as a solution. All one need do to arrive at a 'classical' solution to an economic problem is to solve mechanically a classical mathematical optimization (maximization or minimization) problem.

Clearly this view of the economy as determinate and amenable to mathematical rigor neglects the role of the individual; to put it more emphatically, it invalidates process completely. Yet just as clearly such models as those *actually* promulgated by the classical economists were meant to be simply useful fictions, and so either were never advanced as representations of existing economic conditions, or, if so enunciated, were supplemented by the appropriate caveats (*ceteris paribus* clauses) concerning usefulness and appropriateness.

The paramount reason for the shift in economics toward a general, dynamic method of analysis was the need to account for process and allow for the incorporation within formal analytical models of those variables previously thought of as qualitative and probabilistic, the movements of which may prove significant in that they produce effects which reverberate throughout the system. The necessity to incorporate in economic models elements of change and uncertainty, including the reactions of agents to a temporal, open, non-deterministic environment, in which beliefs are held only uncertainly, derives from a need to provide a more complete and realistic appraisal of the workings of a competitive market economy, accounting of course for the constraints and stipulations under which the model is constructed. Again, the viability of even this form of model in which as many aspects of the environment as may be included are so included remains open to debate. In fact, the degree to which one is willing to accept a mechanical representation of social phenomena is but one of the areas of disagreement which will be reviewed here. Historically, however, the shift from one modeling paradigm to another resulted from the desire to achieve greater theoretical legitimacy and empirical relevance for economic models.

Under a strict interpretation of the writings of the early classical economists, it is difficult to discover one truly convinced of the efficacy of static, partial analysis, except as a pedagogic device. Adam Smith and John Stuart Mill presented lengthy expositions on the dynamics of a general equilibrium economy[19] in which capital, population, and the 'arts of production' (Mill's term for technology) were all allowed to change. Smith's (1789) 'natural price' served the function of an objective and 'real' attribute toward which the economy naturally and continually 'gravitated' (i.e., although it may be 'intuited', the natural price is in a sense a 'tendency',[20] since it is non-measurable but serves as a 'central price'), even in the face of continual disturbances to the general equilibrium of the system (Smith, 1789, Bk.I, Ch.VII, p. 160). Book V of Mill's *Principles* (1871) is devoted to economic dynamics, or a 'theory of motion' of the economy. Specifically, in Chapter III, Section 5, Mill allows technology, capital, and population to change simultaneously, while other chapters take up the question of the tendencies of profits and costs in a general equilibrium framework. Augustin Cournot contemplated the economy as 'a whole of which all the parts are connected and react on each other', and acknowledged that 'for a complete and rigorous solution of the problems relative to some parts of the economic system, it is indispensable to take the entire system into consideration' (Cournot, 1838, p. 127).[21] Joseph Schumpeter (1954), addressing the history of economic analysis, arrived at the conclusion that partial analysis proves inadequate as an analytic, methodological tool applicable to the study of economic phenomena, since it is too restrictive; it removes from consideration those aspects of economic behavior most relevant to (and most interesting for and illuminating of) the study of the behavior of the individual as decision-maker. Its use is nonetheless continued, while at the same time being reviled by theoreticians.[22]

Even Alfred Marshall, adjudged almost universally among economists as an adherent of a static, partial methodology, utilized the method only so far as his mathematical derivation and construction were concerned; i.e., for the sake of simplicity of exposition. His prose is clearly consistent with a dynamic, general framework through which change could be accommodated, with explicit reference to the temporality of economic variables, including expectations and uncertainty. For Marshall, all scientific laws, those of the 'hard,' exact sciences, and those of the 'soft,' inexact sciences, are but statements of tendencies. The line of demarcation between the two is the precision of measurement and the degree of exactitude and continuity of the tendencies. Exact sciences are distinguished as such because their measurements are precise; as practitioners of exact sciences are preoccupied with closed systems, the systems one encounters in experimental situations, the tendencies with which they deal are tantamount to definiteness. Economics, on the other hand, being an example of an inexact science, is distinguished by the degree of uncertainty inherent in its measurement. The vagaries and vicissitudes of the economic environment, the machinations of the individuals acting within that environment, exacerbate an inherent uncertainty, multiplying the variety with which the economist as observer has to deal. As Marshall stated:

> For the actions of men are so various and uncertain, that the best statement of tendencies, which we can make in a science of human conduct, must needs be inexact and faulty.
>
> (Marshall, 1920, Bk.I, Ch.III, p. 32)

This inherent instability in the actor's milieu led Marshall to define an economic law as 'nothing more than a general proposition or statement of tendencies, more or less certain, more or less definite' (ibid., p. 33). While physical laws are precise statements of tendencies, social laws are valid only to a degree of probability. In other words, while physics is an analytic science of closed systems, economics is a contingent science of open systems, its laws not precise statements of cause and effect, but rather imprecise characterizations of process.

The reason for Marshall's reluctance to incorporate probabilistic components

12

into his economic models lay in his view that economic phenomena are incapable of exact measurement. Non-stationarity is the rule with regard to human activity; it is this fact that 'is the source of many of the difficulties that are met with in applying economic doctrines to practical problems' (ibid., Bk.V, Ch.III, p. 347). Human action is not completely reducible to a single class or category; the motives underlying actions, even the actions themselves, are not of a stationary, homogeneous nature, which feature is a prerequisite for the application of the probability calculus. [23] Although some aspects of human behavior may be measurable and reducible to specification as 'laws' of human activity, for the most part such an effort is contingent on the removal from consideration of the non-measurable, unclassifiable vagaries of emotion and caprice and fits of irrationality. [24] The errors of measurement which arise from endeavoring to quantify human actions and behavior combine with the non-measurable aspects of the underlying motivations for this behavior and activity to reduce the effectiveness of any attempted measure. These factors, these elements of exclusion, may in fact be more important from the standpoint of the economist as behavioral scientist than are the elements of inclusion. This Marshall readily understood:

> For indeed there is scarcely any motive so fitful and irregular, but that some law with regard to it can be detected by the aid of wide and patient observation. It would perhaps be possible even now to predict with tolerable closeness the subscriptions that a population of a hundred thousand Englishmen of average wealth will give to support hospitals and chapels and missions. . . . It will however probably be always true that the greater part of those actions, which are due to a feeling of duty and love of one's neighbour, cannot be classed, reduced to law and measured; and it is for this reason, and not because they are not based on self-interest, that the machinery of economics cannot be brought to bear on them.
>
> (ibid., Bk.I, Ch.II, p. 24)

Beliefs and motivations, to take an example, are not variables of a type readily allowing of incorporation in economic models, and so cannot in general be accounted for in any meaningful way, except as is possible indirectly. Motivation is subjective; it is not necessarily correlated with action, and in fact may be purposely concealed (so that the actions perceived seem 'irrational' from the standpoint of the economist as outside observer). One cannot observe the decision process of another; at best one imposes one's own contrived decision algorithm on the outward manifestations of the decisions of others in an effort to promote standardization and objectivity, and to derive rational motivations for perceived actions. What is required from economics as a 'scientific discipline' is a measure of the causal mechanism. This was not for Marshall achievable. Only effects (the consequences of actions) can be observed; causes (or rather the behavioral antecedents of action) are unknowable and perhaps even incomprehensible. They are surely in any event of no consequence since

13

economics in Marshall's view is not a behavioristic discipline. It is on the contrary one which relies on numerical valuation of the phenomena within its domain. Prices and quantities are measurable; money (as in Smith, indirectly) becomes the basis and unit of measurement.[25] But motives, desires, anticipations and the like, while important, are qualitative and hence not measurable, placing them outside the purview of the economist as scientist.

> [Economics] concerns itself chiefly with those desires, aspirations and other affections of human nature, the outward manifestations of which appear as incentives to action in such a form that the force or quantity of the incentives can be estimated and measured with some approach to accuracy; and which therefore are in some degree amenable to treatment by scientific machinery. An opening is made for the methods and the tests of science as soon as the force of a person's motives – not the motives themselves – can be approximately measured by the sum of money, which he will just give up in order to secure a desired satisfaction; or again by the sum which is just required to induce him to undergo a certain fatigue.
>
> (ibid., Bk.I, Ch.II, p. 15)

Yet despite this acceptance that the object of fundamental interest to the economist, the human being as social animal and atomistic behavioral unit, is too complex to be completely understood within the confines of an analytical frame, Marshall felt that there could still be found some round-about method to allow the economist to analyze human motivations and activity. The method involved the applications of the principles of probability theory (as understood at the time), especially the need for the elaboration of a consistent, homogeneous series.

> [E]conomists study the actions of individuals, but study them in relation to social rather than individual life; and therefore concern themselves but little with personal peculiarities of temper and character. They watch carefully the conduct of a whole class of people, sometimes the whole of a nation, sometimes only those living in a certain district, more often those engaged in some particular trade at some time and place . . . .
>
> (ibid., pp.25–6)

> The measurement of motive thus obtained is not indeed perfectly accurate. . . . But yet the measurement is accurate enough to enable experienced persons to forecast fairly well the extent of the results that will follow from changes in which motives of this kind are chiefly concerned.
>
> (ibid., p. 26)

Marshall continued this practice of aggregation and series delineation in his discussion of equilibrium. Marshallian equilibrium is defined as the point at

14

which the demand price equals the supply price, so that production shows 'no tendency either to be increased or to be diminished...' It is stable if, when displaced from the equilibrium point, it 'will tend to return, as a pendulum oscillates about its lowest point...' (ibid., Bk.V, Ch.III, p. 345). Equilibrium as portrayed in the *Principles* is not a static concept; the equilibrium point itself is prone to change as the economy necessarily evolves. But this is not the end of the matter. Equilibrium is defined solely for the aggregate, which itself is a stable, homogeneous collection. It is valid only so long as the series 'behaves.' As the motives of the individual economic agents are not *actually* so constituted as the model requires, as the capricious actions tend in some instances to divergence rather than convergence, the equilibrium of the system, heretofore sustained for short periods when activity is perceived as regular and focused, ceases to hold over the long run. For this reason, in a later explication of long-run phenomena, also in the *Principles*, Marshall explicitly refuted the statical method as an analytical tool:

> In the relatively short-period problem no great violence is needed for the assumption that the forces not specially under consideration may be taken for the time to be inactive. But violence is required for keeping broad forces in the pound of *Ceteris Paribus* during, say, a whole generation, on the ground that they have only an indirect bearing on the question in hand. For even indirect influences may produce great effects in the course of a generation, if they happen to act cumulatively; and it is not safe to ignore them even provisionally in a practical problem without special study.

(ibid., Ch.V, p. 379n)

Dynamics and general equilibrium were from the outset at least implicit (though in many cases stated explicitly) in classical theoretical economic expositions, as was an emphasis on non-determinism.[26] A concern with the question of uncertainty in the perception by economic agents of their circumstances, for instance, was clearly in evidence in these early presentations, although at times only advanced implicitly in order to avoid interfering with the clarity of the exposition.[27] The British classical economists presented essentially 'pure,' qualitative theories aimed at description and understanding, and for the most part held to a clearly defined probability concept as a foundation for those theories.[28] Qualitative theories developed as a means of explaining the rationale behind the decisions of economic agents in an environment characterized as intrinsically unstable and perceived only imprecisely. Conceptual probability served as a vehicle for accounting for this unpredictability, as it provided a theoretical (verbal, rhetorical) basis upon which to structure the classical model.

These 'pure' theories Wesley C. Mitchell asserted are not amenable to quantitative statistical analysis because the problems with which the classical economists dealt were not framed in terms for which mathematical probability analysis is applicable. Mitchell's 'classical theory' was framed entirely in qualitative terms. Should the theory indeed be qualitative, its expression must be verbal, not mathematical; should the variables be incommensurable, as is implicit in qualitative theory, allowance need only be made for tendencies, not precise numerical valuations. As Mitchell stated, 'there is slight prospect that quantitative analysis will ever be able to solve the problems which qualitative analysis has framed, in their present form' (Mitchell, 1925, p. 3). What was absent from the classical theories was a rigorous analytical presentation of the constituents of equilibrium. While explanation and understanding serve a useful descriptive function, the analytics require a more precise axiomatic development and presentation, which serves ultimately to sterilize the concept and so alter its meaning.

To allow more precise analytical (read numerical) development, Mitchell set out to reformulate the classical models, to recast 'the old problems into new forms amenable to statistical attack'. The research program of the National Bureau of Economic Research developed by Mitchell and Arthur Burns underscored the resultant mania for measurement over descriptive and behavioral analysis.[29]

Mathematical modeling and formal deterministic theorizing are in general inapplicable to classical economic theory as defined herein because of the nature of the theory and the inherent qualitative nature of its magnitudes; modeling implies that one has at his disposal quantitative data with which to test the model (or at least have some reasonable idea as to how such data should be collected), and that the universe is one which is closed and so amenable to mathematical expression. Recasting economic theory in deterministic form makes it mathematically tractable,[30] but destroys the essence of the theory, making it sterile if not vacuous. What at once purports to be an explanation of the functioning of a market economy under probabilistic conditions reverts to a Newtonian determinism where all is explainable through reference to well-specified systems of equations. It is this reinterpretation, this redefinition of key aspects of the theory into a mathematically relevant form, which has come to be identified as the 'classical' paradigm.

The works of Kenneth Arrow (1964) and Gerard Debreu (1959) extended the formalism by introducing axiomatic analysis into the corpus of economic modeling. These idealizations of the economic process allowed exploration into the nature and existence of equilibrium, but did so by narrowing its meaning. While accepting uncertainty as a critical aspect of the economic environment, these axiomatizations were nonetheless studies in *static* general equilibrium, much in line with the mathematical general equilibrium model of Leon Walras. Equilibrium became as in the Walrasian model synonymous with zero excess demand. The Arrow-Debreu models (including later variants) utilize the idea of state-contingent commodities to abstract from the dynamics of the decision-making process in an environment of uncertainty. These representations are purported to be consistent with classical statements of economic equilibrium, the equilibrium of Smith and Mill and Cournot, but in fact can pretend to relevancy only as pedagogic devices; they are completely atemporal, and thus not economic models but rather studies in stationary equilibria.[31]

It is the realization that certain variables hitherto excluded from a purely mathematical treatment of the subject could influence significantly the workings of the model as empirical analogue that opened the way for a consideration of methods to allow incorporation of such important elements within essentially deterministic models. It is this realization that allows probability as concept and as measure a role in economic theory. Yet this realization is neither recent nor trivial, for these elements are the stuff of economics.

The importance of accounting for uncertainty (especially epistemic uncertainty) and process in a dynamic, non-deterministic environment was recognized formally in the writings of John Maynard Keynes. Keynes emphasized consistently the inadequacy of any form of modeling process in which extrapolation to policy matters was the goal; his critique of econometric modeling is well known. But his vision was misinterpreted, and so his name is often associated with *ad hoc*, empirically-causal macromodels.

Interpreters of Keynes, excepting some of the latest writers on the subject,[32] restrict their analyses to specific points of emphasis, concentrating on the perceived message of the *General Theory*, ignoring aspects critical to the argument and central to the main arguments of his other works, most notably the *Treatise on Probability*. J. R. Hicks' (1937) exposition of the IS–LM framework, for example, simplified the keynesian[33] model by introducing fixed prices and de-emphasizing the critical role played by uncertainty and expectations. It is here that the keynesian model lost its *Keynesan* flavor (or baggage, depending on the attitude of the reader), and so became amenable to strictly quantitative interpretation. It is this version of the 'keynesian' model that most regard as the authoritative statement of keynesianism; it is the textbook keynesian model. Don Patinkin (1965), Robert Clower (1965), and Robert Barro and Herschel Grossman (1971, 1976) constructed other 'keynesian' models in which the market-clearing paradigm is replaced so as to allow exchanges in a disequilibrium context. Quantity adjustment replaces price adjustment; prices are exogenously determined. The notional–effective (and ex-ante, ex-post) demand and supply dichotomy is used in these interpretations to explain discrepancies leading to disequilibrium (especially as these models concentrate on the labor and goods markets).

These 'keynesian' models, so called because their conclusions suggest a role for policy activism, seen as the *sine qua non* of keynesianism, are mostly *ad hoc*, deterministic constructs, completely out of Keynes's own context in that they de-emphasize process and uncertainty, the role of 'animal spirits' and the probabilistic nature of decision, in favor of specific, quantifiable results. The econometric revolution brought about by attempts at estimating such models, although representing in and of itself a substantial contribution to the applications of theory, is nonetheless fatally flawed by the failure to incorporate among other things environmental elements and any form of decision mechanism that may account for the beliefs, anticipations, learning, etc. of the actors in the system.

Efforts to correct the inadequacies (perceived or real) of the keynesian paradigm led to amendation of the econometric model specifications themselves. John Muth's (1961) Rational Expectations Hypothesis led to a radical restructuring of macroeconomic theory and macroeconometric modeling, away from static models incorporating expectations exogenously, and even dynamic models incorporating very simple types of expectations-formation schema (such as naive and adaptive expectations), towards models attempting an explicit elaboration of the idea that individual decision-makers utilize information efficiently in order to arrive at predictions of future events upon which they may base present and future actions. Although simplistic as theory (supposing that subjective and objective probability distributions coincide), sophisticated mathematical development of these models expanded greatly the computational apparatus at the disposal of the economist. Dynamic programming, linear stochastic difference equations, Bellman optimality, signal extraction, linear least squares procedures, ergodic theory, and other topics from the realms of engineering and pure mathematics entered the lexicon of the economist. Dynamic stochastic models have become the norm.

In the main, however, such a structure as proposed by Muth and the rational expectationists was simply imposed upon an existing model, without regard to the model's rudimentary structure or to its relation to the empirical data generated within the economic environment. Studies in rational expectations equilibria and the search for existence theorems have since the publication of Muth's thesis dominated the literature, and so have become the new mainstream. It may well have been taken for granted that the 'solution' to the problem of uncertainty and expectations in economics had been discovered, with credit going to the new neoclassicists, all that remained being the extension of the theory to fields within economics.

Yet even rational expectations models, dynamic, stochastic, finite- or infinite-horizon constructs exploiting the most powerful techniques of mathematical optimization, cannot account for let alone explain a phenomenon consistently expressed as the fundament of economic theory: an explanation of the *processes* of information utilization and expectations formation by the individual in the theory of choice. They choose in fact to ignore it, treating it as irrelevant to the objectives of the discipline as 'science.' The search for process has not, however, been completely abandoned; it had been at the heart of the classical writings, and is central as well to the economics of the Austrian writers and Keynes. It is still not fully exploited in formal, mathematical constructs nor may it be possible to do so: the intricacies involved limit application. Its existence is and perhaps must be confined almost solely to verbal constructs, usually taking the form of thought experiments.

The inclusion within an economic model of stochastic components means that an explicit expectations structure is forced into the model, and so the

18

model itself becomes a dynamic construct. Although still an artificial construct, such a model provides a somewhat more accurate picture of the economic process than would a static general equilibrium model of the Walras or Arrow-Debreu variety or in fact any non-stochastic general equilibrium model. But even with the inclusion within general equilibrium models of a device for handling random shocks to the system, the acceptance of any form of model implies a belief on the part of the economist in some form of determinism, i.e., a belief that it is possible to represent to a sufficient degree of accuracy the workings of a social collective, a system of individuals acting alone and in concert with others, by means of a system of behavioristic mathematical equations. As will be seen, while this may express the view of mainstream economists, building models incorporating stochastic elements to represent the uncertainty inherent in the system (not the uncertainty of 'perception,' since the mainstream new neoclassical economists accept that an outside observer views the economy and the interactions of its members objectively), it is by no means acknowledged universally as a valid method for analysis. For some economists (Shackle, for one) it is not even valid as an approximation, since the 'true' probabilistic aspects are omitted, and unknown factors, which may exert tremendous influence, are by design outside of reflection.

A truly comprehensive theory of economic choice in a dynamic environment must account not only for behavior expressible through reference to a stochastic distribution function, but also for aberrant behavior, deviations from the norm or behavioral patterns unique and therefore not consistent with any known distribution, and perforce unanalyzable. It must account for learning behavior, to allow agents the possibility of reassessment in the light of new and important information; it must allow for Bayesian (or indeed any other type of) learning.[34] It must account for the truly probabilistic components, unique instances not reducible to a known distribution. In short, qualitative factors play a vital role and should not be excluded simply because they are non-numerical.

That rational expectations models do not and cannot achieve this outcome will become obvious in what follows, and for reasons basic to their paradigm; that Austrian and Keynes's own models do emphasize such aspects is asserted as being for the same reason: the emphasis on probability as measure as opposed to probability as concept and a reliance on quantitative explanation at the expense of qualitative understanding. Only when the models of rational expectations are reformulated to conform with Austrian/Keynes prescriptions are they able to meet the test; but then they no longer fulfill the criterion of rational expectations models, as the term was coined by Muth. It is thus to this distinction that one must turn to comprehend the successes and failures of each economic program.

This is the aim of the following.

THE PLAN OF THE WORK

In what follows it will be argued that probability as measure has been and in some circles continues to be of only limited service in economic theory. When quantitative measurement is possible, e.g., in certain (restricted) areas of value theory, probability values are calculable and have from the beginning been utilized. Where the theory is qualitative, and so requires a description of process not confinable to quantitative measure spaces, numerical probability is inapplicable, but some reference to probability is nonetheless essential, e.g., in the areas of uncertainty and expectations. It is here that what may be termed conceptual probability is more appropriate. This conceptual device may be termed probability *qua* measure of qualitative uncertainty, or qualitative measure. Mathematical probability, game theory, and the applications of econometric techniques to the analysis of empirical data, while important as methods of utilizing the theory of probability, are beyond the scope of the present work, as they incorporate probability from a more practical standpoint, treating it as computational. For this reason alone these approaches will not be considered here.

This essay is divided into seven chapters. Following this brief taxonomic Introduction, Chapter II deals with theories of probability as they developed from efforts to understand the induction problem as put forth by David Hume. It is assumed that the reader has little if any knowledge of this topic, so the presentation is more detailed than would otherwise be required. The purpose of this exercise is merely to elucidate the principal probability types, frequentist, personalist, and necessarian, and to distinguish within each type the method of handling the problem of measurability and the comparability of disparate magnitudes. This is to be accomplished through reference to the major expositors of each position: Simon Laplace, John Venn, Keynes, Emile Borel, Frank Ramsey, and Leonard Savage. In this way theories may be identified with a specific expositor, without attempting to identify an underlying theme presumed held by all writers and practitioners within the school. The advantage of looking at individuals instead of broad categories taken as representations will become obvious from the presentation. Next will be listed the principal axioms of probability theory held here to be applicable to all schools. These are of sufficient generality to be universally applicable and so highlight commonalities, but sufficiently rigorous as to have meaning and usefulness. From these axioms will be derived an important proposition, Bayes's theorem, which is an essential prerequisite for understanding the theories of economics which follow. This too will be shown in later chapters to be universally applicable.

Chapter III concerns the operationalization of the uncertainty notion as interpreted by Frank Knight. Risk is distinguished from uncertainty. This distinction is critical to the analysis of Chapters IV–VI, and serves as a connecting link to the discussion of probability types in Chapter II. Also included as a digression are the paradoxes resulting from attempts at application of probability and utility theories of John von Neumann and Oskar Morgenstern, and Leonard Savage, to qualitative uncertainty and partial belief-orderings, specifically the paradoxes of Maurice Allais and Daniel Ellsberg. These are included here because the Knightian and Keynesan distinctions of risk and uncertainty are at the base of the challenges to utility theory based on axiomatic models.

Chapters IV–VI examine probability as an integral part of Austrian, Keynesan, and Rational Expectations theories, and regard that each is structured on and so can only be understood via a particular interpretation of probability. Austrianism (Chapter IV) is represented by the writings of Carl Menger, Ludwig von Mises, Friedrich A. von Hayek, and G. L. S. Shackle. This is not to deny nor denigrate the outstanding contributions of others working within the Austrian tradition, including such luminaries as Eugen von Boehm-Bawerk, Friedrich von Wieser, Ludwig Lachmann, Murray Rothbard, and Israel Kirzner to name but a few. In fact mention is made throughout of arguments presented by and associated with these scholars and others. However, the primary doctrines enunciated by Menger, Mises, Hayek, and Shackle concern most directly the theme here established, viz., the use of probability in economic theory. Other representations, while important in their own rights, are but reinterpretations of these primary expositors.

Chapter V discusses the economic theories of Keynes in the light of his epistemological position as stated in the *Treatise on Probability*. Keynesanism is here stipulated to refer only to models of Keynes' own design, and so coincides with Axel Leijonhufvud's 'economics of Keynes;' these views are those expressed for instance in the *Tract on Monetary Reform*, the *Treatise on Money*, the *General Theory*, and the 1937 *QJE* article. Later keynesian (Keynes-type) constructs are excluded from consideration as they do not reflect accurately Keynes's own (the *Keynesan*) description of the important aspects affecting economic behavior, but instead reflect the interpretive visions of those purporting to explain Keynes's vision. Where these views are thought important enough to mention (especially as they disagree with the view purported to be Keynes's own), they will be handled through accompanying explanatory notes.

Chapter VI handles rational expectations and the new neoclassical economics. Rational expectations theory is exemplified by the works of John Muth and Robert E. Lucas, Jr., the leading proponents of the theory and among the few to state clearly the theory as theory as opposed to the theory as application. Mention is also made of recent contributions by Douglas Gale and Edward Prescott, and includes recent attempts at reinterpretation of these models in a Bayesian setting by Richard Cyert and Morris DeGroot, and Robert Townsend, and a brief discussion of the literature on sunspots.

Finally, Chapter VII concludes the essay with an examination of the analytical framework developed by the philosopher Martin Hollis dealing with the issue of rationality in economics from Humean and Kantian perspectives. Hollis's thesis is compelling for he portrayed the differences in economic perspectives as consistent with the Humean-Kantian distinctions concerning rationality. The results of the two approaches, the one outlined herein and that of Hollis, are essentially the same, although approaching the issue from very different foundations.

II

THEORIES OF PROBABILITY

Before proceeding with an analysis of the foundations of economic theories from a probability standpoint, it is necessary to set forth the criteria to be employed in the undertaking. Chief among these criteria are the various interpretations of the theory of probability and the significance of the overall problem of induction. A brief summary of the Humean critique of induction is presented as Appendix I to this chapter.

The rationale behind this enterprise to define the 'induction problem' is that induction is employed uncritically throughout the sciences (even the social ones), whatever the degree of determinism involved, and whether the aim is prediction or description. This is especially so with economics. As some would maintain that economics is a predictive science, an account of induction is necessary as a method for the extrapolation of information on future (unobserved) conditions from past and present (observed) tendencies. As others would maintain that economics is a descriptive art, an account of induction is necessary as a method for circumscribing (conditional) causality, i.e., for ascertaining a cause (unobserved antecedent) from an effect (observed consequent).

THE GENERAL (PHILOSOPHICAL) MOTIVATION FOR INDUCTION

The term 'knowledge' has been confined for the most part in philosophical discussions to that which is certain.[35] Knowledge is not dependent upon belief or feeling or any other normative prerequisite. Belief cannot be legitimately held to be a sufficient condition for knowledge. Not even 'true belief' is knowledge, since a true belief may be predicated on a false premise or a cloudy apprehension. What is it then that constitutes knowledge? Bertrand Russell's (1912) definition seems acceptable: 'What we firmly believe, if it is true, is called *knowledge*, provided it is either intuitive or inferred (logically or psychologically) from intuitive knowledge from which it follows logically' (Russell, 1912, p. 139). Frank Ramsey (1929) defined knowledge as a belief which is true, certain, and formed in a reliable way (Ramsey, 1929b, p. 110). Thus we may for the present define 'knowledge' as certain belief which is demonstrable.

To this form of demonstrative knowledge, leading from true premises to a necessarily true conclusion, syllogistic reasoning may be applied from which inferences may be derived through deductive means. Deduction is logical entailment: from p (the antecedent) and $p \supset q$ follows q (the consequent). This is the argument from *modus ponens*. Such inferences as may be derived from deduction, while certain, are however non-ampliative (in Wesley Salmon's terminology): the conclusions derived from the premises are themselves *contained in* the premises; they are nothing more or less than a restatement of the premises themselves (Salmon, 1967, p. 8). No new knowledge can be gained from such an exercise, since the argument itself is structured in such a manner as to limit the content of the conclusion to the content of the premises. This is not to say that inferences so derived (or analytic propositions generally) are vacuous, for they serve to bring hidden structures to the surface, and ensure the completeness of the system.[36] All that is asserted is that such conclusions as are drawn are absolutely certain and add nothing to the store of knowledge.

Any other 'belief' is thus not knowledge *per se*, but is essentially 'opinion.' We may for the time being refer to this type of belief as 'probable knowledge.' Knowledge proper, 'pure knowledge,' allows for the derivation of conclusions the truth (veracity, certainty, legitimacy) of which is beyond question. In the case of probable knowledge, no such certainty as to the veracity of the conclusions derived is allowed; it is simply not possible to draw strict and certain conclusions from stated premises, which premises themselves have not been deemed at the outset true, certain, and reliable, owing to the contingent nature of the propositions. David Hume's (1740) argument on the matter, his critique of the inductive hypothesis, is on this issue most instructive:

> In all demonstrative sciences the rules are certain and infallible; but when we apply them, our fallible and uncertain faculties are very apt to depart from them, and fall into error. We must, therefore, in every reasoning form a new judgment, as a check or controul on our first judgment or belief; and must enlarge our view to comprehend a kind of history of all the instances, wherein our understanding has deceiv'd us, compar'd with those, wherein its testimony was just and true. . . . By this means all knowledge degenerates into probability; and this probability is greater or less, according to our experience of the veracity or deceitfulness of our understanding, and according to the simplicity or intricacy of the question.

(Hume, 1740, Bk.I, Pt.IV, sec.I, p. 231)

Thus, according to Hume, although the rules underlying reasoning may be certain and true, the manner of their apprehension leads us to suspect their validity. We can no longer assume that certain knowledge is even possible, and so we must be content with probable knowledge.

24

Inductive reasoning replaces deductive reasoning in the formation of inferences based upon this incomplete or uncertain knowledge. It is only possible to reach a conclusion through inductive reasoning relative to the data at hand and over the time period and location in question; i.e., induction is sensitive to both temporal and spatial considerations, and is knowledge-dependent as well. Conclusions are accepted as valid *contingently*, not *conclusively*, because we can only form inferences from what is *observed*, this being but a small subset of what it is *possible* to observe. We can on this view say nothing about *unobservables*. The possibility of extrapolation beyond the data is denied; pure empiricism has no basis as a principle of demonstrative inference. Inferences of the sort as are predicated on empirical evidence are non-demonstrative due to the impossibility of deriving necessarily true conclusions from the premises; all that is allowed is the derivation of conclusions valid to a limited degree, to a degree of certainty, or having a relation of some weight[37] to the premises (Carnap, 1950, p. 205; Salmon, 1967, p. 8).

Induction to be valid as a *scientific principle* requires that one be able to extract an ampliative *demonstrative* inference, an inference drawn from established premises which goes beyond the premises and establishes new knowledge. But this requires that some *a priori* condition be stipulated. An *a priori* principle on the order of the principle of the 'uniformity of nature' may provide the requisite rationale for establishing induction as a valid demonstrative principle.[38] If this principle were a synthetic *a priori* truth, then a demonstrative inference could be made ampliative as well (Salmon, 1967, pp. 9–10).[39]

Hume's specific critique of induction extends to any inference involving a synthetic *a priori* proposition.[40] The Logical Positivist position is that only analytic statements can be ascribed the status of *a priori*; they lead to deductive inferences and are non-ampliative. Synthetic propositions are only contingent, and lead to non-demonstrative inferences, but may be ampliative. Thus it became doctrine, at least within Positivist circles, 'that there are no synthetic *a priori* principles in virtue of which we could have demonstrative inferences that are ampliative' (ibid., p. 10).

The acceptance of the Humean proposition that individuals engaged in a decision-making process possess only incomplete or uncertain knowledge means that demonstrative inferences are not possible. Conclusions are valid only to a degree of probability; such conclusions as are drawn have a relation valid to some degree to the initial premises, but this relation is of less than certainty. As a result, a justification for induction as scientific method can be provided by considering it a form of probabilistic reasoning.

The incorporation of probability in economics occurred as the natural consequence of the temporal and spatial nature of the economizing process, the need to make decisions and take actions before one is able to acquire complete (or at times even sufficient) information as to the possibilities available and the potential outcomes of actions taken. The use of probability also gained importance through the recognition that people, even when in possession of 'sufficient information,' do not always use it 'efficiently' or may not always 'accept' the verity of the information. The fact of individuals operating in a dynamic environment requires economists, as analysts of individual behavior, to employ probability, since the economic process itself is one of continuous change, generating a continuous flow of information. Repercussions from actions taken one day are not confined to the single event; they instead lead to efforts at continual re-examination in an effort to account for new data and new situations and the interactions among individuals taking complementary or competing actions. But actions are generally non-repeatable; once taken, they cannot be undone. Therefore, probability as a conceptual device entered into the discipline of economics virtually from the outset as it became evident that the central concern would be with the consequences of individual perception and action; in other words, economics is primarily concerned with the decision-making process, involving the individual in maintaining a necessarily uncertain belief as to the composition of the future.

PROBABILITY TYPES

There is no lack of reference material on the theory of probability or on its history in the various fields to which it has been applied. Isaac Todhunter (1865), J. M. Keynes (1921), Rudolf Carnap (1950), W. Salmon (1967), Leonard Savage (1972), Ian Hacking (1975, 1990), and Roy Weatherford (1982) are but a few of the works treating the development of probability as a device to handle the problems of less-than-complete knowledge and induction (in philosophy), and the problems of gaming (in practical applications).[41]

Regarding classificatory schema, Rudolf Carnap (1950) provided a very useful typology of probability theories, distinguishing between two types, Probability$_1$ and Probability$_2$. Probability$_1$ is the type of probability exemplified (for Carnap) by the work of Keynes; it is an objective concept containing values (conclusions) that are derived relative to a given amount of evidence.[42] This form of probability belongs to the field of inductive logic, and so is independent of empirical frequencies. Instead it applies to arguments which are propositions (or sentences) and asserts a 'partial logical implication' (Carnap, 1950, p. 31). Probability$_1$ is thus analytic.

Probability$_2$ pertains to arguments which are properties, classes, kinds, types, etc. Statements of Probability$_2$ are empirical (ibid., p. 33), referring to long-run, relative frequencies, while the theorems upon which it is predicated are analytic; Probability$_2$ is thus not strictly empirical, but 'logicomathematical' (ibid., p. 34). (Although in relation to the structure of Probability$_1$ it may be viewed as empirical.)

The major difference between the two probability types is in the manner by which they are held to incorporate new information. If a Probability$_2$ statement

26

is shown to be in error regarding its predictive value – if new evidence proves the statement to be a poor predictor of future events – then the statement is simply false; it is factually incorrect. The new evidence will result in an updated statement which will presumably perform better. If a Probability$_1$ statement is shown to be in error, the statement is not erroneous; it is simply irrelevant. As a Probability$_1$ statement is defined with respect to a given evidence set, the new evidence can play no role in altering the conclusions derived from the previous evidence set. The presence of additional evidence necessitates the reconstruction of an entirely new Probability$_1$ statement, superseding the old (ibid., p. 192).

Ian Hacking (1975) in many respects appropriated the Carnap classification, renaming the categories as epistemic and aleatory, i.e., disjoining the overall field into divisions involving degrees of belief (encompassing inductive probabilism) and those involving games of chance (involving frequencies and statistical calculation). Epistemic theories include those of Keynes and Harold Jeffreys at the one extreme (representing logical interpretations) and Frank Ramsey, Leonard Savage, and Bruno de Finetti at the other (representing personalist, belief-based views); aleatory theories include those of Richard von Mises, A. N. Kolmogorov, and John Venn. (This classification, applied not to categories of probability, but rather to uncertainty, will be of central importance in later discussions of import to economic theory.)

A particular probability interpretation may be appraised as both aleatory and epistemic, or belong to neither category; i.e., the two categories are neither mutually exclusive nor exhaustive. Of the probability theories to be reviewed, the personalist theory of Emile Borel, for example, is epistemic (since probability is degree of belief) and also aleatory (measuring probability with respect to betting and the laying of odds).[43] For this reason a different classificatory scheme may be more useful.

Wesley Salmon (1967) considered five types of probability: classical, subjective, frequency, logical, and personal. Weatherford (1982) catalogued four (combining the subjective and the personal). Savage (1972) divided schools of probability into three more explanatory categories: necessarian, personalist, and frequentist. Tony Lawson (1988) divided economic uses of probability into two types: those which regard probability as a *form* of knowledge (the epistemic), and those which regard it as an *object* of knowledge (the aleatory). Those advocating probability as a *form* of knowledge see probabilities as that 'which agents *possess*, or *attach* to particular propositions,'[44] while those advocating probability as an *object* of knowledge view 'probabilities as something to be *discovered*, *learned* about, and *known*'[45] (Lawson, 1988, p. 40). This epistemological division is not that expressed here, not because of a lack of interest or acceptance, but because probabilists and philosophers of science have at hand a readily acceptable classification that is more explanatory.[46] For purposes of the present, it is to the Savage categories that reference will be made, mention being made, in passing, of the classical theory as exemplified in the presentations of Laplace and Bernoulli. Each will be explained in its turn.

PRELIMINARIES TO PROBABILITY

Prior to initiating a discussion of the various definitions and interpretations of probability, it is necessary to establish a set of axioms common in some form to all interpretations, and to state some mathematical preliminaries which will serve as foundations. Later, in the discussions of the specific interpretations of probability, additional axioms and supplementary propositions will be made known that result from the various peculiar specifications.

Given a and b, where a is a hypothesis or conclusion and b is evidence or premises, $P(a \mid b)$ is established as the single 'undefined notion' of conditional probability. Let $A = \{a, b\}$, where a and b are any two hypotheses. The following axioms are stipulated and are for the most part self-explanatory: (see especially Russell, 1948, pp. 345–6):

Axiom 1: there exists a unique value of $P(a \mid b)$ where such a value can be defined; probability is a single-valued function (property of existence)

Axiom 2: $0 \leqslant P(a \mid b) \leqslant 1$ (property of non-negativity)

Axiom 3: if b implies a, then $P(a \mid b) = 1$ (property of certainty)

Axiom 4: if b implies not $-a$, then $P(a \mid b) = 0$ (property of impossibility)

Axiom 5: $P[(a \cap b) \mid b] = P(a \mid b) \cdot P[b \mid (a \cap b)]$
$$= P(b \mid b) \cdot P[a \mid (b \cap b)]$$
(the axiom of conjunction, or the product axiom)

(5a) if a and b are independent propositions, then Axiom 5 becomes: $P[(a \cap b) \mid b] = P(a \mid b) \cdot P(b \mid b)$

Axiom 6: $P[(a \cup b) \mid b] = P(a \mid b) + P(b \mid b) - P[(a \cap b) \mid b]$ (the axiom of disjunction)

(6a) if a and b are disjoint (i.e., if $a \cap b = \varnothing$), then $P[(a \cap b) \mid b] = 0$ and the disjunction axiom becomes the axiom of addition, i.e., $P[(a \cup b) \mid b] = P(a \mid b) + P(b \mid b)$

It should be noted that (5a) and (6a) are not technically axioms, but are postulates derived from the axioms given certain stipulations: independence for (5a) and mutual exclusivity for (6a). The distinction is crucial for the necessarian theory of Keynes, especially in regard to the independence postulate (5a). While all of the axioms are valid universally, the postulates need not be so.

Of course, it should be remembered that these axioms are valid as stated, unqualified, for a finite set of elements of A, i.e., in the case where $A = \{a_1, a_2, \ldots a_n\}$. A *probability measure* is defined then as a function satisfying axioms (1), (2), (3), and (6a), i.e., it is a finite, non-negative, finitely-additive function.[47] In conjunction with the above-listed axioms must be defined the notion of order, partial and total. A binary relation (i.e., one that holds between any two propositions or arguments) R on a set A is defined as a partial order if:[48]

(1) for every $a \in A$, a R a (reflexivity)
For every $a, b, c \in A$,
(2) if a R b and b R c, then a R c (transitivity)
(3) if a R b and b R a, then $a = b$ (antisymmetry)

If the set A is partially ordered, and if for all $a, b \in A$, $a \neq b$, either a R b or b R a (i.e., the set is *connected*[49]) then the set is *totally-ordered*.[50] So it is possible that, under the stipulation of the partial order, for some $a, b \in A$, neither a R b nor b R a obtains (i.e., some a and b may be non-comparable). In what follows, as in most economic applications, the relation R is taken to be the weak ordering '$\leqslant$'.

As Paul Halmos (1944) has shown, finite additivity may be too restrictive an assumption, although Savage (1972) adjudged it well-suited to a definition of probability; countable additivity is in fact a postulate of Halmos's theory of probability, serving only as a special case of Savage's. Countable additivity is valid in defining a probability function so long as it is understood that $P(A) = 1$, i.e., the sum of the probabilities over the entire set equals unity, and that the space upon which P is defined is such that any set of measure zero is identical to the null set.[51] Unless this is admitted, it may be possible to admit that $P(A) = 0$. (Halmos, 1944, pp. 497–9). So, if unique, 'surprise' events are taken as identical in measure to the null set, the countable additivity postulate is valid.

To show the validity of the axioms as stated, one may readily calculate a form of Bayes' theorem, to which reference will be made later.
From Axiom 5:

$$P[(a \cap b) \mid h] = P(b \mid h) \cdot P[a \mid (b \cap h)]$$

It then follows that:

$$P[a \mid (b \cap h)] = P[(a \cap b) \mid h] / P(b \mid h)$$

Now again by Axiom 5:

$$P[(a \cap b) \mid h] = P(a \mid h) \cdot P[b \mid (a \cap h)]$$

Therefore:

$$P[a \mid (b \cap h)] = P(a \mid h) \cdot P[b \mid (a \cap h)] / P(b \mid h)$$

Let the sample space be partitioned into k mutually-exclusive non-null subsets. Then, by definition:

$$P(b \mid h) = U_{i=1 \to k} \, P[(b \cap a_i) \mid h]$$

Now, by Axiom 6 and postulate (6a):

$$P(b \mid h) = \Sigma_{i=1 \to k} \, P[(b \cap a_i) \mid h]$$
$$= \Sigma_{i=1 \to k} \, P(a_i \mid h) \cdot P[b \mid (a_i \cap h)]$$

(by Axiom 5). Finally, combining terms:

$$P[a \mid (b \cap h)] = \frac{P(a \mid h) \cdot P[b \mid (a \cap h)]}{\Sigma_{i=1 \to k} \, P(a_i \mid h) \cdot P[b \mid (a_i \cap h)]}$$

which is Bayes's theorem.

The significance of Bayes's theorem cannot be exaggerated; it is the corner-stone of the theory of probability and fundamental to the theory of decision-making under uncertainty. It will be shown in the discussion which follows that, through an examination of the various interpretations of probability, these being the necessarian, personalist, and frequency approaches, Bayes's theorem is of immense theoretical and practical value as a learning mechanism; in effect, no theory of probability or application thereof has any validity as a guide to action under conditions of uncertainty in its absence. Likewise, usage of Bayes's theorem is necessary (but not sufficient) as a condition for a viable theory of decision and choice. In particular, it will be maintained that such usage entails knowledge of the existence, constitution, and derivation of the prior probability, $P(a \mid h)$. For the three probability types here considered, the prior is either *a priori* or a subjective degree of rational belief (necessarian), strictly a subjective degree of belief (personalist), or is derived experientially (frequentist).[52] In all cases, the use of Bayes's theorem results in a continual refinement in the initial prior probability value, via the use of the calculated posterior probability values, $P[a \mid (b \cap h)]$, which themselves become next-period priors until, through successive iteration, convergence to some value results.

CLASSICAL AND FREQUENTISTIC THEORY

Under the classical interpretation of probability (itself dating back at least to Aristotle),[53] probability is definable as a single, unique value, being the ratio of actual (favorable) to possible types of occurrences in a sufficiently well-defined sequence of events, where each case is assumed *a priori* equally possible.[54] The idea of restricting the appropriateness of probability to a sequence of equally possible cases is of great significance, especially as it applies to games of chance (wherein the possibilities are known in advance, by virtue of the composition of the gaming device) or situations of inherent ignorance. This Principle of Equipossibility, in conjunction with the Principle of Non-Sufficient Reason, which refers to the lack of any method or rationale for preferring (or differentiating) one probability value over any other,[55] are the principal defining propositions of the classical theory of probability.

Of all the writings in the classical tradition, perhaps the most accepted and best-established work in the area is that of Pierre Simon Laplace. In his 1820 *Philosophical Essay on Probabilities* (initiated in 1795), Laplace set forth the definitive statement of classical probability and the doctrine of necessity.[56]

Truth is the basis of Laplacian probability. The universe which the Laplacian posits as the basis for his view of the world is closed and determinate; the world of natural phenomena is reducible to deterministic laws, and these laws are furthermore objective and discoverable. Anyone who is so predisposed may unlock the secrets of nature and so discover for himself these immutable principles. The only barrier to the attainment of 'truth,' to the possession of full and complete knowledge and understanding of the workings of nature, is the constitution of the potential discoverer. The only hindrances which combine to prevent the discovery of truth are the lack on the part of the individual of enough information and the correct type of information, and the capacity with which to process it. Things are as they are of necessity; it is up to the individual to discern the underlying causal reality.[57]

Classical (Laplacian) probability is not concerned with the concrete reality, the necessity of the world as it is; it is concerned specifically and solely with the individual's subjective *apprehension* of this reality. The acceptance that the universe is determinate is reason enough to believe that we are capable of unlocking its secrets. Our inability to do so is a result of our own shortcomings. The classical interpretation of probability, predicated on determinism, on a mechanical view of nature, provided a 'scientific' foundation by which we may eventually 'know' (deductively) that which we accept only as 'belief.'

Among the achievements of classical probability was the elucidation by Jacques Bernoulli, another of the great classical probabilists, of a limit theorem, a 'law of large numbers', by which the 'certainty' of a probability value is assured in the limit, as the size of the random sample (taken as indicative of the total universe) increases; the probability that the sample mean will equal the true mean, differing only by an arbitrarily small constant, is, in the limit, equal to unity. Symbolically,[58]

$$\lim_{n \to \infty} \text{prob}\left[\,|\,(\Sigma_i x_i/n) - \mu\,| < \varepsilon\right] = 1,$$

where μ is the 'true' mean, $\Sigma_i x_i/n$ is the 'sample' mean, and ε is an arbitrary constant.[59]

Bernoulli's theorem has, in classical probability theory, been interpreted as suggesting an underlying empirical order within chance observations. For Laplace, this theorem is not applicable only to games of chance or well-defined experimental situations, but is a general result, applicable to both natural and social phenomena. Single events viewed in isolation from any series from which they may have arisen take on a random character and may be viewed as having arisen by chance. A series of such events over a period of time, on the other hand, possesses a statistical regularity or periodicity which gives the illusion at least of an order arising out of the chaos.[60] Eventually, as the series becomes known, its hidden structure manifests itself. Such regularity is then expressible

31

through reference to natural laws. The universe is determinate, events are characterizable and understandable as the outcomes of specific laws of nature, which are both necessary and immutable.

The reaction to the classical conception of probability was the theory ascribed to the British empirical school, better known as the frequentist school of probability. John Venn, among the best known of the early frequentists and one of the most lucid writers on the subject, established the framework upon which the frequency interpretation rests. In his *Logic of Chance* (1888), Venn defined the concept of a 'series' as central to his version of the frequency theory,[61] where a series is a sequence of events each of which possesses certain notable attributes or characteristics. Probability is understandable only so far as it relates to such an extended (infinite) sequence of repetitive events. The series is a prerequisite for probability as frequency; probability is meaningful only in consideration of the presence of an attribute within a given extended series. Any attempt to determine the probability of the occurrence of an event (i.e., to assign to such occurrence a numerically valued probability) must presuppose the existence of a series of which the event is part. Unique, one-time occurrences are by themselves outside of the realm of reflection as they belong to no discernible series; they are of relevance only so far as they belong to *some* extended sequence which can be defined and constructed.[62] Probability may then be defined with respect to the ratio of favorable to possible cases in an empirical series of infinite length. Probability is the limiting value of the 'relative frequency with which certain events or properties recur' within a sequence of observations, wherein the sequence is of infinite length (R. von Mises, 1957, p. 22).[63] The superiority of the frequency conception of probability over the classical interpretation lies in abandoning reliance on the *a priori* condition of equipossibility; it allows for the possibility of bias and indeterminism (Venn, 1888, p. 163).[64]

Probability as frequency is applicable to a series which 'combines individual irregularity with aggregate regularity' (ibid., p. 14). The single events of experience may seem completely random (read 'patternless') but the series of which they are part is stationary and regular. Systemic order prevails out of individual chaos.[65] But this begs another question: Is the eventual stationarity true of *all* sequences of events, or are there characteristics which must hold for this position to be valid? In other words, are there some series which are by their very nature non-stationary? Venn's 'answer' required that he distinguish between 'natural uniformities' (empirically observable series occurring in nature) and those uniformities arising from games of chance. The distinction centers on the question of stability: ' . . . whereas natural uniformities at length fluctuate, those afforded by games of chance seem fixed for ever' (ibid., p. 16). Only the latter type of series is truly amenable to analysis on the frequency view. In games of chance, scientific inference is possible because such an aggregate regularity (in fair games) is readily apparent; chance affords an objective, homogeneous, stationary series. In empirically observable series, on the other hand, series chosen from a potentially unstable natural environment, such homogeneity and regularity may not be in evidence. One cannot *a priori* assume stability; rather one must be alert to the possibly chaotic nature of any empirical series which may, over the short and the long run, generate patterns for which a probability distribution does not exist or one which generates no discernible pattern whatsoever.[66] Too many unobservables may impinge on the series under investigation, and account is not easily taken of these extraneous elements. Well-behaved, homogeneous, objective series are amenable to analysis; behavioral series, by their nature subjective, may be too 'noisy' to allow even modest inferences to be derived.

Initially, the two types of series appear alike; only later, in the ultimate stages of the processes, does divergence occur. Both series

> are alike in their initial regularity, alike in their subsequent regularity; it is in what we may term their ultimate form that they begin to diverge from each other. The one tends without any irregular variation towards a fixed numerical proportion in its uniformity; in the other the uniformity is found at last to fluctuate, and to fluctuate, it may be, in a manner utterly irreducible to rule.
>
> (ibid., pp. 16–17)

In referring to the use of probability in the realm of human behavior, Venn noted this peculiarity of empirical series, viz., that it is not always possible to measure accurately an individual's subjective degree of belief in an argument or proposition due to the influence of emotions, surprise, passion, caprice, etc., defining aspects of the person which cannot be removed from the human constitution. There are simply too many states and countervailing tendencies to allow for the complete enumeration of a homogeneous reference class necessary to parameterize beliefs. Even if it were possible, Venn thought the cost to be too great, since then it 'would be almost equivalent to saying that whilst we profess to consider the whole quantity of our belief we will in reality consider only a portion of it' (ibid., p. 125). The extraneous constituent parts would have to be constrained, resulting in a series which, while purporting to deal with the constitution of human behavior, in effect represents only a (perhaps) inconsequential aspect.

Coincident with the impossibility of accounting for uniqueness or uncertainties which may influence belief is the 'complexity and variety of the evidence on which our belief of any proposition depends' (ibid., p. 126). It may be impossible to gauge accurately at any given point in time the true nature of any single belief 'so that we can scarcely even get sufficiently clear hold of it to measure it' (ibid., p. 126).[67]

This difficulty with measurement required Venn to modify slightly his definition of a series, to create what is in effect an 'ideal' series for which measurement could then be applied:

The series we actually meet with are apt to show a changeable type, and the individuals of them will sometimes transgress their licensed irregularity. Hence they have to be pruned a little into shape, as natural objects almost always have before they are capable of being accurately reasoned about. The form in which the series emerges is that of a series with a fixed type. This imaginary or ideal series is the basis of our calculation.

(ibid., pp. 119–20)

... it is to be recognized as a necessary substitution of our own for the actual series, and to be kept in as close conformity with facts as possible. It is a mere fiction or artifice necessarily resorted to for the purpose of calculation, and for this purpose only.

(ibid., p. 120)

Subjective considerations must enter when the situation involves actual decision-making among alternatives.[68] Objective frequencies alone are not sufficient as a basis for action. In this instance, probability valuation (the calculation of the frequency of occurrences) provides only a criterion upon which judgment and action may be based. It is up to the individual to decide how to incorporate the probability values into a decision matrix. As Venn stated:

... all which Probability discusses is the statistical frequency of events, or, if we prefer so to put it, the quantity of belief with which any one of these events should be individually regarded, but leaves all the subsequent conduct dependent upon that frequency, or that belief, to the choice of the agents.

(ibid., p. 137)

The entire notion of a scale of rationally-determined degree of belief was for Venn not conceivable without recourse to experience, since such beliefs could not otherwise be proven either correct or erroneous. What was required was some tangible reality to which the degree of belief could be associated, and thereby checked for validity.

The degree of belief we entertain of a proposition may be hard to get at accurately, and when obtained may be often wrong, and may need therefore to be checked by an appeal to the objects of belief. Still in popular estimation we do seem to be able with more or less accuracy to form a graduated scale of intensity of belief.

(ibid., pp. 138–9)

Experience will test whether any proposition is true so long as the degree of belief in the proposition is such as to be inconsequential: tests of scientific hypotheses are (and must be) conducted irrespective of the belief of the investigator in the veracity of the proposition under investigation. In this respect the individual may be said to have 'full belief' in the proposition. Even in games of chance where the object (die, coin, card, etc.) is of such a constitution as

34

to allow mathematical calculation of the chance of occurrence (so that a probability value could be assumed *a priori* based on the form and design of the object), there must be still recourse to experience, owing to the myriad of outside effects and influences which may serve to force deviations from the probabilities otherwise calculable in the case of an ideal object.

Even the Principle of Sufficient Reason as set forth by Venn, that, given that certain instances (events) occur equally often, combinations of these instances will as well occur equally often, was not to be taken as an *a priori* law, but rather as a principle empirically derived and verifiable (ibid., p. 83). Although its use was to be restricted initially to narrow limits, it was seen as possible to extend it to less narrowly defined limits, and then to infer universal validity by reverting to the 'rule by Induction and Analogy' (ibid., p. 83). In these instances, however, the best that can be achieved is 'a qualified assent' (ibid., p. 84).

Partial belief is of a different type. In the case of a single event 'no justification of anything like quantitative belief is to be found' (ibid., p. 143). No event will partially occur; even mathematical expectation gives no answer.

Single events, as alluded to previously, are capable of examination only insofar as they are part of a well-defined and homogeneous series or, more accurately, a homogeneous reference class. The single event has for Richard von Mises, another of the leading expositors of the frequency view, 'no "probability" at all', since the collective of which it is a part has not been defined (R. von Mises, 1957, p. 19). When addressing the probability or improbability of events, reference must be made to the series or the collective or the reference class. For Venn, unique events, although belonging to a possible infinity of series, or to no series whatever, are capable, notwithstanding the lack of a specified reference class, of being so ordered has to allow justification of a type of belief (Venn, 1888, pp. 147–8).[69]

> ...the different amounts of belief which we entertain upon different events, and which are recognized by various phrases in common use, have undoubtedly some meaning. But the greater part of their meaning, and certainly their only justification, are to be sought in the series of corresponding events to which they belong; in regard to which it may be shown that far more events are capable of being referred to a series than might be supposed at first sight.
>
> (ibid., p. 150)

There are some elements, however, which must be eliminated from incorporation into series which determine the formation of inferences, except when they are such as may constitute a uniform series. One such group considered for exclusion includes all those ideas and beliefs which are termed collectively 'emotions.' However, the element of 'surprise' may not be excluded due to its constant conjunction with other elements comprising the notion of probability. As Venn described it, 'surprise' behaves in a quite uniform manner and is essentially 'free from that extreme irregularity which is found in most of the other mental conditions which accompany the contemplation of unexpected events' (ibid., pp. 157–8). Venn noted further that

> ... our surprise ... having no proper claim to admission into the science of Probability, is such a constant and regular accompaniment of that which Probability is concerned with, that notice must often be taken of it.
>
> (ibid., p. 158)

The distinction between 'emotion' and 'surprise' is then that emotion refers to a mental state while surprise is contingent upon the occurrence of an event and is a concomitant of the event; the degree of surprise therefore reflects an indication of the degree of belief held in the possibility of the occurrence or non-occurrence of the event (or in the truth of a proposition), expressible after it is known whether the event has or has not occurred (or after the veracity of the proposition has been shown).

Statements for which the frequency interpretation is of value are those which are independent of any type of belief; such statements are true or false irrespective of whether they are believed to be so, and so are of a completely objective nature. The frequency interpretation is thus completely devoid of any reference to the degree of belief or knowledge concerning the outcome of a future event.

NECESSARIAN (LOGICAL) THEORY

The logical or necessarian theory of probability[70] is most closely associated with John Maynard Keynes's 1921 *Treatise on Probability*, itself an enlarged version of his 1909[71] fellowship dissertation at King's College, Cambridge. In order to fully appreciate Keynes's contribution to the theory of probability, it is important to recognize from whence he came. At the time Keynes wrote on the subject, probability was dominated by the work of the frequentists. The most dominant among these writers was Venn. Keynes criticized Venn in particular and the frequentists in general for having identified 'probability' with 'statistical frequency' (Keynes, 1921, p. 103).[72] The calculation of the frequency of the attributes in a given series or reference class was for Venn the only valid definition of probability, since other uses of the term involved invoking subjective motives and beliefs which were neither measurable nor especially interesting. Keynes's criticism of the frequency view centered on his supposition that incomplete knowledge necessitates recourse to an *a priori* principle (or some such similar criterion) from which may be deduced an initial probability value, and through which a comparison of propositions may be entertained. The frequency interpretation (unlike the classical one) needs no *a priori* proposition as a base; neither can it support one. Instead it relies solely on experience and empirical phenomena for the determination of a probability value. While acknowledging the valuable role played by experience, Keynes felt it insufficient by itself to serve anything but a supporting function; experience could not form the foundation of a probability theory. A theory of probability, because it represents a method by which one intuits a conclusion based on incomplete knowledge, cannot rely on calculations arising from a reference class which is itself imperfect; a probability theory must be founded upon a firmer, more precise foundation: 'Where our experience is incomplete, we cannot hope to derive from it judgments of probability without the aid either of intuition or of some further *a priori* principle' (ibid., p. 94). In many situations, experience is unlikely to provide a ready stationary and homogeneous series.

To this objection Keynes provided a ready solution. This solution revolved around probability as part of the field of logic. Keynesian probability is essentially a *relational* calculus. According to Keynes, logical arguments are of two types, conclusive and inconclusive. Conclusive arguments are those of which the certainty of a proposition (the conclusion) is intuitive or demonstrative; the conclusion is certain and is entailed by the premises. This is the realm of pure knowledge (as distinct from belief). Inconclusive arguments are those in which a proposition (the conclusion) stands in a relation of less than certainty to the evidence while still possessing a claim to some *degree* of certainty. The 'belief' held in a proposition lies somewhere along a continuum extending from 'pure ignorance' to 'pure knowledge'. 'Rational belief' is coextensive neither with certainty nor with truth; such a belief may be certain or only probable.[73] A rational belief may then be held about a proposition the truth or falsity of which is unknown. Only when rational belief is certain is it to be regarded as knowledge, and for this reason knowledge in Keynes's system is fundamental, gradations of rational belief being defined in relation to it.[74]

All judgments of probability are relative to the knowledge possessed about a given proposition, while the probability relations are logical constructs.[75] Let h represent the premises of an argument; that is, h represents the complete available knowledge (full information) set of the individual (not to be confused with the certain knowledge of a proposition) at any point in time. (h then is termed an *evidential proposition*.) Let a represent the conclusions. Then a stands in relation to h, i.e., a R h. The evidential statements are easily seen to be inseparable from the conclusions derived. Specify R as the relation of probability, P. Then a P h represents the primitive, undefined, *conditional* probability relation.

The proposition a, which Keynes termed the *primary proposition*, may be known directly or indirectly through knowledge of a set of evidential propositions or premises, h. The primary proposition is derivative from the evidentiary statement. The connecting link is the *secondary proposition*, $a \mid h$; it is an assertion that a probability relation exists (ibid., p. 11). Knowledge, in contradistinction to probability, requires that one possess direct and certain apprehension of the proposition a (so that a is self-evident) or, failing that, that the proposition h be known with certainty and that a secondary proposition is

37

known which states a certainty relation. The proposition a is known in this second instance with certainty, but this knowledge is indirect; it is gained by argument. Keynes termed this, the direct or indirect certain knowledge of a, the knowledge *of* the proposition a (ibid., pp. 11–15, 17). In this instance, $P = 1$. Probability, or the degree of rational belief in a proposition of less than certainty, is less well-defined, but appears to be also of two forms: either the secondary proposition is known with certainty and nothing is known about a, or h is known as certain but the secondary proposition is a probability relation.[76] The *probability relation* itself, it must be stressed, does not depend upon the evidence; the *magnitude of this probability* is, however, determined relative to evidence. This Keynes termed knowledge *about* the proposition a (ibid., p. 13). Here, $P < 1$.

Keynes defined the conditional probability of a given h, $a \mid h$, as equal to α, where α is the degree of rational belief in the conclusion a brought about through knowledge of its relation to the premises h.[77] As h represents the complete relevant information or knowledge of the individual, he will not entertain a degree of rational belief of less than α; the degree of rational belief depends on *all* of the evidence available at the time the judgment is made. To illustrate, let $h_1 \subset h$ (i.e., h_1 is an alternative set of premises representing incomplete knowledge for an individual at a given point in time, while h is complete and absolute knowledge of this same individual). Then the degree of rational belief in a proposition based on such incomplete knowledge, for the present termed α' $(= P(a \mid h_1))$, is inconsistent with the degree of rational belief, α, based on more complete information (Russell, 1948, pp. 376–7; Keynes, 1921, ch.1). The partial evidence h_1 can then only be defined as the complete relevant knowledge of the individual at a different (earlier) point in time.

For Keynes, probability is not a concept amenable to categorization as objective or subjective, but comprises elements of both. Probability is a subjective concept in the sense that a proposition is capable of standing in relation to knowledge in varying degrees and is therefore dependent upon the knowledge to which it relates; the circumstances in which the actor finds himself are subjective. It is objective in that once the evidence is given, probability judgment is no longer 'subject to human caprice'.[78] The objective component pertains to the probability relation itself. Once the facts are in, what is probable is determined objectively via the probability relation, the secondary proposition, and not related solely to opinion. Probability values are in a sense the product of a mechanical 'black box' process. 'The theory of probability is logical, therefore, because it is concerned with the degree of belief which it is *rational* to entertain in given conditions, and not merely with the actual beliefs of particular individuals, which may or may not be rational' (Keynes, 1921, p. 4).

The subjective element in Keynes' interpretation enters through the choice (circumstances) of the premises ('evidence,' in Carnap's terminology) with respect to which the conclusion (hypothesis) is related with a degree of rational belief. This degree of rational belief is not itself subjectively determined; the subjectivity is reflected primarily in the differences in evidence (or knowledge) existing among and between individuals; it is reflective of differences in circumstance. This evidentiary differential affects perception and apprehension and hence the derivation of the degrees of belief in the propositions. The premises may then be termed knowledge-dependent. That this is so is evident from Keynes's remarks, wherein he wrote explicitly of the inherently subjective nature of opinion and knowledge:

> We cannot speak of knowledge absolutely – only of the knowledge of a particular person. Other parts of knowledge – knowledge of the axioms of logic, for example – may seem more objective. But we must admit, I think, that this too is relative to the constitution of the human mind, and that the constitution of the human mind may vary in some degree from man to man. What is self-evident to me and what I really know, may be only a probable belief to you, or may form no part of your rational beliefs at all. And this may be true not only of such things as *my* existence, but of some logical axioms also.
>
> (ibid., p. 18)

> What we know and what probability we can attribute to our rational beliefs is, therefore, subjective in the sense of being relative to the individual.
>
> (ibid., p. 19)

Keynes made it clear in advancing his epistemological position that knowledge is not absolute since it is impressed upon the mind through sensation or perception, which must of course differ among individuals as their cognitive and perceptual skills differ. All knowledge is subjective, unique to the individual; even knowledge of the axioms of logic so far as it is relative varies according to the intellectual capacities of the individual and the composition of the individual's belief system. The axioms are under this interpretation perceived 'relative to the constitution of the human mind' (ibid., p. 18). Yet the subjectivity and relativity of knowledge and opinion do not obviate the existence of a logical structure upon which arguments can be constructed:

> But given the body of premises which our subjective powers and circumstances supply to us, and given the kinds of logical relations, upon which arguments can be based and which we have the capacity to perceive, the conclusions, which it is rational for us to draw, stand to these premises in an objective and wholly logical relation.
>
> (ibid., p. 19)

Although a particular universe of reference may be defined by considerations which are partly psychological, when once the universe is given, our theory of the relation in which other propositions stand towards it is entirely logical.

(ibid., p. 142)

The meaning of these statements is clear: although the premises of an argument may be subjectively ascertained, the conclusions derived are objectively determined through the use of the logical calculus. [80] In this regard Keynes followed Gottfried Leibniz, who suggested the application of syllogistic logic to the study of probabilities. It is for this reason that Keynes's probability theory may be termed subjective epistemic necessarianism. [81]

It may be objected that Keynes is involved in a contradiction as to the logical nature of probability, and indeed objections along these lines have been raised by, among others, F. P. Ramsey (1926) and R. B. Braithwaite (1973). The objections highlight an inconsistency as to the status of the probability relation, viz., whether the probability relation is objective and the probability value subjective, or whether the probability relation itself is subjective. Rod O'Donnell (1989) claimed to have 'resolved' the apparent contradiction by asserting that, as with Keynes, individuals possess but limited logical ability or insight (O'Donnell, 1989, pp. 64-6). He could then contend that no contradiction would ensue if it were accepted that (1) the perceptive powers of individuals in regard to logical analysis are not uniform, but differ among them; and (2) there may be a general limitation on the powers of individual reason. This is significant in explaining Keynes's insistence that even knowledge of the axioms of logic is relative. The logical relations of probability may be objective, but are perceived subjectively. [82]

There must then be three aspects to Keynesian probability: the logical relation, which is objective; the *knowledge* of this relation, the manner in which it is perceived, which is relative and subjective; and the knowledge of the central propositions or premises of an argument (the evidence), from which conclusions are derived with respect to the probability relation, which is also subjective (Keynes, 1921, p. 19). The objective aspect of Keynesian probability is thus defined solely with respect to the probability relation itself. The *relation* is objective; the *judgment* is subjective. The probability relations are neither certain nor probable; only their relation to knowledge is expressible in these terms (ibid., pp. 3-4).

Central to Keynes's general theory of probability is the notion that probability cannot be restricted in definition to being a measurable function, [83] and so it is not sufficient to confine it definitionally (as did the frequentists) to such a restrictive class of functions. Probability in the most general sense (which was the way in which Keynes viewed it) allows for the inclusion of elements of measure zero, i.e., it allows for the possibility of unique instances, which cannot be eliminated from the set of probable events. In short, it accommodates surprise. It also needs account, at least at a philosophical (epistemological) level, for unknown measures for which even the relation of probability is beyond comprehension.[84] There may be instances in which we simply do not possess sufficient mental prowess, i.e., a sufficient outfit of powers of intuition, to allow for apprehension of the probability relation. Numerical measurement in general as applied to such situations for obvious reasons Keynes believed untenable.[85]

Thus a justification for the construction of a 'probability-relation' must require more than simply the measurability accepted by classical and frequency theorists (and, as will be seen, by the personalists as well). It requires an acuity on the part of the individual sufficient to intuit the underlying relation:[86]

> We might, that is to say, pick out from probabilities (in the widest sense) a set, if there is one, all of which are measurable in terms of a common unit, and call the members of this set, and them only, probabilities (in the narrow sense). To restrict the term "probability" in this way would be, I think, very inconvenient.
>
> (ibid., p. 36)

So, in Keynes's theory the finite-additivity postulate, upon which much mainstream probability theory is based, is replaced by countable additivity in the general construction, and a measure space is then defined as but a partition of the totality.

Even given his agnosticism as to the valuation of probabilities, Keynes did not wish to suggest that one should rule out completely any comparisons of probabilities, nor did he deny the possibility of comparisons of non-numerical probabilities. Comparisons are possible between non-numerical and numerical probabilities 'by means of *greater* and *less*, by which in some cases numerical limits may be ascribed to probabilities which are not capable of numerical measures' (ibid., p. 132). The most that could be said is that the elements of comparison are capable of standing in an order relation: 'Objects can be arranged in an order, which we can reasonably call one of degree or magnitude, without its being possible to conceive a system of measurement of the differences between the individuals.' (ibid., p. 22). Although numerical measurement may be neither practical nor possible in the majority of instances in which probability is viewed as an appropriate mode of analysis, some form of order may be so.[87]

Such an ordering, whereby a standardized scale is constructed and probabilities (non-numerical or numerical) are placed in relation to it, affords only an approximation, not an exact numerical series. Once the ordinal scale is constructed and probabilities ordered, then, as an analogue to numerical measurement and comparison, one may obtain a close approximation. Continuous verification of such an analogue may lead to an ever closer approximation, or a 'practical certainty' in a proposition which, although not amenable to the logical calculus in a way in which logical certainty is (i.e., the contradictory is not impossible), is still of sufficient validity to warrant belief approaching (as a limit) certainty (ibid., p. 177).

Keynesian probability is therefore also definable as an order (a hierarchy) calculus (the probability relation is itself not definable; it is a primitive relation),
but not of the unidimensional form typically considered (i.e., as measured
along a linear continuum [0,1]); rather Keynesian probability is multidimensional. Yet given multidimensionality, i.e., the simultaneous existence of multiple series of probabilities, even the existence of an order relation is by no
means assured. Keynes himself maintained that probability relations may not
even be 'comparable in respect of more or less' (ibid., p. 37).[88] There may well
be inherent tensions or inconsistencies among the various alternatives presented
to the actor for reflection. An event may be equally well represented as
belonging to any of a number of reference classes, each of which will allow for
the calculation of a different value of the probability of occurrence.[89] The alternatives may, for instance, belong simultaneously to more than one (intersecting) series, or belong to mutually-exclusive (non-intersecting) series, or
belong to no series whatsoever. An order may also not be feasible, if the propositions and the probability relation are beyond the comprehension of the individual, or if there is no unique, discernible reference class. Only where a
probability relation is known, and a unique and homogeneous reference class
is manifest, is an order possible.[90] Comparisons of such a type are only feasible
between probabilities 'when they and certainty all lie on the same ordered
series' (ibid., p. 38).[91] Transitivity, for instance, as a defining characteristic of
a partial order, and as a decision axiom (to be discussed in Chapter III), maintains validity only for such a unidimensional comparison. Any and all alternative series consisting of common (coincident) events are non-comparable. All
that is certain when multiple, intersecting series are active is that probability
lies somewhere between certainty and impossibility; along which continuum
and in what relation to other values of probability are questions not readily
answerable.

This led Keynes to stipulate certain properties of ordered series which he
believed were central to his system. These are (ibid., p. 41): (1) every probability lies between certainty and impossibility, and the whole forms an ordered
series; (2) the series is not necessarily or even in most instances compact since
'betweenness' is not a necessary property of a series; (3) the same probability
can belong to more than one series; and (4) if ABC and BCD are ordered series,
where $A < B < C$, and $B < C < D$, then ABCD is also an ordered series. The
consequence of these conditions is that each set of degrees of rational belief
comprises an ordered series, ordered by the relation 'between'; all probabilities
lie between 0 and 1 (designating impossibility and certainty, respectively); and
if A lies between 0 and B (this being termed AB) then $B > A$ and 0A and A1
are true for all probabilities (ibid., pp. 42–3).

Ordering relations and measurability provide principles for a comprehensive
theory of probability. Nevertheless, since mathematical probability is a subset
of the general theory, account must be taken of and allowance made for its
existence and incorporation. To facilitate mathematical probability, Keynes

proposed a set of requirements consistent with the general axioms of probability theory, those of compactness, existence, finite additivity, and independence, requiring that each be defined explicitly. [92] The independence postulate is for Keynes one of the cornerstones of mathematical probability theory; in fact, it holds more importance than measurability.

> Unless, therefore, we are dealing with independent arguments, we cannot apply detailed mathematical reasoning even when the additional probabilities are numerically measurable. The greater part of mathematical probability, therefore, is concerned with arguments which are *both* independent *and* numerically measurable.
>
> (ibid., p. 176)

Keynes' general theory of probability could then be reduced to complementarity with the frequency theory by the inclusion of a few simple axioms and definitions, including specific axioms of addition and multiplication. [93]

Finally, Keynes required a new form of the Principle of Indifference (what had been termed by the classical probabilists the Principle of Non-Sufficient Reason) to act as an *a priori* proposition in respect to the establishment of equipossible alternatives. The Principle as it had been applied in classical and frequency probability maintained that in the absence of any reason for assigning unequal probabilities to each of several propositions, given the state and degree of our knowledge concerning the alternatives, equal ones should be assigned. Here was provided a rationale within the classical interpretation (and the frequency interpretation, where it is termed the Principle of Sufficient Reason) for the numerical measurement of probability. Such a principle presupposes (as, e.g., in Venn) that there exists a complete enumeration of alternatives, and that every probability value is either greater than, less than, or equal to any other; in other words, it presupposes the existence of a complete, total order relation.

Keynes's solution to the problem of requiring an *a priori* condition as a consistency postulate was to distinguish between two types of probability based on evidence and conclusions: (1) situations in which the evidence is the same, but the conclusions reached in respect of the evidence differ; and (2) situations in which the evidence differs, but the conclusions reached are the same (ibid., p. 58). The first type is a judgment of preferences, comparing $x \mid h$ to $y \mid h$. In the case where $x = y$ (more correctly, where $x \mid h = y \mid h$, i.e., when the conclusions are equivalent based on the same evidence), the two are indifferent. Otherwise, there exists a preference for the one over the other.

The second type is a judgment of the *relevance* of the premises, comparing $x \mid h$ to $x \mid h_1 h$. If the addition of h_1 to the existing evidence h makes no difference to the conclusion, h_1 is termed irrelevant. Otherwise, h_1 is relevant and adds *weight* to the conclusion. [94] The notion of weight was of particular interest to Keynes since it related conceptually to the degree of confidence one could

43

express in a probability judgment as a guide to conduct: the greater the weight, the greater (or more intense) the preference.

It should be mentioned that additional evidence in Keynes's interpretation of probability does not alter the probability based on the evidence initially available; it instead elicits an entirely new probability relation, much in the sense of Carnap's Probability$_1$. The previous relation based on 'yesterday's news,' although valid at the time of its calculation (intuition), is no longer relevant to the situation of today. The change in the evidentiary proposition must lead to a completely different relation. Even so, whereas any additional relevant evidence may increase or decrease the degree of *belief* in a proposition (in the sense of inducing the formation of a new probability 'value'), it will always have the effect of increasing the *weight* of the argument; i.e., there is in the accumulation of additional evidence always 'a more substantial basis upon which to rest our conclusion' (ibid., p. 77). Increased weight, then, is perfectly consistent with increased, decreased, or unchanged values of probability, of degrees of belief; but increased weight always increases the degree of confidence in any conclusion drawn. [95] In other words, increased weight leads *pari passu* to increased validity in the efficacy (but not necessarily the truth) of the proposition; it allows it a greater audience. Weight is a function of the completeness, not the volume, of the evidence. The degree of uncertainty in a proposition can be reduced by the acquisition of more information (i.e., relevant knowledge) and hence lead to an increase in the confidence level, while it is unclear as to the effect of this increased confidence on the probability value. [96]

Keynes's new Principle of Indifference relates directly to the relevant evidence on hand and is therefore applicable to comparisons based on indifference and irrelevance. For the Principle to hold, therefore, '[t]here must be no relevant evidence relating to one alternative, unless there is corresponding evidence relating to the other; our relevant evidence, that is to say, must be symmetrical with regard to the alternatives, and must be applicable to each in the same manner' (ibid., p. 60). To clarify, let $\phi(x)$ and $f(x)$ represent propositional functions, and $x = \{a,b\}$. Then given the propositions $f(a)$ and $f(b)$, $\phi(a)$ and $\phi(b)$ will possess equal credibility (Russell, 1948, p. 387). That is, $P(\phi(a)\,|\,f(a)) = P(\phi(b)\,|\,f(b))$. [97]

Similar considerations apply to Keynes's view of induction. All experiential knowledge is derived inductively. To this end, Keynes seemed receptive to the Humean and Baconian arguments against pure induction, arguing in favor of a form of Baconian 'induction by analogy.' Hume, Keynes maintained, had relied too heavily on the uniformity of instances in his critique of induction; Keynes argued for more variance in the non-essential characteristics, i.e., those characteristics of instances which are not themselves relevant to the subject under study, a consideration ignored by Hume. This Keynes termed the 'negative analogy.' Keynesian induction by analogy therefore involves increasing the *differences* among the instances, increasing the variation among the non-essential characteristics, strengthening the negative analogy (Keynes, 1921, pp. 243, 260).[98] Induction then becomes synonymous with the number of experiments; analogy with likeness. Induction commences with numerous observations, each constituted of similarities to and differences from the others. The Keynesian experimenter concentrates on those elements of likeness, extrapolating likeness in other respects to unobserved cases (ibid., p. 244). Induction by analogy is scientific method; pure induction, induction by enumeration, is the 'crude' method of experience (ibid., p. 260).

Regarding the formal construction, if $\phi(x)$ and $f(x)$ are again propositional functions, each valid for all x, then the functional $g(f,\phi)$ is a 'generalization' about ϕ and f. If a and b satisfy ϕ, then there exists an analogy between them. Specifically, let $p = \phi(a)$ and $q = \phi(b)$ be propositions. Then p and q exhibit a 'positive analogy' since both satisfy ϕ. Now let p be compared to not-q (i.e., ϕ is satisfied by a but not by b). Then, since b does not satisfy ϕ, while a does, there exists between them a 'negative analogy'.[99]

Now let ϕ and f be completely analogous. Then, if ϕ exists, the assertion can be made that f exists also. This is 'induction by analogy.' The functions ϕ and f are analogous (coincident), so the unknown f can be extrapolated from the known ϕ (ibid., p. 249).

PERSONALISTIC THEORY

The personalistic theory of probability, sometimes also referred to as subjective[100] probability, has its genesis (at least in terms of codification) in the work of Emile Borel (1924) and Frank P. Ramsey (1926), and was later refined and expanded upon by Leonard J. Savage (1972).[101] It is this variant of probability theory which is at the heart of current micro- and macroeconomic analysis (i.e., rational expectations as well as the game-theoretic analysis of choice).

Borel's 'A propos d'un traité de probabilités,' published in the *Revue Philosophique* in 1924, is the seminal, albeit virtually completely neglected, statement of the principles of a subjective theory of probability. In this pioneering paper, Borel, as did Keynes, began by differentiating objective from subjective probabilities. Objective probabilities Borel defined as those 'common to the judgments of all the best informed persons,' and may also be referred to as 'probabilities of events' (Borel, 1924, p. 50). These are the probabilities within the domain of the frequency theory; they are but a ratio calculable by anyone and everyone in an identical manner given the requisite reference class and the class of attributes of interest. Such probabilities are constants, given the conditions governing their calculation, but are modifiable through the process of discovery and the acquisition of additional knowledge through the use of Bayes's theorem. Subjective probabilities, on the other hand, are defined as 'those which particularly interest Mr. Keynes,' (ibid., p. 50)[102] and are characterized as having 'different values for different individuals.' These take a less structured form, more on the order of opinion.

Such probabilities are dependent upon the differences in information between individuals, or, in those instances in which the information is identical, the differences in conclusions reached based upon this information.

Probability is then 'relative to a certain body of knowledge . . . but not such that the same abstract knowledge constitutes the same body of knowledge in two distinct human minds' (ibid., p. 51). In this Borel is in agreement with Keynes, and admitted as much:

> This remark of Mr. Keynes is incontestably correct in principle: it is not to be doubted that all of those who reflect and write about probabilities admit it implicitly . . . Observe however that there are cases where it is legitimate to speak of the probability of an event: these are the cases where one refers to the probability which is common to the judgments of all the best informed persons, that is to say, the persons possessing all the information that is humanly possible to possess at the time of the judgements.
>
> (ibid., p. 50)

The most important aspect of Keynes's theory for Borel is that the subjective nature of probability leads not merely to greater precision in the calculation of the probability judgment, but instead leads to its replacement:

> For any modification in the system of knowledge in relation to which probability is defined has as a consequence the modification of this probability. It is no longer a question of making more perfect or precise this probability, but of substituting for it another probability which is entirely different.
>
> (ibid., p. 51)

Probability statements are not to be viewed as augmented or augmentable through the incorporation of additional knowledge. Rather, the new knowledge renders the old probability statement obsolete and replaces it with a new one. Thus far there is agreement between the two positions.

The primary point of contention between Keynes and Borel involves the quantitative aspect of probability judgments, i.e., whether numerical valuation of probabilities is practically feasible. Borel countered Keynes' claim that in the main probabilities are unmeasurable by establishing a situation where subjective judgments could be quantified through the use of betting: 'I can offer a choice between two bets procuring the same advantages in the case of gain . . . . The same method can be applied to all verifiable judgments; it allows a numerical evaluation of probabilities with a precision quite comparable to that with which one evaluates prices.' (ibid., p. 57). Qualitative probability (degrees of rational belief) becomes subject to quantitative evaluation through the imposition of an experimental mechanism which allows for the denotation of a scale of comparison.

Thus Borel sought to establish a method by which, contrary to Keynes's

46

view, probabilities were measurable; those few instances in which a measure could not be obtained were not of great enough interest to warrant a revision of the theory of probability or deny the value of partial measures. 'If these exceptional cases are numerous enough to be worth the trouble, then a new theory must be developed for them besides the classic theory' (ibid., p. 59). Apparently for Borel, they were neither sufficiently numerous nor bothersome.

Frank P. Ramsey expressed a view of probability similar to that of Borel, emphasizing specifically the measurability of probability relations and the elicitation of probability values via the use of behavioristic experimentation; i.e., he stressed reliance on betting procedures[103] as a means of eliciting beliefs. In his 'Truth and Probability' (1926) Ramsey suggested that a probability theory which was dependent on logical relations without itself being a logical relation was preferable to Keynes's system: 'We should thus have a variety of ordinary logical relations justifying the same or different degrees of belief.' (Ramsey, 1926, p. 61). Even so, this was not the type of probability theory Ramsey felt was applicable to experimental situations designed to elicit responses relating to choices among alternatives. A logical theory had its advantages, but in his view one could only measure belief by examining behavior.

Thus at the outset Ramsey established as a goal the task of developing 'a purely psychological method of measuring belief' (ibid., p. 62).[104] Actions are the result of attempts to maximize individual utility, where utility is meant to include all conscious and unconscious desires. Further, such an endeavor must include all forms of belief and not attempt, as Keynes had suggested, to restrict the analysis of probability to that part of belief amenable to numerical measurement. In particular, utility is not restricted to a crude Benthamite pleasure calculus. On the Ramsey view, all belief is measurable; it makes no sense to distinguish between measurable and non-measurable components (risk and uncertainty)[105] since, even were the distinction relevant from a theoretical standpoint, it is not of sufficient import to prevent quantification of that segment of rational belief which is capable of being measured.[106] In essence, all that is required is consistency.

Ramsey did concede, however, the difficulty involved in such a task, allowing two reasons why beliefs may be apportioned different values: (1) 'some beliefs can be measured more accurately than others;' and (2) measurement is ambiguous, and results in 'a variable answer depending on how exactly the measurement is conducted' (ibid., p. 63). To remove these difficulties, the form of measurement to be used had to be precisely defined. Ramsey's solution held that at a minimum a system for the measurement of beliefs had to be one which would allow the experimenter to (1) 'assign to any belief a magnitude or degree having a definite position in an order of magnitudes' (ibid., p. 64), and to (2) 'assign numbers to these degrees in some intelligible manner' (ibid., p. 64). Thus initially Ramsey accepted that to attempt psychological measurement in a manner analogous to that of physical phenomena, a numerical scale had to be constructed which would correspond with what he judged to be the additive properties of degrees of belief.

Ramsey discussed two ways in which such a measurement could be constructed. The first involved the use of subjective degrees of belief; degrees of belief would be equated with 'feeling of conviction' or 'belief-feeling' (ibid., p. 65). This he rejected as leading to values which were non-numerically comparable, and as being (possibly) even counterintuitive.[107] The second proposal dealt with degree of belief as a measure of the individual's preparedness to act upon his belief, i.e., his willingness to accept a 'wager' or 'bet.' It was the latter proposal which Ramsey considered a viable method for the eliciting of degrees of belief.

To account for the ambiguity of measurement, as well as the inherent impossibility of measuring something as vague and indefinable as 'feelings', many of which are not acted upon and therefore are not observable, Ramsey concentrated on effects, the consequences brought about by acting on beliefs. Probability must then deal with 'belief *qua* basis of action' (ibid., p. 67). The beliefs for which probability is appropriate are 'dispositional,' not 'actualized' (ibid., p. 68). They are the beliefs we hold, perhaps unconsciously but which nonetheless are action-oriented. More to the point, they are not the beliefs of the moment, which may be fleeting; they are the beliefs upon which we depend for guidance. Measurement of these beliefs may be undertaken by relating such actions to the willingness of the individual to accept odds in a betting situation similar to that suggested by Borel, but not of the crude monetary variety.[108] For Ramsey, the problem with studying behavior by examining responses to a series of monetary wages was that this method was 'insufficiently general' and too 'inexact' to be practical. In its place he proposed one look at 'goods' and 'bads', which presumably were subject neither to diminishing marginal utility nor risk-avoidance or risk-attraction. The Ramsey measure is instead a psychological one, relating 'goods' to 'bads' and taking note of the odds.

Having established the more practical aspects of his theory, i.e., the manner in which degrees of belief may be elicited and measured, Ramsey then felt obliged to refine his method, specifically dropping the additivity and measurability assumptions in favor of an axiomatization based on the concept of an 'ethically-neutral' proposition. An 'ethically-neutral' proposition is defined as a proposition the truth or falsity of which is irrelevant to the individual as it enters into propositions which are important (ibid., p. 73). This proposition is given a value of 1/2. Based on a series of axioms and theorems which stipulate relations between 'worlds' ('states') and the ethically-neutral proposition, Ramsey formed a basis for measuring beliefs. Preference gives an ordering relation which Ramsey concluded is in a one-to-one correspondence with the real numbers (ibid., p. 75). Measurability is accomplished with relatively few restrictions, and probability theory is placed on as logical a foundation as is mathematics.

Being a theory of decision-making based entirely on 'feelings' or 'convictions' as to the propositions in question, Ramsey needed no *a priori* justification. He could then dispense with any Principle of Indifference altogether:

> we do not regard it as belonging to formal logic to say what should be a man's expectation of drawing a white or a black ball from an urn; his original expectations may within the limits of consistency be any he likes; all we have to point out is that if he has certain expectations he is bound in consistency to have certain others.
>
> (ibid., p. 85)

Consequently Ramsey precluded any knowledge *a priori* of the probability of a proposition; he allowed only that present beliefs coupled with a knowledge of observational evidence could lead backwards to the initial belief. This initial belief is therefore determinable *a posteriori*.

Leonard J. Savage's 1972 *Foundations of Statistics* presented a form of personalism which extended the theories of Borel and Ramsey beyond an analysis of propositions and events to account for decision-making as it concerns the relation of acts to consequences (and justifies behavior through an appeal to consistency) under conditions of uncertainty; this theory is thus not so much a theory of probability as it is a theory of expected utility. Much of Savage's theory is based on the form of personalism developed by Ramsey in conjunction with the theory of utility developed by John von Neumann and Oskar Morgenstern (1953).[109]

In their *Theory of Games and Economic Behavior*, von Neumann and Morgenstern postulated an individual possessing complete information and a totally-ordered preference set, i.e., an individual 'who, for any two objects or rather for any two imagined events, possesses a clear intuition of preference' (von Neumann and Morgenstern, 1953, p. 17). As in Venn, not only will single events be comparable, but also combinations of events. Since cardinal utility[110] was to be the focus of von Neumann-Morgenstern utility theory (as opposed to the ordinalism of Keynesian probability), the frequency theory became essential in order to provide 'the necessary numerical foothold' (ibid., p. 19).[111] Cardinality requires that values be defined only up to a linear transformation; uniqueness guarantees the existence of a numerical scale.[112] However, subjective probability was not completely discounted as invalid, since they noted that it could be incorporated into a theory of utility provided 'the two concepts (probability and preference) can be axiomatized together' (ibid., p. 19n2).[113] *If* the choices are *consistent*, i.e., the decision-maker accepts as a valid description of his behavior the total order relation (specifically, if his ranking is complete and transitive), a cardinal index may be constructed as easily as if the probabilities were objective (i.e., Vennian). This simultaneous axiomatization of utility and subjective probability is precisely that attempted by Savage; Savage needed only the weaker definition of monotonicity, but could retain cardinality.[114]

The difference between the two utility concepts (Savage and von Neumann-Morgenstern) is not consequential. The von Neumann-Morgenstern axioms refer to comparisons among *utilities*; the Savage axioms weigh comparisons among *acts*. For Savage, an act is a function attaching a consequence to each state of the world; an act is thereby identified with its consequences: 'If two different acts had the same consequences in every state of the world, there would . . . be no point in considering them two different acts at all.' (Savage, 1972, p. 14).

A 'consequence' Savage defined as 'anything that can happen.' Let Ω be the set of states of the world (capable of being completely enumerated) and F be the set of consequences. Then an act f is such that $f{:}\Omega{\rightarrow}F$, the act is a function mapping states to consequences. It is this mapping which is central to Savage; the reliance by frequentistic probabilists on consequences leads to a preoccupation with risk as opposed to uncertainty and to reliance on ordinal utility, which Savage classified, after George Stigler (1950), as 'probability-less' theory (ibid., p. 96).

As did von Neumann and Morgenstern, Savage expressed some interest in the possibility of a partial ordering to account for instances of noncomparability, but rejected it in favor of a more restrictive total ordering thought necessary for consistency: 'This [the partial order] would seem to give expression to introspective sensations of indecision or vacillation, which we may be reluctant to identify with indifference' (ibid., p. 21). Savage did not in fact define an ordering with respect to reflexivity; his definition requires only connectedness and transitivity. He maintained that reflexivity played a role only in the partial order, i.e., only for non-comparable elements. Irreflexivity, whereby either $a < b$ or $b < a$, but not both, is the appropriate basis for the definition of a total order relation. It is, however, the partial order which is essential to Keynes; the total order, being more restrictive, guarantees comparability.

This comparability is achieved through a reduction of the universe of possibilities. Savage noted that the universe of propositions under consideration (the 'world') may be reduced in size and complexity by ignoring the non-fundamental distinctions between states of the world, thus allowing elements judged to be of little or no possibility (of measure zero) to be considered as equally unlikely and therefore to be ignored for the purposes of the decision-making process (ibid., pp. 9–10). Nothing in the formal definition of a probability measure would preclude elements of measure zero. [115] However, Savage (as well as Paul Halmos (1944), and A. N. Kolmogorov (1950)) defined probability in such a way that any two subsets of an event set are to be considered identical whose difference has probability zero. The relevant σ-algebra is thus reduced by identifying elements of zero measure with the null class of elements which by definition have probability zero. Savage needed only finite additivity for this obvious reason.

The Savage postulates (P1 to P5 in Savage, 1972) can then be reduced to three relations (leading to implications similar to those of the postulates) to allow compliance with the above-listed established axioms of probability theory. 'Qualitative probability' is then a relation '$\leqslant$' holding for all events B, C, D if and only if (ibid., pp. 31–2):

1 $\leqslant$ is a total ordering
2 if B∩D = C∩D = $\varnothing$, then B $\leqslant$ C iff (B∪D) $\leqslant$ (C∪D) (D does not affect the value of the preferences if it accompanies B and C symmetrically)
3 0 $\leqslant$ B, 0 $\leqslant$ Ω, where Ω is the universal set

Savage defined conditional probability in a similar fashion. If '$\leqslant$' is a qualitative probability (as defined immediately above), and 0 < D, then B $\leqslant$ C, given D iff (B ∩ D) $\leqslant$ (C ∩ D) (ibid., p. 44). This implies that, since an act maps states to consequences, and an event is a set of states, one need consider only events and not consequences. Savage's postulates applicable to acts are then reducible to conditions applicable to events because of this correspondence.

Qualitative probability, in conjunction with the postulate concerning the partitioning of a set (Savage's postulate P6') allows for the numerical measurement of probability (ibid., pp. 33–40).[116] As with Keynes, it is the additional postulate which is necessary to provide the foundation upon which numerical probability (and hence mathematical statistics) may be based.[117]

REMARKS

In the Introduction, the distinction was made between the terms probabilistic and stochastic, and this distinction was said to be crucial for economic modeling.[118] To reiterate, the term 'probabilistic' in the present context refers to incommensurable or measure zero events or propositions, belonging possibly to an infinity of delineable reference classes or to none. In those instances, in which a probability relation is definable, the events (propositions) are representable via an order relation (even though a possible infinity of series may serve as convenient representations). In general, little can be said in regard to comparisons of probability values since the series are multidimensional. These probabilities are the rudimentary probabilities of Keynesian epistemic necessarianism.

'Stochastic' refers to numerical (measurable) probabilities, representable as part of single well-defined series of random events. For such a series a probability relation is defined, and the probability values handled easily via the mathematical probability calculus. This is the area of probability for which the tools of the frequency and personalist interpretations are suited, but is also representative of a subset (albeit a small one) of Keynesian necessarianism. In fact, probability is definable under the frequency and personalist theories only with reference to well-defined measures.

The category 'unknown' is rather more complex. As defined above, as part of the Keynesian interpretation of probability, from which it derives its validity, it implies that knowledge of the logical relation itself, not simply the propositions linked by the relation of probability, is beyond the apprehension of the individual. Not even an order is possible since there is no basis upon which an order may be founded. The 'values' of probability, should they exist at all, are non-measurable and non-orderable because the relation is unknown. Further, it is by no means certain that in this context the concepts of order and measure have any meaning. This area, the 'unknown,' while outside the scope of probability theory proper, is still important in theoretical discussions, and is especially important with respect to Keynesan and Shackelian economics, and must therefore if only for this reason not be neglected. It must be considered if only for completeness.

The term 'uncertainty' has already been employed in this work in two very different contexts: the manifest uncertainty of the environment and the uncertainty of our *apprehension* of the environment (or rather of the signals *generated* by the environment). This is, in other words, a distinction between the mechanical occurrence of the event, and our belief that the event will occur. The terms systemic uncertainty and epistemic uncertainty have been introduced here as descriptive labels, respectively, of these general forms of uncertainty.

However, another, somewhat more descriptive classificatory scheme presents itself which is very similar to that of the above-mentioned one. This scheme divides overall uncertainty into epistemic and aleatory components, and is employed in conjunction with the risk/uncertainty dichotomy to be introduced in the next chapter.[119] Following Lawson (1988), the terms aleatory and epistemic reference probability types, viz., probability as an object of the environment, and probability as a form of knowledge, respectively. Risk and uncertainty denote the degree of commensurability. We have thus four categories: aleatory risk, epistemic risk, aleatory uncertainty, and epistemic uncertainty. 'Aleatory risk' is descriptive of events which fall within the confines of the frequency probability interpretation of Venn; it refers to the intrinsic nature of chance events numerically measurable and thus definable with respect to a stationary, homogeneous series. We may represent this form of uncertainty as having the constitution of a stochastic process. 'Epistemic risk' is descriptive of Keynes's Principle of Indifference (as an *a priori* principle), and the personalist interpretation of probability; it refers to beliefs and apprehensions of chance (random) events which the individual can evaluate and internalize by the subjective application of the numerical probability calculus. We are aware that an event may transpire, and, further, we can each individually arrive at a degree of belief as to its potential for occurrence, for each state of the world can be *a priori* assigned a probability value of occurrence. 'Aleatory uncertainty' would include unique, empirical events for which a reference class may not exist at all; it was referred to above as systemic uncertainty, or the uncertainty of the occurrence of a specific event, such as a natural disaster or a sudden climatic change. The event may have a 'facility' of occurrence, but has not done so in fact (or at the least if it has it is beyond our knowledge). 'Epistemic uncertainty' includes Keynes's general probability interpretation; it takes account of the situations in which we are not capable of forming any belief or opinion due perhaps to the incompleteness of the data set at our disposal. We simply have no reason to conclude that an event is possible let alone probable, for we have no mechanism for ascertaining a reference class, irrespective of whether one actually exists. 'Ignorance' is then the final category of unknown probabilities, and connotes incommensurability as well as the lack of knowledge of the secondary proposition (also part of the Keynesian view of probability). We are ignorant if we not only cannot determine whether a reference class exists for the particular event or proposition, but are equally uncertain about the *procedure* for determining this fact.

Given these definitions, it must be noted that aleatory uncertainty is only strictly defined with respect to the risk category, and epistemic uncertainty seems more tractable as a single category itself. Aleatory means 'depending upon chance,' while epistemic means 'the act of knowing.' Chance implies risk; uncertainty implies lack of knowledge. Therefore, in an effort to avoid confusion, systemic uncertainty will be used to signify the uncertainty in the environment itself and so will encompass aleatory risk and aleatory uncertainty. The terms epistemic risk and epistemic uncertainty, will, however, be employed to denote those instances in which apprehension is limited by information deficiencies (but a personal valuation may be forthcoming), and those instances in which there is no mechanism by which we may arrive at a valuation of belief, respectively. Similarly, aleatory risk and aleatory uncertainty will be employed to denote those instances in which events are serializable and those instances in which they are single, non-seriable occurrences, respectively, when the context is unambiguous.

Finally, a third classification, not dissimilar to the one preferred here, is that advanced by Fritz Machlup. In volume III of his treatise on knowledge in economics, *Knowledge: Its Creation, Distribution, and Economic Significance* (1984), Machlup distinguished between statistical and subjective probability, and the possibility of surprise. Statistical probability (essentially the frequency view) is advocated by those 'with a strongly numerical-empirical bent'; it is 'based on frequencies of occurrence that are assumed to be of enduring significance' (Machlup, 1984, p. 271). Subjective probability is the tool of those 'inclined towards methodological subjectivism' wherein emphasis is placed on 'the businessmen's intuitive judgment' (ibid., p. 271). The difference between the two 'lies in the fact that the former refers only to one given type of occurrence or to outcomes of one given type of action repeated or replicated any number of times.... Where the situation changes rapidly, where conditions in many markets are apt to change, the "probability" of outcomes of particular actions is a subjective, not a mathematical expectation' (ibid., p. 271). The third category, surprise, is that advanced by G. L. S. Shackle. 'Surprise' implies that an outcome occurs which was not contained in the list of all possible alternative outcomes. This will be explored in depth in the chapter on Austrian economics.

The probabilistic and stochastic measures will be the focus of the remainder of this work, the unknown category being confined for the most part to Keynes (although its importance will become manifest in the discussion of Shackle's economics and the Austrians). The importance of these classifications for the comparative study of economic theories will become evident in later chapters.

APPENDIX I

HUME'S STATEMENT OF THE PROBLEM OF INDUCTION

Any discussion of induction and the theory of probability (or more accurately of 'theories' of probability) must include at least a mention of the foundation, the classic statement, of scientific inference, that promulgated by Scottish philosopher David Hume. His 1740 *Treatise of Human Nature* is widely regarded as the classic statement of the problem of induction, for there Hume identified the problem and more importantly stressed the difficulties involved in attempts at solution.

For Hume, induction was not simply inverse deduction, which, were it so, would lead to certain, general laws derivative from particular events or observations. It is not the case that one need simply collect enough evidence over a sufficiently restricted domain (a reference class), with the resultant synthesis being termed a law or statement of causality. Simple induction by enumeration is not a valid method for the derivation of causal relationships. Given a series of observations, one cannot assert that future events (even within the same restricted reference class) will continue in the same pattern, since the observed and unobserved are not logically connected. [120]

Inductions are only contingent, probable conclusions from the event to the reference class. Sensory and experiential phenomena are apprehended only imprecisely, impressing themselves upon the human mind imperfectly and, at times, incongruously. The very nature of human action, human apprehension, militates against any causal necessity, making generalizations at best tenuous: 'Necessity is regular and certain. Human conduct is irregular and uncertain.' (Hume, 1740, Bk.II, Pt.III, sec.I, p. 451). Probable reasoning is conjectural. Uncertainty is an irremovable aspect of human life, it is perhaps even a defining aspect, so that reasoning (discerning) a cause or a general law from observed phenomena (including, most especially, observed human behavior) with certainty is not possible. Applied to the vagaries of human life, probability is the most that can be expected.

The probability ('reasoning from conjecture') Hume described is divisible into two types, cause and chance, the defining characteristic being the degree of certainty appertaining (i.e., the determinateness of the relation). Cause is merely constant conjunction, from which derive beliefs: A is seen to occur always and everywhere in tandem with B, and therefore A may be said to cause B. Causation Hume defined as that 'which produces such a connexion, as to give us assurance from the existence or action of one object, that 'twas follow'd or preceded by any other existence or action' (ibid., Bk.I, Pt.III, sec.II, p. 121). 'Cause' is not an innate relation, but is itself an inductive notion. This, the relation of cause (A) to effect (B), cannot advance knowledge since 'by this means we . . . can only multiply, but not enlarge the objects of our mind' (ibid., sec.VI., p. 136).

Chance by contrast leads to indeterminism. There is no reason to suppose that what we perceive as correlative is in any way causal. A and B may occur together (or follow in temporal succession), but an unseen C may be the causal link. Whereas experience allows for a determination of cause and effect, chance 'is merely the negation of a cause' (ibid., sec.XI, p. 175). As ideas and events are separable, necessary connection cannot be had, especially in the empirical realm. If conjunction is not constant, only likelihood (probability) is possible. Even with constant conjunction, inference to future behavior from past is not with certainty assured, for although two objects have been constantly conjoined in the past, this does not constitute a valid reason to assume they will continue to be so paired in the future; constant conjunction is not enough to justify an inductive inference (ibid., sec.XII, p. 189). It is 'necessary connection' which is most important to causality. Since no cause can be inferred in a situation of chance, indeterminateness and skepticism are the only recourses.

Probable knowledge was distinguished further by Hume in the manner of its apprehension. The distinction is as to whether the environment within which the individual must function is truly uncertain, and so discernible only incompletely, or whether that which exists is known as certain but *perceived* as uncertain. The individual may not fully comprehend his environment, but yet will formulate conjectures based on experience. Probability then is a function of the perceptual and cognitive abilities of those individuals making such judgments as to the character of the 'facts' (ibid., Bk.II, Pt.III, sec.IX, p. 490). It is conditional on the constitutions of those making judgments as to that which they perceive; it is relative to apprehension, not comprehension, for comprehension connotes knowledge while apprehension connotes a less complete belief.

A necessary condition for the existence of Humean chance is not that a causal factor does not exist, but that it be unknown; one cannot ascertain a determinateness from what is presented. This requires a criterion allowing for such a judgment of indeterminateness to hold. Humean chance accepts such a criterion by requiring as an axiom equipossibility and therefore indifference: there can be nothing favoring the occurrence of one event over another, else the favorable factor be taken as a causal one. 'A perfect and total indifference is essential to chance, and one total indifference can never in itself be either superior or inferior to another.' (ibid., Bk.I, Pt.III, sec.XI, p. 176). But still 'there must always be a mixture of causes among the chances, in order to be the foundation of any reasoning' (ibid., p. 177).

But ultimately Hume did not think chance to be of any value: ' . . . what the vulgar call chance is nothing but a secret and conceal'd cause.' (ibid., sec.XII, p. 181). Certain knowledge is therefore possible, if only because it is within our power to divine cause and effect. It is the multiplicity of instances which brings us to the conclusion of certainty. The judgment known as probability is therefore only an ephemeral one, being a judgment held tenuously, as an interim belief, from the procession from ignorance to certainty.

> . . . philosophers observing, that almost in every part of nature there is contain'd a vast variety of springs and principles, which are hid, by reason of their minuteness or remoteness, find that 'tis at least possible the contrariety of events may not proceed from any contingency in the cause, but from the secret operation of contrary causes. This possibility is converted into certainty by farther observation.
>
> (ibid., sec.XII, p. 182)

APPENDIX II

DID KEYNES CAPITULATE TO RAMSEY?

In 1931, Keynes published a tribute to Ramsey in the *New Statesman and Nation*. Part of the tribute reads:

> Ramsey argues, as against the view which I had put forward, that probability is concerned not with objective relations between propositions but (in some sense) with degrees of belief, and he succeeds in showing that the calculus of probabilities simply amounts to a set of rules for ensuring that the system of degrees of belief which we hold shall be a *consistent* system. Thus the calculus of probabilities belongs to formal logic. But the basis of our degrees of belief – or the *a priori* probabilities, as they used to be called – is part of our human outfit, perhaps given us merely by natural selection, analogous to our perceptions and our memories rather than to formal logic. So far I yield to Ramsey – I think he is right. But in attempting to distinguish "rational" degrees of belief from belief in general, he was not yet, I think, quite successful. It is not getting to the bottom of the principle of induction merely to say that it is a useful mental habit.
>
> (Keynes, 1931, p. 407)

Much has been made of this statement, for instance by Bradley Bateman (1988), who insists that it implies a capitulation on the part of Keynes of the very essence of his view of probability, and his subsequent acceptance of the position of Ramsey. Others, for instance Rod O'Donnell (1989), disagree, saying that Keynes's later writings belie any change in his underlying probability theory, which after all was the venue for the elucidation of his epistemology.

As we have already seen, for Keynes the probability *relation*, the secondary proposition, had to be objective; it had to be of the nature of a Platonic reality, the existence of which holds irrespective of experience. It is the linchpin of the Keynesian theory of probability, and the reason for the theory being referred to as a logical theory. By the same token, it is the degree of belief in a given proposition, based on the evidence, which is subjective, and this subjectivity is fundamental. While we may be unable to perceive the probability relation, perhaps due to our 'limited' logical abilities or insights, it is nevertheless always present. This is, noted the Cambridge philosopher G. E. Moore, just as certain as that the wheels of a train do not vanish simply because we no longer see them upon boarding. Conclusions stand objectively in a relation to premises. The subjective beliefs we hold in these conclusions, the *essential* aspect of probability, depends on the nature of the individual.

While Keynes agreed with Ramsey that the basis of degree of belief is subjective, while at the same time believing that 'the calculus of probabilities belongs to formal logic,' he need not have changed his position to arrive at another consistent with Ramsey's. This distinction merely defines the objective and subjective components of probability already in Keynes's theory. What Keynes did not yield is more fundamental: he did not concede that the distinction between belief and 'rational' belief had been established conclusively by Ramsey. Specifically, Keynes did not accept the pragmatic nature of Ramsey's critique. Keynes did not, in other words, think that Ramsey had successfully disaggregated formal from human logic. This is the principal distinction which, if accepted by Keynes, would have marked his departure from his own theory of probability and his acceptance of the ideas of Ramsey and Wittgenstein and Borel, and his acceptance of the philosophy of logical positivism.

III

PROBABILITY AS A
FUNDAMENTAL CONCEPT IN
ECONOMICS

The acceptance in classical economic literature of 'risk' as an economic factor
to which measures could be applied led to efforts at definition, classification,
and characterization. To the classical economists risk was held to be an objective
factor. From Smith to Marshall the general opinion held that systemic uncertainty, although for the most part incommensurable, could, under certain circumstances, be reduced to a measure of risk should the units employed be
properly defined. However, this equation of risk with uncertainty was by no
means accepted completely and unquestioningly. For example, despite the fact
that at times Smith equated uncertainty with risk (1789, esp. Bk.I, Ch.X, Pt.I),
it is not at all clear that this risk was believed measurable quantitatively; the
existence of risk for Smith implied nothing more than the existence of a
non-deterministic environment. The vagaries of the environment within which
economic activity takes place places prohibitive barriers in the way of accurate
economic calculation. Seasonal, cyclical, accidental, and coincidental variation
combine with errors of omission and commission to drive the economic
(cross-sectional) series to randomness.

John Stuart Mill expressed an overall position on economic measurement and
calculation consistent with that of Smith in that both emphasized the value to
be extracted from an analysis of empirical cross-sectional and time-series data
(although they disagreed as to whether unvarying measures were calculable).
An example of such a definable empirical economic series is profits. Profit,
defined by Mill as affording 'a sufficient equivalent for abstinence, indemnity
for risk, and remuneration for the labour and skill required for superinten-
dence' (Mill, 1871, Bk.II, Ch.XV, p. 406), is not a uniform series, but is rather
a composite of disparate series which vary within and among the different
employments of capital. Consistent with a Vennian description of the behavior
of a random empirical series, Mill argued that this particular composite
reference class, while not strictly homogeneous, could be shown to exhibit
stationarity. As Mill stated:

> But though profits thus vary, the parity, on the whole, of different modes
> of employing capital . . . is, in a certain and a very important sense,

maintained. On the average (whatever may be the occasional fluctuations) the various employments of capital are on such a footing as to hold out, not equal profits, but equal expectations of profit, to persons of average abilities and advantages.... If the case were not so, if there were, evidently, and to common experience, more favourable chances of pecuniary success in one business than in others, more persons would engage their capital in the business.... The expectations of profit, therefore... tend to a common average, though they are generally oscillating from one side to the other side of the medium.

(ibid., p. 412)

Averaging smooths the fluctuations in the time series of profits; this smoothing allows comparisons of disparate series whose individual components may be non-comparable between and among series.

But the averaging process is not appropriate to all cases. Economic series differ depending upon the conditions underlying their generation. Some series are more homogeneous than others. In the case of monetary aggregates, the fluctuations are regular and so the series is readily characterizable as a stationary reference class exhibiting stable long-run fluctuations. In the case of agricultural data series, seasonal fluctuations affect the stationarity of the series and so adjustments are required. The non-stationarity dictates that attention be given to short spans to which a correction procedure can be applied. Averaging lengthy series of this type before adjustment is inappropriate and leads only to measurement errors since the seasonal components do not enter the series in a fit and regular manner.

The averaging process alone is also not sufficient to guarantee the degree of stability and homogeneity desired from an empirical data series, both characteristics which are required as prior conditions for the employment of mathematical probability. Neither is the averaging process appropriate to all areas of risk and uncertainty. The uncertainty inherent in the classical model is not reducible to a measure of risk; the series components do not comprise a stochastic process, where a stochastic process is defined as a set of random variables indexed over time or contingencies. The environment of the classical model is not structured, but is instead non-patterned, so that even the term 'stochastic' is inapplicable.

The problems in classical economics with the concept of uncertainty lay in the precision with which the definition of uncertainty and its subsequent calculation may be achieved and the manner of its quantification. This is not to imply that classical thinking held systemic uncertainty to be completely discountable to measurable (aleatory) risk, for clearly the opposite is true. Direct measures of uncertainty were thought neither possible nor valid even at a theoretical level. It is rather to suggest that *indirect* measures were thought more appropriate devices for expressing qualitative, incommensurable variables in quantitative terms.[121] One may at best approach some fixed standard which may be defined for all practical purposes as a measure of systemic uncertainty, as well as a measure of the uncertain manner in which we perceive the environment and the signals generated therein (epistemic uncertainty).

Yet before the close of the classical age, reappraisal was apparent. John Haynes, for example, defined risk as 'chance of danger or loss' (Haynes, 1895, p. 409), but included in this category all aleatory risks and uncertainties, discountable and not. Risk became synonymous with uncertainty. He then divided the general risk category into static and dynamic risks, static risks being those which are atemporal (natural causes, carelessness, moral hazard, ignorance), with dynamic risks being definable temporally (changes in attitudes and changes in technology) (ibid., pp.412–13). It was in the identification and calculation of these risks that Haynes' work, although long since forgotten, showed promise, for here he enunciated a method that accounted explicitly for subjective, not simply objective (market), valuations.

> The amount of probable gain must equal the amount of possible loss, not in the mere objective amount as represented by market values, but according to the subjective valuation of the person who is about to risk his capital or other valuable thing.
>
> (ibid., p. 433)

Despite the inclusiveness and subjectivity of Haynes's risk concept, it did not and does not provide a complete catalog of all aspects of uncertainty. Haynes did not, for instance, believe that absolute certainty was attainable, but left no provision for the residual (after calculating risk proper) which is itself an important subset. He appeared interested only in measurable risk, neglecting error as incalculable, disregarding non-measurable variation from even theoretical consideration. In effect, however, there is in such a presentation (and in a similar presentation by John Bates Clark (1892)) a place, albeit concealed even from its expositor, for an uncertainty beyond objective risk, since the subjective probability calculation affords greater latitude in the measurement of risk. This subjective component can readily be seen as a precursor of probabilistic economics. The subjective calculus affords a platform upon which may be constructed a more formal theoretical apparatus.

RISK AND UNCERTAINTY IN KNIGHT

The publication in 1921 of Frank Knight's *Risk, Uncertainty, and Profit* affords a starting point for the genesis of a truly probabilistic economics, as uncertainty as an essential concept gained significance and refinement, [122] as well as a degree of operationalization, with its publication. [123] The primary thesis of Knight's work is that uncertainty as expressed in the classical literature has in fact two components, 'risk' and 'true uncertainty', account of which must be explicitly taken in order to fully comprehend the role of the entrepreneur in the capitalist market economy, the nature of profit in such a system, and the interaction of economic variables in the determination of output.

Knight was not the first to recognize the risk–uncertainty distinction. Richard Cantillon (1755) was one of the first economic writers to identify uncertainty as a necessary condition for the existence of profit. Johann von Thünen, in his *The Isolated State* (1850), defined profit as subject to claims in three areas: interest on invested capital, insurance premia, and the salaries of supervisory personnel. The remainder accrues to the entrepreneur as a surplus, the 'entrepreneurial gain' (Dempsey, 1960, p. 246). While the first three components are calculable payments to factors, known in advance of production and hence discountable, the surplus exists as a positive residual, available because of the inability of the entrepreneur to calculate accurately and insure sufficiently against any and all possible contingencies. This surplus is a form of aleatory uncertainty; account of which cannot be ignored, but which is for all practical purposes beyond calculation. There is no method of accounting for every situation of risk, so a portion of profit must be set aside as payment against unforeseen, uninsurable contingencies (ibid., p. 69).

Frederick Hawley, writing in 1893, recognized a place for the residual (i.e., profit) as a payment to a fourth productive factor, risk-taking. Hawley's theory is one of risk-uncertainty, but is not so explicitly stated. Risk is insurable, but not completely eliminable. It is rather transferred to one willing to assume the burden and who seeks, not 'a definite and predetermined reward,' as would accrue to someone assuming risk proper, but rather 'a residue for his remuneration,' i.e., a reward for the uncertainty of repayment (Hawley, 1893, p. 465). Uncertainty determines the end-value of the reward for assuming the risk, and is not eliminable until the production process is completed; risk is, however, subjectively determinable: ' . . . the subjective value is at least capable of computation, while the excess over it necessarily remains uncertain until the complete ending of the productive process . . . .'(ibid., p. 466).

Irving Fisher advanced a more complete theory that in many ways was a presage of things to come. Fisher, in his *Nature of Capital and Income* (1906), predicated his theory of risk and uncertainty on the classical Laplacian theory of probability. Briefly, Fisher held that an event either occurs or does not. (As with Keynes, a proposition is either true or false). This objective reality demands a true–false, existence–nonexistence universe devoid of probabilistic interpretation. It is a theory applicable to the knowledge of *things*, not *truths*. Either something is or it is not; it is nonsensical to consider that anything empirically existent is only partially so.

The problem is that *subjective* considerations determine whether, and if so to what extent, the individual can have knowledge of the existence of the object of reflection, or in the occurrence of the event. Although undoubtedly some event will *objectively* have occurred *ex post*, this can only be known *subjectively*, as perceived by the individual, *ex ante*.[124] By way of explanation, Fisher presented the example of a coin toss. An individual forms a *subjective* probability, i.e., a degree of belief, in the proposition that the coin has landed heads (or tails), while the coin is *objectively either* heads or tails (for it cannot be both or neither, nor can it be partially one or the other), and this objective fact is knowable (and is discovered by the individual *ex post*). The outcome of the coin toss is in fact known with certainty by the person tossing the coin. So while an objective certainty exists, for all practical purposes one apprehends this only to a degree of certainty.

Fisherian risk is then simply 'lack of foresight,' and so is nothing more or less than an 'expression of ignorance' (Fisher, 1906, p. 291). It is epistemic risk. For Fisher, risk is an inescapable constituent of economic reality, since economic decisions are by definition made with reference to the future, which is itself indeterminate and indeterminable. But this risk is not an objective, measurable magnitude that all conceive of uniformly. It is rather a subjective estimate of future returns and outcomes contingent upon the occurrence of specific states of nature; it is dependent upon one's beliefs and knowledge *today* as to the structure of the world *tomorrow*.

Finally, it should be noted that Marshall also recognized the dichotomy between risk and uncertainty. From the *Principles* we have: 'Thus, though when we have counted up the average receipts of a risky trade, we must not make a separate full allowance for insurance against risk; though there may be something to be allowed as a charge on account of uncertainty.' (Marshall, 1920, Bk.V, Ch.VII, p. 400). In his *Economics of Industry* (1899), Marshall also commented on the distinction between risk and uncertainty and the means of dealing with the two. [125] In remarking on the labor market, for instance, Marshall wrote:

> We should obviously start by taking the earnings of an occupation as the average between those of the successful and unsuccessful members of it; taking care to get the true average. We then obviate the necessity of making any separate allowance for insurance against risk; but account remains to be taken of the evil of uncertainty . . . . Uncertainty, therefore, which does not appeal to great ambitions and lofty aspirations, has special attractions for very few; while it acts as a deterrent to many of those who are making their choice of a career. And as a rule the certainty of moderate success attracts more than an expectation of an uncertain success that has an equal actuarial value.
>
> (Marshall, 1899, p. 264)

Risk is measurable and manageable; uncertainty is non-measurable and insidious. [126]

Marshall may then be said to have provided a place for uncertainty and expectations in economics for he laid the foundation upon which a more thoroughgoing analysis of economic activity in an uncertain environment could be constructed.

In all of these early contributions to the theory of uncertainty, there appears to be a mischaracterization as to the term itself. Uncertainty in economics is fundamentally an epistemic concept: the conditions and circumstances in which the economic actor finds himself generate within him a feeling of uncertainty. The environment is uncertain only in the manner of its perception and apprehension. Insofar as we may speak of a systemic (aleatory) uncertainty, uncertain events are only relevant for economics to the extent that they affect decision-making: as these events are unanticipated, systemic (aleatory) uncertainty implies epistemic uncertainty (but the direction of implication is unidirectional). At times, however, the classical economists (excepting Marshall and Fisher) wrote as if uncertainty were a physical aspect of the environment. A situation is uncertain on this view if there cannot be identified a series to which it is a constituent member. This type of uncertainty exists irrespective of apprehension. This may explain the preoccupation of classical writers with numerical valuation and the equation (at times) of uncertainty with risk. In any event, the concept of uncertainty was (and is) not well defined, which is the reason for simplifying matters by defining epistemic and systemic uncertainty as two distinct concepts.

Even Knight did not fully comprehend the difference between uncertainty as an objective description of the environment and uncertainty as a description of the degree of our apprehension and belief. He thus built his theory of risk and uncertainty on an aleatory definition of the terms (unlike Keynes, whose theory is predicated on epistemic uncertainty).

Knight's contribution to the debate lay in his emphasis on the uncertainty–risk dichotomy as the central concept in a theory of profit, with his technical redefinition of uncertainty and risk. Specifically, Knight divided uncertainty into 'reducible' and 'irreducible' components. Reducible uncertainty is defined as (aleatory) risk; irreducible (aleatory) uncertainty is the 'true' uncertainty. Risk is analyzable according to the laws of mathematical probability; true uncertainty is outside the bounds of numerical probability theory.[127] Yet the two categories are neither mutually exclusive, nor are they independent, and cannot be considered as separate or separable components (thus the rationale behind their being defined as components of the single, all-encompassing category, systemic). That which had been previously regarded as uncertain may under some circumstances be internalized as a risk if it can be serialized and then reduced to a numerical value.[128] 'The fact is that while a single situation involving a known risk may be regarded as "uncertain," this uncertainty is easily converted into effective certainty' (Knight, 1921, p. 46), this being accomplished through a statistical grouping of like cases, the distinguishing of a homogeneous reference class, and the delineation of a random empirical series. Through the statistical laws of chance this procedure allows that the error term from prediction (or rather its expected value) approaches zero (as suggested by Bernoulli's theorem in classical probability and by Venn and the frequentists).

Knight was not satisfied with the possibility of reducing uncertainty to *effective* certainty, to a quasi-determinism; he rather needed the further reduction to *absolute* certainty and so the guarantee of *absolute* determinism. Should it be true that a 'quantitatively determinate probability' exists to which uncertainty could be reduced, then this uncertainty 'can be reduced to complete certainty by grouping cases' (ibid., pp. 231–2). The result is that 'in attempting to "act intelligently" we are attempting to secure adaptation which means foresight, as perfect as possible' (ibid., p. 238).[129] All this implies that particular outcomes of a process, and particular actions and even consequences of actions, behave in a similar fashion, and can to an extent be classified within certain broad categories; they may be reducible to Vennian series. This is not to imply that the events under consideration are identical or even similar in every respect; it is to say simply that the data set (i.e., the set whose elements are specific manifestations of events) is consistent in certain respects which 'matter.' The outcomes, actions, and consequences comprise reference classes of an acceptable degree of homogeneity. To justify considering the reference classes as homogeneous and thereby validating the use of some form of probability theory as a basis for analysis, Knight reverted to a form of the (Keynesian) Principle of Limited Independent Variety as an *a priori* principle, similar in form but derived independently of that put forward by Keynes.

> It must be possible not merely to assume that the *same* thing will always behave in the same way, but that the *same kind* of thing will do the same, and that there is in fact a finite, practically manageable number of *kinds* of things.
>
> (ibid., p. 205)

> For our limited intelligence to deal with the world, it must be possible to infer from a perceived similarity in the behavior of objects to a similarity in respects not open to immediate observation.
>
> (ibid., pp. 205–6)

Individuals in attempting to arrive at a decision in a rational manner must make reference to such a principle; i.e., they 'must use the principle that things similar in some respects will behave similarly in certain other respects even when they are very different in still other respects' (ibid., p. 206), while it is evident that under some conditions '[w]e require the further dogma of identical similarity between large numbers of things' (ibid., p. 205). Again the influence of Venn is clearly in evidence, as is the more than apparent similarity to Keynes.

This is not to imply that all uncertainty is so reducible, and so probability as frequency is by itself inapplicable generally to a Knightian environment. Knight classified probability into three types (ibid., pp. 224–5): (1) *a priori*; (2) statistical; and (3) estimates. Regarding the *a priori*, an initial probability value is established through recourse to 'general principles', e.g., the Principle of Insufficient Reason. The classical theory of probability clearly falls within this category, as does the necessarian, since both posit as a necessary condition an initial principle of this type. In the 'statistical' category, probabilities are empirically-determined through reference to a given stationary and homogeneous series. This is simply a restatement of the frequency view, holding valid so long as there exist series upon which frequencies can be based. In the case of 'estimates', there may be included here those instances of unique events not categorizable through reference to a series; in this category fall those subjective elements for which 'there is *no valid basis of any kind* for classifying instances' (ibid., p. 225). Estimates require the formation of the probability of a probability.[130] An empirical frequency ratio requires an extended series of the type Knight thought existent. However, no allowance is made in such a series for the effects of unique events constituting the true uncertainty, of which no knowledge is possible.[131] All the frequency theory can provide is a means for analyzing a risk-series composed of quantitatively-measurable, objectively-determined events; it must therefore neglect possibilities considered as *virtually* impossible, i.e., probabilities below some *a priori* given critical value. These 'irrelevant probabilities' are nonetheless the important, critical elements of true uncertainty, the elements comprising the field for which 'estimates' is the valid class.[132]

Knight then applied his dichotomy to the analysis of profit. With complete measurability there is no opportunity for profit; all contingencies are reducible to risk, and so are insurable. Change, i.e., an alteration in the environment, be it temporal or structural, itself is also not a sufficient condition for the existence of profit, nor is an unpredictable change which is reducible to a statistically-measurable process. The change must be of a truly unpredictable nature for it to be of consequence; it must have a truly non-measurable or non-patterned component. This requires simply a divergence of that which is expected from that which actually occurs. More importantly, the fluctuations (or the divergences) must also be unpredictable (and not merely unpredicted) in order for profit to arise, so that allowance is provided for ignorance on the part of the decision-maker as to the constitution of future conditions.[133] Knight expressed it as follows:

> It is necessary to stipulate that the fluctuations must be of sufficient extent and irregularity that they do not cancel out and reduce to uniformity or regular periodicity in a time-interval short in comparison with the length of human life.
>
> (ibid., p. 38,n.1)

For indeed if change is uniform or mathematically calculable, 'the future may be foreknown as accurately as if there were no change' (ibid., p. 315). The entrepreneur 'could operate and base his competitive offers upon accurate foreknowledge of the future if quantitative knowledge of the probability of every possible outcome can be had' (ibid., p. 199); i.e., he could discount completely the effects of an uncertain future to a quantifiable risk-factor or discount factor. The result would be that the entrepreneur could then have at his disposal the pure chance series for which Venn considered that probability values were calculable. Once such calculations are made, the aleatory risk, the quantified systemic uncertainty, can be shifted as a burden to parties willing and able to bear it, viz., through the medium of insurance. [134]

The necessary ingredient for change, and hence profit, is that the relevant reference class be of such a length that no pattern is discernible. Entrepreneurs must *anticipate* future actions on the basis of unknown, unanalyzable prospects. Once a pattern is recognizable, everyone will immediately take it into account, discounting it to risk, much as chance is reduced to cause in Hume. If the anticipations prove correct, these prescient, far-sighted individuals (as they are apt to be called) gain windfalls; if not, they fail to so realize any such extra-economic gains and so are in effect losers. It is the prospect of enormous gain from uncertain future prospects that motivates the process. [135]

Uncertainty in Knight depends upon change; in fact, change and uncertainty as expressed in *Risk, Uncertainty, and Profit* presuppose one another. Equilibrium depends upon certainty; these two concepts are likewise interdependent. In Knight, it is only in a static environment, one in which change is absent, that knowledge of the future may be secured with certainty. [136] Here the potential for perfect foresight ensures the existence of a stationary competitive equilibrium. Under conditions of certainty, deviations from the stationary equilibrium position may occur, but such deviations represent measurable, statistically-calculable events which may be internalized and discounted and thereby reduced to certainties. By contrast, under conditions of uncertainty wherein stationarity cannot be assumed to hold, perfect competition, as expressed by the classical economists, is no longer feasible since anticipations and results do not necessarily coincide, anticipations of the future being based on past (and present) conditions.

Yet 'the mechanism of price adjustment is the same as in any other market' (ibid., p. 274). So the difference between the two situations, the situations of certainty and uncertainty (or stasis and change), is the difference between 'doing things' and 'how to do things.' When the environment is characterizable as certain, 'doing things' becomes of utmost importance.

> [I]t is doubtful whether intelligence itself would exist in such a situation; in a world so built that perfect knowledge was theoretically possible, it seems likely that all organic readjustments would become mechanical, all organisms automata.
>
> (ibid., p. 268)

The *individual* as decision-maker is ignored in the perfect-information model in favor of the *system*; the analysis is objectivistic, treating the economy as a physical system tending to equilibrium.

Under conditions of uncertainty, 'doing things' becomes of secondary importance; 'the primary problem is one of deciding what to do and how to do it' (ibid., p. 268). Under these conditions, the individual is provided the central role. Decision making is the focus of the analysis, not the end result of the decisions made. The analysis is subjectivistic, treating of the individual as he interacts with others in the economizing process.

DIGRESSION ON ALLAIS-ELLSBERG PARADOXES

The Knightian risk–uncertainty dichotomy continues to play an important role in clarifying certain conceptual issues in the area of choice theory, particularly as they concern the axiomatizations of utility and preference of von Neumann-Morgenstern and of Savage.[137] The problems with the use of expected utility approaches to utility and the theory of choice are readily apparent when one approaches them from the positions of Knight and Keynes, as expositors of theories relying for their plausibility on the partial-order as a representation of the underlying decision space.[138] In these presentations, the principal concession is that not all possibilities (alternatives) are comparable in terms of more and less, preference and indifference.

The principal axioms of consumer choice theory are exactly those presented in Chapter II as defining a total order relation. This should not be surprising, given that preferences order consumption bundles. These axioms, to repeat, are connectedness and transitivity. Connectedness implies that the individual expresses a preference from among any two alternatives (the ordering is complete), and that in fact a choice is made;[139] transitivity is employed as an axiom of rational behavior. The axioms are valid for a theory of utility if and only if, in addition, a function $U: A \rightarrow \mathbb{R}$ exists for all commodity bundles $(a, b) \in A$, and is continuous,[140] such that $a \leqslant b$ if and only if $U(a) \leqslant U(b)$; in other words, the axioms of utility theory are valid if and only if supplemented by the condition that a utility function exists.

Note that a separability criterion, such as the independence axiom or Savage's 'sure-thing' principle, is not considered here as a 'core' axiom of utility theory,[141] where independence is defined as requiring that, if a and b are weakly ordered preferences, then any convex combination with a third, irrelevant, alternative is also weakly ordered; i.e., for all choices $a, b \in A$, if $a \leqslant b$, then $[\gamma a + (1 - \gamma)c] \leqslant [\gamma b + (1 - \gamma)c]$, for $0 \leqslant \gamma \leqslant 1$.[142] This criterion is, however, necessary for the existence of a specific type of utility function, viz., an expected utility function of the von Neumann-Morgenstern variety. Its acceptance, in fact, ensures that the expected utility function is linear in probability. The contention here is that it is not a requirement that the utility function *in general* be linear in probability.[143]

The von Neumann-Morgenstern and Ramsey-Savage axiomatizations of utility under uncertainty each rely on these principal axioms (postulates) of consumer choice theory as a foundation, supplementing them with ancillary propositions (sometimes also expressed as axioms), the most notable (or notorious) being the separability axiom or proposition. The principal difference between these interpretations is that von Neumann-Morgenstern utility theory is positive, while Savage's theory is open to normative interpretation (Savage, 1972, p. 97), and Ramsey's by contrast is descriptive, neither normative nor prescriptive. Irrespective of the probability basis of their construction (von Neumann-Morgenstern based on the frequency interpretation, Ramsey-Savage on the personalist) these axiom systems were shown by Maurice Allais (1952) and Daniel Ellsberg (1961) to exhibit paradoxical results in experimental (and so through extrapolation actual choice) situations; i.e., they allow behavior inconsistent with the axioms. Since the two results are similar (the difference being that Ellsberg's paradox is more closely associated with Keynesian probability and the incompleteness of preference orderings), the focus will be on the Ellsberg paradox, with brief mention being made at the outset of the theory of Allais.

Allais reasoned that the axioms of von Neumann-Morgenstern and Savage (among others) restrict severely the options available to decision-makers by limiting the probability measure to single values. For Allais, rationality is behavior that is not self-contradictory, conditional on logically consistent ends and appropriate means (Allais, 1952, p. 69). His complaint with standard utility theory lay in the apparent neglect by those of the 'American school' (identified with the axiomatizations of von Neumann-Morgenstern and Savage) of higher moments of the probability distributions, and their acceptance of the separability criterion. Allais's theory can be described as an attempt at reconciliation of theory with application, achieved by constructing a pure theory of risk in which use is made of the concept of the 'dispersion of psychological values' (ibid., p. 55).[144] It is not enough for Allais to restrict the theory of choice under conditions of uncertainty to a measure of psychological values or subjective measures; any single-valued measure he deemed inapplicable to actual decision processes.

No mention was made by Allais of Keynesian 'true' epistemic uncertainty (or Knightian 'true' aleatory uncertainty) except implicitly in his inclusion of the entire probability distribution function instead of relying on specific point values of probability (or expected utility). His insistence on cardinality in fact implies that any true uncertainty (aleatory or epistemic) is neglected, since any possible contingency is assumed to be included within the given probability distribution functions, the contingencies are measurable, and further that such distribution functions are assumed to exist.[145] For cardinality to be viable, there must exist a preference among all sets of alternatives; there can be no non-comparability. So while rejecting a part of the Bayesian approach (the 'sure-thing' principle of Savage), Allais accepted what is arguably the most significant aspect, the postulate asserting the existence of a total order.

Ellsberg pursued a different approach to the solution of the problems inherent in the personalist (Bayesian) interpretations of probability and utility.

Ellsberg observed that the axiomatic approaches to probability and utility of von Neumann-Morgenstern and Savage inadvertently operationalize the Knightian distinction between risk and uncertainty in that such approaches suggest that, for individual decision-makers, 'with respect to certain events they did not obey, nor did they wish to obey – *even on reflection* – Savage's postulates or equivalent rules' (Ellsberg, 1961, p. 646). This is the nature of the Ellsberg paradox.[146] Although each axiom can alone be accepted as a reasonable account of rationality, as a system they lead to inconsistencies in decision-making; the axiomatization comprises an antinomy.

To illustrate the Ellsberg paradox, contemplate the following decision problem.[147] Consider two urns, each containing 100 black and red balls. Urn II contains 50 red and 50 black balls; Urn I has an unknown ratio of the two.

Let an individual (the 'subject') make a 'draw' from an urn, preceded by the placement of a bet as to which color he favors. He then receives $100 if his desired choice obtains, $0 if not.

There are then four possible pairs of outcomes ('gambles') to consider:

(1) draw a red ball from Urn I or a black ball from Urn I
(2) draw a red ball from Urn II or a black ball from Urn II
(3) draw a red ball from Urn I or a red ball from Urn II
(4) draw a black ball from Urn I or a black ball from Urn II

Between cases (1) and (2), the subject in experimental situations is indifferent; each provides for the possibility that prob(black) = prob(red). Between cases (3) and (4), most subjects preferred drawing a red ball from Urn II over drawing a red ball from Urn I, and black from Urn II over black from Urn I. But this is clearly a violation of the Savage axioms. Choosing red from Urn II implies that the subject assumes prob(red II) > prob(red I), while at the same time choosing black from Urn II implies that prob(black II) > prob(black I). But if it is accepted that prob(red II) > prob(red I), then it must be true that prob(black I) > prob(black II). Since prob(red II) = prob(black II) = 0.50, then the choices imply that prob(red I) < 0.50 and prob(black I) < 0.50. Savage's (1972) postulate 2 (known in the literature as P2), which states that for all acts f, g and state B, either f ≤ g or g ≤ f given B, is violated. Since the resulting choices are not representative of probability judgments, P1 (the total order postulate) is also violated (Ellsberg, 1961, pp. 650–1).

Those who violate the axioms do not do so as a result of the relative desirability of payoffs or likelihood of the events obtaining; they do not violate the axioms because of internal inconsistencies. They rather appear to violate the axioms because of information uncertainties: 'the nature of one's information concerning the relative likelihood of events' (ibid., p. 657). The problem is that, for the individual, no preference ranking from among the given alternatives is possible; the situation is indeterminate. Thus as Ellsberg noted, such choice criteria as minimaxing, etc. are useful in cases of total lack of knowledge of probabilities, while the Savage axioms are useful in the face of a lack of uncertainty, i.e., where the probabilities are known, and where all uncertainty is reducible to risk and thus measurable, so that choice takes the form of choice among known probability values or distributions. Ellsberg was able then to redefine uncertainty so as to distinguish between uncertain, ambiguous processes (unique events, 'surprises') and uncertain, unambiguous events (e.g., games of chance). [148]

Howard Raiffa (1961) accepted that (in his experimental situations) there were instances in which, when subjects were not presented with numerical probabilities (or likelihoods), the results were inconsistent with the Savage axioms. But instead of noting the failure of the axioms to elicit from the subjects the 'correct' responses, he concluded that his subjects were ill-informed as to the fine points of decision-making under uncertainty. They were in essence deemed ignorant of what was in 'their own best interests,' and so required instruction in the use of the decision axioms: 'There is a need to teach people how to cope with uncertainty in a purposive and reflective manner, and to break down the taboo that probabilities should only be assigned if one has clear-cut relative frequency data at hand' (Raiffa, 1961, p. 692). It is not, on this view, the theory which is defective; it is the computational and conceptual deficiencies of the subjects which lead to the inconsistencies, the paradoxical results.

Savage himself readily accepted that there were difficulties with his theory of probability (especially following the critiques of Allais and Ellsberg). He acknowledged, for instance, the importance of non-measurable uncertainty as a real-world problem, but thought it could be ignored on the grounds of practicality. The 'vagueness' of individual preferences means, for Savage, that for actual decision-making, complete rankings are impossible to achieve. It may be the case that only in an ideal environment is a supposition such as completeness valid, and may then be stipulated as a decision axiom; applicability requires certain abstractions be made, that in effect the environment be treated *as if* the ideal applied. [149] These difficulties moreover do not seriously affect the theory's validity. The decision-maker may behave in a manner inconsistent with the dictates of the theory (which even Savage admitted to doing) but, once given the opportunity to re-examine his choices in the light of his preference-rankings as provided for by the theory, it is perfectly legitimate for him to change his rankings and so return to consistency: [150]

> ... the behavior of people is often at variance with the theory. The departure is sometimes flagrant, in which case our attitude toward it is much like that we hold toward a slip in logic, calling the departure a mistake and attributing it to such things as accident and subconscious motivation.
>
> (Savage, 1972, p. 20)

The connection to Keynesian probability theory is obvious and straightforward. Although Keynes placed great emphasis on the non-measurability of probability, this was only one of the objections which he expressed concerning numerical valuations and comparisons. Two of the other reasons given (probability measures may exist but are unknown, and such measures are not practically determinate) can be accommodated in the light of the Allais-Ellsberg objections to the von Neumann-Morgenstern/Savage axioms. This is easily accomplished by replacing the total order (of von Neumann-Morgenstern/Savage) with a partial order, and redefining the decision axioms accordingly. [151] Use of the partial order is necessitated by the belief that it is not always possible for an individual decision-maker (the 'rational agent') to compare acts; it is not always the case that individuals are consistent in their behavior concerning choices among actions. Given the acceptance of a partial order, and the possibility that even the partial order is too restrictive, given that for multidimensional comparisons intransitivities may be evident, it is no longer necessary to assume that the decision-maker has established preferences over the entire set of acts, nor that he be cognizant of the set of consequences of all possible acts. [152] It is perfectly reasonable for the individual to arrive at a decision which is valid based on his conceptual abilities and access to information regarding alternatives, although the decision may be less than optimal or even, in the end, erroneous, without being judged irrational. (This thus invalidates much of expected utility theory in that the connectedness and transitivity requirements may no longer hold.)

This notion had, of course, been acknowledged outside of the context of Keynes. Ellsberg (1963) emphasized abandoning reliance on the total order as essential to any true comprehension of the uncertainty of the environment; the rationale for such a belief is that actors do not in general have unidimensional probability distributions: 'the set of probability distributions compatible with (not excluded by) all our definite probability judgments at a given moment typically contains more than one member' (Ellsberg, 1963, p. 338n.5). This provides a justification for using a partial order, and so is in contrast to Allais's suggestion of accepting the total order but expanding the form of the probability measure (from point values to probability distributions) incorporated in the decision-maker's choice function. The result is a form of probability measure consistent with the conceptualization of Knight and the probabilism of Keynes. [153]

RISK AND UNCERTAINTY AGAIN

'Uncertainty' as a focal point in economic theory is, as per Knight and Keynes, compounded of two variants: measurable and non-measurable. Measurable uncertainty, more commonly denoted as risk (be it aleatory or epistemic), is a quantitatively calculable [154] subset of the totality of uncertainty, one which is expressible by numerical values representable as summary statistics. This treatment of uncertainty is the sole domain of what is defined herein as stochastic economics. There exist well-defined probability distributions for events subsumed under this category, with known means and variances; it is accepted that events are representable as members of a clearly defined series (albeit perhaps unique to each individual). Elements within the domain of measurable uncertainty are characterizable through reference to specific generating functions. Were economic agents to exist in an environment wherein all aleatory and epistemic uncertainty is measurable and seriable, and so reducible to a measure of risk, in which economic (consumer) behavior develops in accordance with a given, known distribution function, their anticipations of future economic activity could be reduced to numerically-valued quotients subjectable to the normal laws of statistical error; such expectations as were formed could then be rank-ordered or represented as weighted, numerical values. Certainty equivalents would then serve within economic models to guarantee the existence of equilibrium conditions which would be stable and well-behaved. The ergodic theorems guarantee convergence to equilibrium.

Non-measurable uncertainty is, by contrast, qualitative, non-quantifiable and thus not amenable to the probability calculus; it is the 'true uncertainty' [155] of Keynes and Knight. 'Surprise' is regarded as forming the largest component of this form of uncertainty; it is the ultimate undiscountable externality. One is completely ignorant of the probability distributions of these events, that a distribution in fact exists, or whether the events (signals) perceived are even seriable, and hence one cannot assert that a particular generating mechanism even exists let alone can be discovered which will replicate these events. Agents working in an environment characterizable as 'surprise-laden' (one in which 'surprise' components are asserted to have substantial impact) can have little accurate knowledge of the path of the future course of events; they cannot extrapolate from past experience anything that may be of relevance to the prediction of the future, nor can they even discount the consequences of such events since a suitable discount factor is incalculable. Economic agents do not as a rule even possess any knowledge of how to form estimations of future events in a truly epistemically-uncertain environment (in the manner of Keynes), since by the nature of the term 'surprise' any such event may be (but need not be) in the nature of a unique, one-time occurrence (in the manner of Knight). The presence of 'surprise' as a spontaneous, unique occurrence, or as a previously unperceived opportunity, acts as a 'shock' to the economic system. Further, such non-patterned events are (presumably) in continuous occurrence, although they are by definition not of such a constitution as to be considered representable as members of any defined homogeneous series (in the sense of Venn); it is impossible to enumerate all conceivable outcomes given the fact of unknowability. The result is that the economic environment and our apprehensions of it cannot be asserted to be either inherently stable or as exhibiting a tendency to an equilibrium position since such shocks cannot be considered as behaving in a manner representable by a series (since their distribution is unknown and unknowable) which would then be amenable to statistical evaluation; these elements cannot be appraised as being normally-distributed random events of the type required for statistical analysis. [156]

To provide a theoretical justification within economics for the acceptance of the Allais-Ellsberg critiques and to allow a place (albeit indirectly) for Keynesian probability considerations, the classical decision axioms, the rationality postulate, must be amended. Herbert Simon identified three modifications to the classical economic assumptions of perfect information and foresight which allow for limitations on the classical rationality postulate, for replacing classical rationality with bounded rationality. The first modification substitutes stochastic elements for deterministic ones. [157] Random variables with well-behaved distributions known by decision-makers replace the exogenous, fixed parameters of the classical model; first and second moments are used explicitly in choice calculations. The advantage gained by this alteration lies in the accounting within the strictures of the 'classical' economic model of the essential non-determinateness of the choice process; it allows inclusion within the basic classical structure of an element of risk. As the environment within which the actor operates is an open one (i.e., the environment is non-structured), it is perceived uncertainly. The inclusion of a risk factor serves as a mechanism for handling the measurable aspects of this uncertainty. The problem with this change is that it simply moves the decision-makers' task to another level: 'the assumption of the actor's perfect knowledge of these functions has been replaced by the assumption that he has perfect knowledge of their distributions' (Simon, 1982, p. 410).

A second modification allows that the actor possesses only limited or incomplete information as to the available alternatives. [158] The complete set of actions is open to the actor (i.e., he is not precluded from taking any of the actions of which one may conceive), but he is not assumed to have full and complete knowledge of this list. He is only aware of a limited set of available actions, and so must choose from this constrained set. The agent is, in other words, engaged in a search from among a set of known alternatives. Moreover, he knows quite a deal about the alternatives within this constrained set. This again involves the agent in a stochastic maximization problem, as he 'knows' the relevant first and second moments, but the problem is one which involves maximization over an incomplete set.

Thirdly, there is the problem of constraints which prevent any best-choice calculation from being made. The individual choice functions themselves are not of the linear or quadratic variety, or too many constraints apply to allow for a first-best calculation. One can approach the optimum, but the resultant choice may only be of a second-best nature (ibid., p. 411).

Simon deemed the type of behavior exemplified by the Savage axioms to be 'programmed' decision-making, characterized by (1) a given frame of reference, (2) a pre-established set of alternatives (possible actions), (3) a preference-ranking among possible consequences, and (4) a relationship (deterministic or stochastic) between possible actions and consequences (ibid., pp. 382–3). This characterizes the expected utility model, sometimes (confusedly) referred to as the classical model of rational behavior. Acts are analyzable outside of the process of their determination. This type of decision-making corresponds to Simon's 'objective' or 'substantive' rationality. In Savage's terms, behavior must correspond to the dictates of the decision axioms (which guarantee consistency) in order to be adjudged rational. It is not necessary to know the rationale behind the decision, since only the decision itself is relevant. In Simon's view, this type of decision model allows 'strong predictions to be made about human behavior without the painful necessity of observing people' (ibid., p. 321).

By contrast, 'non-programmed' decision-making posits that the individual must function within a dynamic, patternless environment. The full range of alternative actions is not deemed known to the actor, there do not in general exist preferences among all possible consequences, and the relationship between actions and consequences is generally neither known nor well understood. This type of decision-making is consistent with Simon's definition of 'subjective' or 'procedural' rationality, whereby emphasis is placed on the rationality of the decision-maker. Subjective desires and expectations determine and serve to drive actions; the actions are not analyzable outside of the process by which they are generated. The rationale behind the decision is of the utmost concern; it is the *sine qua non* of this type of decision model. This form of rationality, with its emphasis on process, is implicit, at least, in Keynes's probabilism, and is the reason for labelling his theory of probability as subjective epistemic necessarianism. It is also the basis of Keynes's and Knight's economics (and, as will be seen, the economics of the Austrians as well). The individual may be considered as rational without being forced into consistency with decision postulates or behavior axioms, which tend to an objective nature, so long as his decision has *some* basis.

It remains to see whether and how these distinctions, between expectation and outcome, between uncertainty and measurable risk, between stochastic and true probabilistic interpretations of 'shock' parameters, have been incorporated into economic doctrine. To do so, the Austrian, Keynesan (not keynesian), and Rational Expectations schools of economic theory will each be examined in an effort to determine if, and the extent to which, each has accepted (1) the dichotomy between risk and uncertainty, and more importantly, (2) a need to incorporate explicitly within the models some form of the probability concept.

IV

AUSTRIAN ECONOMICS

The economic theory classified as Austrian is not a monolithic paradigm, but is rather a loose amalgam of theories each of which holds to a core set of consistent beliefs and ideals.

Within the tradition of Austrian economic thought is an emphasis on process, the operation of those factors which drive the individual decision-maker to an intended goal. For the economists of the Austrian school, motivations, knowledge, subjectivism, time, and the individual are of central concern; they are the core elements of a theory of human action of which the discipline of economics is but a part of the larger study of the entire social milieu. The concern for the individual and his subjective apprehensions of his environment, of the manner in which he arrives at (perhaps idiosyncratic) actions, are in fact the principal foci of this philosophy. Motivations, tastes, and expectations need be accounted for, but are subjective and qualitative inducements to behavior; they are by definition neither conducive to measurement nor representable as an order relation.

'Knowledge' *per se*, in the Austrian ideal, is not amenable to measurement or order since it falls in the same general category as tastes and expectations as a subjective quality. Subjective knowledge allows that each individual in the system is autonomous and possesses a mental apparatus, a system for information collection and processing, peculiar to his personal beliefs, experiences, perceptions, apprehensions, etc.; each and every individual can (and will) formulate a different degree of rational belief as to the outcome of any given situation (e.g., as to the future value of the rate of inflation or the possible selling price of a proposed product line) based upon his unique information set and his cognizance of the situation and his place in the general scheme of things. This 'knowledge' or 'reason', constrained and modified by reference to the aforementioned motivations, tastes, and expectations, then dictates choice and action. It is the filter, the rose-colored glasses through which the Austrian (and Kantian)[159] actor perceives his environment, and so serves an organizing function, superimposed on the external reality. In Ludwig Wittgenstein's (1921) terms, this subjective apparatus is a pre-existent 'picture' of the world which precedes the perceptions of empirical phenomena, and so serves as a precondition for what is typically regarded as knowledge.[160] 'Action' and subjective choice derive through reference to this *a priori* mental 'filter', but themselves are viewed as supreme in the Austrian model; deterministic positivism is *ipso facto* rejected. At the extreme a form of solipsism is maintained.

Since there is not a single Austrian economic view, it is necessary to synthesize an Austrian 'belief-system' which will allow discussion of the beliefs of the leading intellectual lights writing within the paradigm. It is not possible within the confines of the present study to discuss fully all of the works of those writing in the Austrian tradition; the present topic is not broad enough to accommodate such a nicety. A restriction is made to center on those leading figures of Austrian economic thought whose work maintained the fullest discussion of the subject of probability in economics and decision-making.[161] For the purpose of the present study, the four leading influences in this regard are taken to be Carl Menger, Ludwig von Mises, Friedrich A. Hayek, and G. L. S. Shackle.[162]

MENGER

Carl Menger, the founder of Austrian economics and among the early enunciators of subjective value theory, maintained that economic valuation could not be constrained to that which is objectively measurable, while still being construed as unique to the individual. An objective measure presupposes complementarity and comparability among the actors and their plans of action, which is not a characterization which Menger was willing to concede. Value is defined with respect to the beliefs and motivations of the individual actor and is determined subjectively; as each of us possesses different abilities as regards the apprehension, accumulation, and interpretation of economic and social data, it is difficult to see how it could be otherwise. It is equally perplexing how an objective and interpersonal measure of this highly personalized valuation process, itself only vaguely understood, could be forthcoming. Once we accept that the individual is central to value theory, and that individuals cannot by virtue of their individuality be taken as constituents of any homogeneous class (i.e., each is unique in composition and constitution), we preclude comparisons for the very same reason we preclude comparisons between disparate non-homogeneous reference classes: we cannot confine correspondence to like qualities and so have no hope of an objective comparison. This inability to identify subjective valuation as representable by an objective, value-free measure which would allow interpersonal comparisons requires that the measure of value itself be subjective, unique to each individual.

> The *measure* of value is entirely subjective in nature, and for this reason a good can have great value to one economizing individual, little value to another, and no value at all to a third, depending upon the differences in their requirements and available amounts . . . .
>
> Hence not only the *nature* but also the *measure* of value is subjective.

Goods always have value *to* certain economizing individuals and this value is also *determined* only by these individuals.

(Menger, 1871, p. 146)

Goods therefore have no intrinsic worth whatever, but have value simply by virtue of the fact that they are perceived as being valuable, as having some utility, as providing a satisfaction. The valuation process occurs ultimately in the mind of the individual actor. The manner of this determination from the standpoint of the outside observer is quite irrelevant. Value is

a judgment economizing men make about the importance of the goods at their disposal for the maintenance of their lives and well-being. Hence value does not exist outside the consciousness of men.

(ibid, p. 121)

Objective measures of value are thus further inappropriate because non-existent; as 'values' have no objective independent existence, no basis exists for which a precise and unvarying numerical value may be defined. Similarly with manufactured goods, being comprised of a number of disparate inputs, each differing qualitatively, each valuable singly but not comparable collectively;[163] the goods cannot be valued other than by a subjective measure of the utility they provide.[164] This determination of utility likewise occurs in the mind, i.e., in the imagination.

As the Mengerian individual 'learns' of his environment, or 'matures,' his apprehensions of value necessarily change. Indeed it would be difficult to imagine cases in which the individual's valuations remained constant throughout his life-span. The environment tomorrow is different qualitatively from that of today; needs continually change as do requirements for their fulfillment; the perceptions and apprehensions by the actor of those needs also evolves. With this continual re-evaluation of prospects and re-interpretation of desires follows a change in subjective valuations. This process affects not only individual rankings of goods values (as the utilities are ordered), but also inter-personal rankings as perceived from a more objective vantage, the value in exchange.

Notwithstanding this characterization of Menger's view of valuation as subjective, he was not a strident ideologue; he was not above allowing objective considerations to enter the decision calculus. Values of satisfaction Menger deemed dependent on the degree of importance to men's lives and well-being, yet allowed that (in modern terminology), owing to the possibility of 'defective knowledge' and even 'defective constitutions' (which could lead to misapprehensions of economic signals and to epistemic confusion), some individuals may arrive at satisfaction rankings which are in contradistinction to their 'true' valuations and hence harmful to their overall welfare.[165] Even duplicity cannot be ruled out as a motivating factor (although Menger seems not to have considered this possibility). This is not to suggest that the resulting actions are irrational; it is rather to point out that knowledge is not a sufficient condition for 'rational' calculation. Knowledge itself is a limiting factor. Those individuals who strive to behave consistently according to the dictates of the decision-calculus, in an effort to avoid the pitfalls associated with ill-trained observation and unstructured thought (much in the manner of Savage and Raiffa, *et al.*) may, due to the very constitution of the human mind, still find themselves in a position of erroneous calculation:

> Even individuals whose economic activity is conducted rationally, and who therefore certainly endeavor to recognize the true importance of satisfactions in order to gain an accurate foundation for their economic activity, are subject to error. Error is inseparable from all human knowledge.
>
> (ibid., p. 148)

Under conditions of 'complete Mengerian rationality' the individual is still prone to erroneous valuation of goods; e.g., he may incorrectly estimate goods availability and even his own wants and desires (ibid., p. 120). He is also prone to erroneous calculation of possible future events and the course of economic activity, since the future is not an object of perception and Mengerian rationality is not synonymous with perfect foresight. Even when calculation is not erroneous, i.e., when we have at our disposal all information which can be had (and is in fact needed) for a 'correct' calculation, it is still possible that expectations will prove incorrect since it is impossible to account for each and every contingency. As with Carnap and Keynes, the calculation may have been 'correct' at the time it was made, but events have conspired to make it irrelevant. There is an element of ignorance inherent in any calculated decision; this ignorance is so ubiquitous and pervasive that it may be said that decision is impossible in its absence. Ignorance may be said to be a more important motivation to action than knowledge: knowledge leads to action, but ignorance defines ultimately the consequences of that action, viz., whether the action has for the individual the intended consequences. [166] The fact that an action leads to an unintended outcome is not an indication of the irrationality of the actor or the act, but is merely indicative of a lack of sufficient knowledge upon which to form a judgment. It is nothing but a sign that uncertainties and fate (outside influences beyond individual control because unfathomable) have conspired to play a greater role than could have been anticipated. The presence of uncertainty in apprehension requires the redefinition of rationality to allow for the potentiality that actions undertaken with a promise of gain may in the end prove disappointing. The consequences of an action may diverge considerably from the promise, the anticipated outcome, which motivated the decision, without the decision itself being irrational. No probability calculus can rectify the situation; not even a consistency calculus (e.g., of the Borel-Ramsey-Savage variety) will have the effect of reducing to a satisfactory level the error held by Menger to be inherent in the act of decision-making. Menger's apprehensions maintain validity despite protestations by personalists who require consistency as a postulate ostensibly to prevent the making of a 'Dutch book'; in fact, Menger's critique appears especially prescient in respect to numerous criticisms of personalist probability theories, notably those of Keynes, Shackle, and Arrow.

Economic applications of Menger's Austrian epistemology reiterate the above-mentioned themes of subjectivism, individuality, and the exploitation of error. Menger insisted that the concept 'national economy' was *per se* a fiction, for the aggregation necessary to bring to the concept any substance removes from consideration those aspects of the choice problem which are the most relevant and interesting. Instead of examining economies in their totality (the macroeconomy) the Mengerian economist should view economic phenomena in terms of atomistic units. Thus developed the notion (in economics generally and in Austrianism in particular) of the primacy of the individual. These individual 'economizing units,' being the primary components of a larger, more comprehensive, but less comprehensible system, are the only form of economy amenable to understanding; the basic principles upon which economics is constructed (the microfoundations) may be apprehended only with respect to these elemental, atomic units.

Mengerian economic valuation is therefore first and foremost subjective; it is determined simply by the relation between the availability of goods and individual requirements and desires for said goods, given that the individual is cognizant of his dependence on the good in question for his satisfaction, and coupled with his apprehension of his own wants and desires and knowledge of the environment. Valuation is entirely epistemic. 'Value is therefore nothing inherent in goods, no property of them, but merely the importance that we first attribute to the satisfaction of our needs, that is, to our lives and well-being, and in consequence carry over to economic goods as the exclusive causes of the satisfaction of our needs.' (ibid., p. 116) The valuation process must therefore be assumed to take place entirely in the imagination; in other words, the subjective values are intuited. It is because of this highly personal value process that reduction of interpersonal values to any single probability measure is not only inappropriate but also quite impossible. For this reason alone, that no single probability measure is appropriate for the Mengerian valuation process, the personalist and frequency interpretations of probability are not deemed here as being compatible with Mengerian Austrianism. Something 'Keynesian' is required.

MISES

As the founder of the analytic variant of the Austrian school, Ludwig von Mises placed great emphasis on the rationality of the individual economic actor in an arena of inherent epistemic uncertainty, to a far greater extent than did Menger. With Mises, rationality of the actor achieved central significance and importance for all of Austrian economics. His magnum opus *Human Action* is widely regarded as the defining work of the strict rationalist variant of Austrianism, itself a rather small but significant segment of the school,[167] the importance and influence of which cannot be denied.

For Mises, the fact of human action is co-extensive with the uncertainty in our perceptions of the future; the two cannot be separated, the one implies the other (Mises, 1966, p. 105).[168] The implication of this correspondence is that the individual must act with but partial knowledge of the totality of possibilities, and necessarily limited comprehension of the potentialities of the consequences of his actions; the actor is neither insightful enough nor well-enough informed to discern the composition of an exhaustive list of potential actions. As one is never fully cognizant of all potential actions at one's command, neither can one enumerate a complete catalog of all possible ramifications resulting from any actions taken. Imprecision with respect to the totality of acts and consequences enters into the definition of human cognition; there is, in short, no basis for the construction of a 'decision tree' whereby acts are associated with consequences arranged in accordance with the probability of occurrence.

Any empirical theory put forth as an explanation of human activity requires the explicit consideration of an individual possessed of less-than-certain knowledge. It must further be predicated on subjective apprehension of signals and subjective belief. In other words, a theory of action implies a theory of contingent truth. Thus Mises's economics suggests a two-track, disjointed approach, one track being concerned with 'apodictic certainty,' the other with 'epistemic uncertainty.' Truth and certain knowledge fall within the domain of epistemology proper, and within the domain of Mises's praxeology; uncertain and probable knowledge fall within the domain of Mises's applied economics.[169]

Individual actors in Mises's scheme are assumed to possess knowledge in different degrees and to process the information differently, depending upon their individual situations at the moment, and their apprehension of their situations within a larger context both spatially and temporally. The Mengerian subjectivist still holds sway. These differentials in knowledge possession and information-processing potential are for Mises essential ingredients in the functioning of the market.

> In an economic system in which every actor is in a position to recognize correctly the market situation with the same degree of insight, the adjustment of prices to every change in the data would be achieved at one stroke.
>
> (ibid., p. 328)

Certainly the market that catallactics deals with is filled with people who are to different degrees aware of the changes in data and who, even if they have the same information, appraise it differently.

(ibid., p. 328)

The market is continually in a state of 'agitation', so that the *expectation* of profit, for instance, is always a factor in the motivation of the entrepreneur. It is the inherent epistemic uncertainty and instability which makes it so, which makes expectation a necessary precondition to motivation and action. Without such individualistic, subjective appraisals of the information generated by the market, the market economy as such would cease to exist. In its place would be substituted a mechanistic, abstract market as it involves the Walrasian auctioneer in the provision of complete and perfect information leading to the possibility of the attainment of complete and perfect knowledge on the part of the individual actors in the economy and the attainment on the part of the macroeconomy of a constant state of equilibrium. The decision tree model would gain credibility as a representation of the decision-making process, with mathematical expectation (and hence the subjective expected utility model) being granted special status. The subjectivity requirement ensures for the Austrians that uncertainty and differentials in information processing and information possession remain an integral part of the market process, with the result being that market outcomes are fundamentally indeterminate and that equilibrium, which implies an end-point to process, is meaningless.

This indeterminateness in our perceptions of the economic signals generated by the environment requires that economic analysis be conducted in a probabilistic form; the subjectivity of the valuation process alone requires this be so. For although Mises's praxeology and Menger's ideal laws are deterministic – they allow the deduction of absolutely true conclusions based on stipulated premises – in actuality the requirement is for a means to reduce the degree of non-determinism. To develop this theoretically, Mises considered the existence of two types of probability, much as did Venn, categories dependent upon whether the elements of inclusion are representable as series or are simply unique, unstructured, unclassifiable events. These categories Mises labeled *class probability* and *case probability*. [170] Class probability refers to knowledge of the behavior of a class of events, a reference class, without acknowledgement as to the singular elements of the class. The class itself is treated in its totality (ibid., p. 107). An example of similar usage is that of the frequency theory and mathematical probability, which is concerned with classes of events, not particular elements within the class or series; in application the equation with insurance arrangements is rather obvious. [171] This probability-type is amenable to numerical measurement because of the pre-supposed existence of a clearly defined stationary homogeneous series (collective) comprised of delineable (seriable) components. Case probability, by contrast, refers to knowledge of particular events, and is fundamental in human activity. Each event may be an element of a particular reference class or series, but the specific class or series to which it belongs is unknown; or the events may not be classifiable at all. To case probability the mathematical probability calculus is inappropriate (as in Venn) for the reason that nothing more is known about the event beyond that it has occurred. Frequencies cannot be calculated because there is a lack of a suitably defined reference. 'Here any reference to frequency is inappropriate, as our statements always deal with unique events which as such – i.e., with regard to the problem in question – are not members of any class.' (ibid., p. 111).

This Misesian dichotomy is but a variant of the Knightian distinction between calculable (aleatory) risk and non-calculable (aleatory) uncertainty. It is not at all clear that risk and uncertainty are to be confined to the epistemic, so as to suggest a kinship with Keynes, since Mises gives examples to suggest an aleatory reading as well. All that is certain is that Mises believed that well-behaved series for which reference classes are determinable are amenable to investigation through the application of the mathematical probability calculus; single, unique, perhaps non-seriable events are by definition exclusive of any representable series, or they may be considered as by themselves constituting series consisting of unique events, and so the calculus is inapplicable. For Mises, then, the appropriate method of handling uncertainty (be it epistemic or aleatory) is not that of the frequentists with its emphasis on the pre-existence of a homogeneous reference class; something more encompassing is required, something capable of handling non-measurable uncertainties. This 'something' is a probability-type such as that developed by Keynes, an all-encompassing general theory of probability for which non-measurability and non-comparability are of paramount importance, the specific realm being inconsequential.

In the area of economics proper, specifically monetary economics, Mises's general theme of subjective valuation of incommensurable magnitudes achieved a degree of concreteness. Money is not an objective measure of goods-value or price; subjective valuation of the type Mises championed precludes objective measurement. All that subjective valuation produces is an ordering of goods, a static relationship based on comparative valuation (Mises, 1953, pp. 38–9).[172] 'Subjective value is not measured, but graded.' (ibid., p. 47). (In this sense Mises clearly held to an epistemic view of uncertainty.) Money serves the function of reducing reliance on an inordinate number of exchange-ratios; it allows exchange to take place in the absence of a continual re-calculation and re-evaluation of ratios of exchange. In effect, money plays a role in enhancing our ability to apprehend economic signals, thus reducing our degree of confusion with respect to the myriad of external influences acting to alter our perceptions. Money serves the role of an indicator of interpersonal valuations. In a sense, it serializes disparate signals. The sole function of money is as an index of value; its indispensability in this regard suggests to many that it may be termed (albeit erroneously) 'a measure of prices' (ibid., p. 49). This concession to objectivity is acceptable to Mises provided that at heart we 'know better.'

HAYEK AND SHACKLE

Friedrich Hayek and his student G. L. S. Shackle emphasized themes some-what different from those advanced by Menger and Mises. It is this re-emphasis on the purely epistemic nature of risk and uncertainty which allows the language of probability a more integral role in the Austrian tradition.

Hayek believed that the perfect competition model propounded in academia, the pedagogical competitive model, is not one with application to 'real world' problems. In fact, it serves as nothing more than an exercise in logic.

> *If* we possess all the relevant information, *if* we can start out from a given system of preferences, and *if* we command complete knowledge of available means, the problem which remains is purely one of logic.
>
> (Hayek, 1945, p. 77)

The formal analytics of 'equilibrium economics' has little to contribute to economics as an empirical discipline dedicated to the understanding of the society 'as it is.' For Hayek, the economic problem is not the distribution of scarce resources or the production of goods and services, but rather is 'the utilization of knowledge which is not given to anyone in its totality' (ibid., p. 78). The equilibrium perfect competition model is simply not structured to deal with this problem. In fact, it is only valid conceptually under one of two conditions: (1) when the analysis is restricted to that of a single individual, whose actions are part of a single, coherent, structured plan, and in which outcomes are all decided upon simultaneously; or (2) when multiple actors are allowed, their expectations are predicated on a commonly-held data set, and are fully compatible one with another and perforce known *ex ante* (Hayek, 1937, pp. 33–6). Both conditions imply full knowledge and the ability to act upon this knowledge.

> It appears that the concept of equilibrium merely means that the fore-sight of the different members of the society is in a special sense correct. It must be correct in the sense that every person's plan is based on the expectation of just those actions of other people which those other people intend to perform, and that all these plans are based on the expectation of the same set of external facts, so that under certain conditions nobody will have any reason to change his plans.
>
> (ibid., p. 41)

If this mutual compatibility of intentions were not given, and if in consequence no set of external events could satisfy all expectations, we could clearly say that this is not a state of equilibrium.

(ibid., p. 40)

In the perfect competition model, according to Hayek, equilibrium is guaranteed as a consequence of the *ex ante* compatibility of the individual plans of action without however there being any basis for such a postulate (ibid., p. 37).[173] The perfect competition model then can only define the Pure Logic of Choice.

Hayek noted further the inconsistency of the prevailing economic orthodoxy in advancing the postulates required for the perfect competition model to be valid; there is a fundamental contradiction in the traditional model of orthodox neoclassical economics. Knowledge must be static in order for equilibrium to hold, since a change in the data alters the action-plans of the participants in the process; but, for equilibrium to apply, the actions of the market participants *must* take place *over time*. Otherwise there is no *process*. Epistemologically, equilibrium is an atemporal concept in the orthodox paradigm; however, as physical analogue, it is only understandable as a temporal process. Hence the contradiction, with the result being that the entire concept of a perfectly competitive equilibrium collapses. (See especially Hayek, 1937, p. 36).

The problem for the economist who wishes to resolve the contradiction is to reject the perfect competition dogma and attempt to understand the mechanism behind the workings of the market. For Hayek, the market has no objective existence; it is defined through its consequences, i.e., it is defined solely as the process of the interactions of individuals in their activities of buying and selling goods, services, information, etc. The task of the economist is to understand 'how the spontaneous interaction of a number of people, each possessing only bits of knowledge, brings about a state of affairs... which could be brought about by deliberate direction only by somebody who possessed the combined knowledge of all those individuals' (ibid., p. 49). The accepted orthodoxy has become increasingly objectivist. The formal analytics of mainstream economics was (and is) predicated on an 'as if' basis: subjective valuation and interpersonal comparisons of value and utility can be avoided by stipulating formal characteristics common to physical systems which could be applied to the economic system (since it must be accepted that all systems have certain common attributes). The economy could then be analyzed 'as if' it were a physical analogue.

Instead of advancing the accepted 'as if' doctrine and so continuing in the direction of the perfect competition model, Hayek chose to take a different route and explicate the use of knowledge and information as the centerpiece of a theory of economics, and to contemplate the manner in which the interactions of individuals possessed of different temperaments conspire to create order 'spontaneously.' The creation of this 'spontaneous order' Hayek insisted (in 1933) had been accepted even by those practicing in the natural sciences; there it is the prevailing opinion that 'different tendencies may produce what we call an order, without any mind of our own kind regulating it' (Hayek, 1933, p. 130).[174] As with Menger, Hayek's view of the economic process is one in which the imagination is given center stage.

'Equilibrium' can then only be understood as a tendency which is 'relative to that knowledge which people will acquire in the course of their economic activity' (Hayek, 1937, p. 53). It is a result of the unco-ordinated actions of individuals who have little if any communication with one another as to their desires, wants, needs, abilities, means, etc. Equilibrium is a process, and so temporal in nature, which identifies the movements of the individuals in the economy as they seek to acquire knowledge, to apprehend the signals generated by the environment. 'Competition' is likewise a 'process' whose function is to induce in the system coherence and structure (Hayek, 1946, p. 106). Equilibrium and competition are not institutions which can be imposed upon an existing collective; they are terms economists attach to self-generating, independent processes.

Prices play the role in this process of information-dissemination mechanisms. The dispersion of knowledge throughout the economy, each individual actor possessing only that information relevant to the furtherance of his actions, requires a device for co-ordination (Hayek, 1945, p. 85). Prices perform this function. They serve, to reassert the language of the theory of probability, as partial-information priors which, through the interactions of the individual actors in the everyday pursuit of seemingly unconnected and unco-ordinated goals, to generate (in perhaps a Bayesian fashion, although Hayek never presented his theory of learning and the evolution of the market in these terms) over time new and more complete, i.e., more information-laden, values. It is not necessary that the information presented in the price signals be accurate; all that is required is that the prices reflect the information being generated by the market (i.e., by the spontaneous activities of the actors in the economic sphere in the pursuit of their individual goals). The more recent prices, in the language of Keynesian probability theory, have greater 'weight' than the old ones, allowing the actors a better basis upon which to decide: better, but not necessarily more accurate.

The Hayekian market is an information network. As the actors continually update their information sets, the economy is led to a tendency to a position of equilibrium. This equilibrium is not an end-point, a position to which the economy will ultimately be driven; it is the manifestation of the process of interactions among a large number of actors each possessed with subjectively held plans of action and disparate (and so not necessarily coincident) data sets. Just as the market for Hayek is not an objective entity, but the outcome of activities of interacting individuals, equilibrium is but a name to be given to this temporal learning process. It has no end; it is solely means-driven.

Yet the irony is that, while Hayek presented a theory of the market in which learning is the single most important attribute, and while it can be asserted that the mechanism behind this learning is explainable as a Bayesian process, the subjectivity of the theory implies that the one cannot model the decision processes of the economic actors in any empirical way. The problems identified by Hayek make the use of the classical probability calculus wholly inadequate. Even the personalism of Borel, Ramsey, and Savage has nothing to contribute, since the data to which an outside observer would presumably have access, the objective signals of the environment, does not necessarily coincide with the data which is employed in the decision-making of the actors in the process. Hayek eschewed 'as if' theorizing of the kind necessary for the application of personalist probability in favor of a descriptive model of the market, one which attempts to show the preconditions for the establishment of a market. Yet at bottom, Hayek's theory is not amenable to quantification since the market itself is not amenable to contemplation.

In many ways Shackle is intellectually the direct descendent of Hayek. Shades of Hayek are evident throughout Shackle's numerous writings, especially notable in the emphasis he places on the role of knowledge and the importance of epistemic uncertainty in the apprehension and collection of knowledge as the foundation for a theoretical 'scheme' of economics. Shackle extended the overarching theme of subjectivism within the Austrian theory of economics, embracing an extreme, almost solipsistic, variant. Whereas Mises identified problems with the measurement of economic variables, emphasizing the role of uniqueness as it affects the decision-making process, and Hayek's work is concerned primarily with the role of information and knowledge as attributes structuring the market, Shackle concentrated on the very nature of uncertainty itself; the temporal dimension, as an integral component of uncertainty, assumes fundamental importance for economic analysis.

Of special significance to Shackle's theory is his integration (albeit unknown to Shackle at the time of his articulations) within the Austrian subjectivist model of the Keynes-Knight distinction between risk and true uncertainty and his further acceptance of the centrality of Keynesian epistemic uncertainty. Shackle revived the distinction, in effect making it his own, distinguishing between what he termed distributional and non-distributional uncertainty, corresponding to measurable and non-measurable distribution functions, or to Mises's class and case probability (or what is defined in the present context as stochastic versus probabilistic measures).[175] Distributional uncertainty refers to the attention by economic agents to uncertain events as seriable, and so classifiable and categorizable into a number of exclusive and exhaustive groups; a system finite and closed is implied.[176] This form of uncertainty is descriptive of situations involving divisible, seriable experiments and is thus amenable to the frequency form of probability. It is the stuff of stochasticism. Non-distributional uncertainty, by contrast, allows of a possible infinity of imaginable outcomes, and is thus not to be seen as a means of event-classification or categorization, but rather as an expression of possibility. It refers to our inherent inability to assert a structure on our apprehension of the environment. This form of uncertainty is descriptive of non-divisible, non-seriable 'experiments' and is thus amenable to a probability approach emphasizing degrees of feeling or belief. It is truly probabilistic, as the term implies the existence of a non-patterned environment.

There is in such a classification a basis for a theory of utility, upon which may be founded a theory of action. Shackle described his own utility theory (theory of decision-making under uncertainty) as non-additive and non-measurable (non-distributional). He held that only in this context could a theory of utility have any relevance to the analysis of beliefs, in contrast to the prevailing frequency-ratio probability which he deemed (as did L. von Mises before him) applicable only to numerically-measurable, completely additive, divisible cases (i.e., to cases involving aleatory risk) whose application to utility assumes commensurability. He adjudged probability of the frequency-ratio type as being 'quite unsuitable for describing mental states of uncertainty' (Shackle, 1949–50, p. 70), and for this reason proposed as its replacement a measure of 'potential surprise' by which the standing of alternative hypotheses could be conceived as independent and not necessarily summable to unity (where independence is a critical requirement, in fact an axiom, of orthodox, i.e., frequentistic, probability theories).[177] The concept of potential surprise allows for a clearer apprehension of the nature of true epistemic uncertainty.[178] On Shackle's view, even the postulate of countable additivity is not a sufficient condition for the acceptance of a frequency interpretation of probability for use in decision theory, for any interpersonal or intrapersonal comparability is denied. As the list of rival hypotheses facing the actor expands, an acceptability criterion based on belief becomes unworkable because too many hypotheses compete for the positive values of belief; as additional hypotheses occur to the actor, the degree of belief expressed in previously determined hypotheses must be reduced to allow for their consideration (ibid., p. 70). 'Perfect possibility' of a hypothesis exists when the hypothesis 'appears to a person to be wholly consistent with all that he knows about the relevant situation' (ibid., p. 70). If another hypothesis is entertained which is deemed also to be 'perfectly possible,' the actor need *not* diminish his degree of acceptance of the first hypothesis.

'Potential surprise' is offered then by Shackle as an alternative, subjective assessment, distinct from expression as mathematical probability or even measure, but capable of ordinal ranking (Shackle, 1939, p. 443). A 'perfectly possible' hypothesis has a degree of potential surprise of zero. Zero potential surprise is equivalent to 'perfect possibility' as perceived by the actor: there are no perceived obstacles to the attainment of the hypothesized outcome. Expectation then takes on an entirely new meaning. An 'expected' *hypothesis* is one having either zero expected surprise attached to it and all rivals, or one having attached to itself zero expected surprise while others have attached positive expected surprise. An expected *event* is then an event having zero expected surprise. An unexpected *event*, by contrast, is one having never occurred to the actor in the first place (Shackle, 1953, pp. 112–13). This measure is obviously a qualitative one, applicable only to single events and non-repeatable experiments (Shackle, 1972, pp. 403–4).[179] This is an expression of uncertainty for which Keynes's theory of probability is most relevant, especially the Keynesian idea of weight.

'Possibility' (or, as Shackle (1949–50) preferred, its inverse, 'disbelief') treats of sets of mutually-exclusive alternatives which are not representable as series: the acceptance of any one proposition as true immediately denies the truthfulness of the remainder. Possibility

> is a reaction or response of the individual to a suggestion, whether made by himself or another, the suggestion that some specific evolution of affairs as they affect his interest can be the sequel of some course of his own action.
>
> (Shackle, 1979, p. 72)

Any perceived obstacle to possibility must be met by measures aimed at its removal. The ease or difficulty attendant to this removal causes one to ponder the existence of a continuum of possibility (ibid., p. 73). Along this continuum there may be an infinity of possible choices, which fact makes it difficult if not impossible to choose the 'most likely' possible (or most probable) outcome by applying the traditional devices of probability theory. Mathematical expectation is not applicable to Shackelian probability or utility theory (which are inseparable in Shackle's view: utility is an explicit form of the probability calculus) since its use presupposes a search from among a finite list of alternatives. Shackle's desire was to replace this determinateness by invoking the imaginative process as a means for the expression of choice. There is no need to have at one's fingertips an exhaustive list of alternatives, each member of which is assigned a numerical value as to its likelihood of occurrence. The imagination chooses from among the possible; it is in this sense that Shackelian utility theory is manifestly a discovery process (ibid., p. 79).

Shackle's utility theory is a *possibility* calculus, not a *probability* calculus (Shackle, 1972, pp. 21–3).[180] The distinction is more than semantic. Probability as Shackle perceived it as referring to the frequency view, assumes that (1) there exists a complete and exhaustive list of all contingencies (alternatives), (2) the sum of all probabilities equals unity, and (3) there exists a distribution function which is knowable. The system is closed and determinate. Frequency ratios are then calculable and employable in the determination of a numerical probability value. Possibility requires only that (1) the number of contingencies is not only unknown, but is strictly unknowable, and (2) there does not exist a distribution for the magnitudes in which we are interested. The system is open and indeterminate. This redefining of the calculus allowed Shackle to express the distinction between risk and uncertainty in a less ambiguous way than did Knight, i.e., in a set-theoretic form.

As classical and neoclassical economics are concerned with the logic of choice (Shackle accepting the position of Hayek), the decision-maker of these models must be assumed to have an end in view, and must attempt the attainment of that end through appropriate action, given that he possesses complete information as to all conceivable alternatives; he must by postulate in the neoclassical paradigm be designated an omniscient being.[181] This defines for Shackle the rational actor of classical economic theory. There must then exist a one-to-one correspondence between actions and states of mind for the choice to be rational and not merely an arbitrary happenstance. 'Choice is *rational* when it conforms to a perfect knowledge of all circumstances which will affect its relevant outcome.' (Shackle, 1965, p. 12). The classical theory is atemporal, since only in the past or the present can the rational actor have at his disposal all the information upon which a rational decision need be based; even general equilibrium variants which pretend a comprehensiveness *must* be static since they consist after all of a series of simultaneous equations in a necessarily timeless universe: the models assume that all choices and actions have been predetermined and are representable via a closed Newtonian framework. Decision tree analysis is under these conditions indispensible as a guide to the dissection of choice. Neoclassical dynamic stochastic general equilibrium models fare no better, for while they incorporate explicitly a time dimension which, through the use of variable-parameter equations and the inclusion of various possible learning schema, allows adjustment to be studied, specific outcomes are still incalculable.[182]

Even considering the economic system over time, traditional value theory can neglect any influence exerted by uncertainty in perception and apprehension and imperfect knowledge on the part of the individual by specifying the length of the period, or by specifying certain ancillary assumptions which lead to a convergence to equilibrium once exogenous forces have disturbed the system. The analysis of the traditional value theory is period-to-period, equilibrium-to-equilibrium, irrespective of the process motivating the movement. But the process *over* time does not coincide with the process *in* time, since the movement from equilibrium to equilibrium (characteristic of a Walrasian tatonnement process) assumes perfect foresight and the complementarity of plans. Error is eliminated axiomatically; rational behavior has triumphed. The end is the equilibrium of the system; the problem for the economist is reduced to an examination of how, theoretically, to construct a model to achieve that end (Shackle, 1972, p. 128).

As price serves the information function in Hayek's theory of the market, for Shackle money becomes *the* element which allows for the consolidation of uncertainty; money would be unnecessary in the economy of perfect foresight governed by Walrasian general equilibrium since 'prices' (values) would be determined instantaneously and would be expressed in terms of goods ratios. [183] By the same token, equilibrium is invalid conceptually in a monetary economy, since the presence of money, and indeed the presence of any form of credit market, generates not a unique equilibrium but multiple equilibria price vectors. [184] The existence of money implies that individuals differ with regard to their expectations of the movements of the economy, and have imagined different paths toward achievement of the ends they desire; money allows them to forestall making choices (ibid., pp. 233–5).

Classical rationality, or 'rational response' (as Shackle defined it), necessitates the full and certain knowledge on the part of the market participants of the outcomes of any given act. Arguments must be in a very real sense demonstrative; all relevant premises must be known, *ex ante*. Should that foresight be absent, rational choice in its classical guise breaks down. There is then a lack of sufficient premises upon which to base a conclusion. [185] In consequence, the entire realm of expectation is excluded from serving any meaningful purpose in the perfect-knowledge classical model, for expectation implies (requires) that the future be unknown and that the outcome of any course of action taken today will be indeterminate (ibid., p. 156).

The solution for Shackle was to abandon the rationality postulate as he considered the classical economists to have defined it, viz., in terms of perfect foresight and the complete ordering of alternatives within an atemporal framework. For Shackle, the end of the process (essentially the 'discovery' process) is not even imaginable; it is impossible to proceed in the formation of expectations covering any appreciable length of time beyond the immediate future with anything approaching a reasonable degree of certainty. Too many permutations are possible for the individual to take into consideration anything but his own choices consistent with reasonableness in attempting to reach a desired outcome. This clearly limits the domain of that information deemed to be of relevance to the act of decision-making. The constriction of the amount of information available to the actor limits his ability to form a 'rational' judgment, and so restricts his universe of potential actions. 'To act by reason, a man must be fully informed of his circumstances so far as they bear on the outcome of his action.' (ibid., p. 91). Any situation restricting the actor to less than full and complete knowledge of outcomes must result in his being uncertain as to the consequences of any action. Therefore, the economic actor can be nothing but irrational in the classical economic sense of the term. The type of static optimization at the heart of classical economic theory, that which asserts rationality by postulate, is in this situation of no value. [186]

This reduction in information availability forces the actor to accept other, less reliable, mechanisms for the attainment of reasoned decisions. In the 'kaleidic' world of Shackle: [187]

> . . . all endeavours can still be supposed to be directed by reason (deliberative or intuitive), but by reason basing itself on a flow of suggestions rather than on well-jointed information, a flow which occasionally

achieves coherence for all participants at once (though not necessarily, or even with the smallest probability, the *same* coherence) and leads to a state of affairs which has some public air of being generally co-ordinated.

(ibid., p. 125)

In order to have any content, economics must assume that the universe is open and non-determinate, that perfect foresight is non-existent (Shackle believed the condition of perfect foresight to be irrational), and that uncertainty is bounded (since a truly chaotic universe is one lacking any causal relationships). Shackle's kaleidic world is not, after all, completely chaotic or indeterminable; on the contrary, the reliance by agents on 'suggestions' implies a coordinating mechanism which serves to channel beliefs and actions towards a convergence. It must be kept in mind that a kaleidoscope does not work by forming unique, one-time, irreproducible patterns; it instead produces a limited number of *random* patterns which are readily seen to recur periodically. [188] Causal factors are at work to produce order from chaos in this simple child's toy as they are in the economic system. We do not fully comprehend their workings, although we are reasonably certain that outcomes will fall between certain intervals (not distinctly different from the confidence intervals of Neyman-Pearson statistical analysis). In other words, while it is not the case that the universe of actions is mechanical, neither is it entropic. Decision is then characterized as 'choice in face of bounded uncertainty' (Shackle, 1969, p. 5).

Shackle referred to the horizon over which an individual has formed expectations concerning the occurrence or non-occurrence of events in the future as the 'expectational vista' (Shackle, 1939, p. 442). The 'vista' need not consist of a unique contingency, but may encompass a number of conceivable scenarios, none of which is construed as being more likely to occur than any other at the instant in which they are fabricated. Each scenario may be viewed *a priori* as having an equiprobability of realization. [189] Each scenario may, however, differ in content and 'degree of surprise' should any in fact become actualized (ibid., p. 442). We may be cognizant that one of the scenarios comprising our vista will indeed occur (although even this is not necessarily so: we may have unwittingly excluded some scenarios from the set comprising the vista), but as to which we know not; when one specific scenario does occur, we are genuinely surprised. Should the set of acts and consequences be constrained, however, so that each act has attached a single, unique consequence, the decision process is no longer creative; it is mechanical. We are no longer then engaged in discovery, but in inevitability.

If, for each available act, he [the individual] sees one and only one outcome, and if also he assumes that an act necessarily has an outcome, and if further he can order all the outcomes (one for each act) according to his greater or less desire for each, then we say that his choice amongst the available acts will not involve decision, but will by contrast be a mechanical and automatic selection of that act whose outcome he most desires.

(Shackle, 1969, p. 4)

But choice is constrained as referring only to the imaginable, i.e., to that which is desired: 'Choice amongst outcomes takes place in the individual's imagination.' (ibid., p. 9). As imagination is a creative process, that which is imaginable is possible. Choice is effective. It is this constraint on choice which is destructive of the rational-actor model postulated in classical and neoclassical economics.[190] It is this constraint which is responsible for creativity and learning.

> Men imagine outcomes which come into their minds we know not whence; these outcomes can be *new* in the most absolute and radical sense, untraceable to the individual's past or present, sprung from nowhere.
>
> (ibid., p. 10)

> Decision is an operation of an individual mind, and for such decision only those things count which belong to that mind, which are available to it and are sanctioned by it.
>
> (ibid., p. 11)

Any outcome which is 'real', in the sense of having actually been experienced, is a datum and thus beyond the realm of choice. If an event has already taken place, then a choice must already have been made; choice can no longer become a consideration outside of the mental act of selection from a list of possible alternatives. Choice is creative.

Shackle could then define 'expectation' as 'Imagination constrained to congruity with what seems in some degree possible.' (ibid., p. 13). Quite a similar view as this concerning the subjectivity of expectations was well expressed by Ludwig Lachmann (1943): Expectations 'are largely a response to events experienced in the past, but the modus operandi of the response is not the same in all cases even of the same experience. This experience, before being transformed into expectations, has, so to speak, to pass through a "filter" in the human mind, and the undefinable character of this process makes the outcome of it unpredictable.' (Lachmann, 1943, p. 14). This well expresses the Kantianism inherent in the philosophy of Shackle and others of the Austrian school; it is a theme to which attention will be turned in the conclusion to this essay.

REMARKS

The Austrians as depicted above, especially Mises, Hayek, and Shackle as representative of at least a variant of Austrianism (and assumed here to be working unknowingly with a form of Keynesian probabilism), reject the use of probability measures, specifically frequency measures, for handling uncertainty. The Austrians as a group question the relevance of using probability theory to deal with what may be individual, unique events, i.e., choices of the individual decision-maker not based upon any prior event or subsumed under any other such classificatory scheme. For such events as these, no probability measure can be applied.[191] Yet only Shackle has attempted explicitly a fashioning of a suitable replacement calculus, reworking the Keynesian logicism, substituting 'possibility' for 'probability' and basing his concept on the notion of 'potential surprise.'

Menger, Mises, Hayek, and Shackle agree as well on the role in the decision process of the imagination – the thoughts and beliefs entertained by human decision-makers and the meanings attached to such thoughts and beliefs – as the basis of human action and hence the foundation of the science of economics. This is an outgrowth of their views of the utility of probability measures. Further, they all characterize the environment in which decision-makers interact as one lacking constancy in any dimension. Continual flux is the norm in virtually all aspects of the economic and social milieu affecting the decision process. It is this lack of a structured environment that allows for choice, since choice can only meaningfully take place among *possibilities*, not among data which, being known values existing *ex post*, are beyond the influence of the decision-maker.[192]

V

KEYNESAN ECONOMICS[193]

The economic theories of John Maynard Keynes descend in large measure from his views on the nature of uncertainty, probability, measurability, and the theory of knowledge as presented in the *Treatise on Probability*. This single, uninterrupted influence is readily recognizable throughout his theoretical economic writings as well as his policy pronouncements and excursions into areas other than the economic (e.g., population control and social policy matters). The main ideas derived from the *Treatise* which are consistent throughout Keynes's economic writings, in particular those discussed here, viz., *A Tract on Monetary Reform*, the *Treatise on Money*, the *General Theory of Employment, Interest, and Money*, and the 1937 *Quarterly Journal of Economics* article, 'The General Theory of Employment', are the notions of the non-measurability of beliefs and the non-seriable quality of many empirically-observed events, and the uncertainty of individual perceptions and apprehensions of the economic, political, and social environments. In other words, Keynesan economics is predicated on an understanding of *systemic* and *epistemic* uncertainty (with the emphasis on the epistemic) as fundaments of a theory of choice in an open system. Keynes was consistent in his conviction that individual, subjective choice among alternative courses of action could not be understood within the context of a deterministic environment. Non-determinism, a realization of the importance of the individual, and a general rejection of a condition of stasis as a description of the economic milieu are persistent and crucial notions appearing throughout his work. Taken in concert with an advocacy of subjectivism, the result is a theory in many ways consistent with that of Austrianism.

A TRACT ON MONETARY REFORM

Evidence of Keynes' belief in open systems may be gleaned from his repeated allusions to the need to account for the effects on beliefs and expectations of empirical non-seriable events and the manner in which the individual economic actor internalizes these influences. The possibility that non-quantifiable 'shocks' to the economic system – situations which give rise to an atmosphere of 'true' epistemic uncertainty – may have severe consequences for the economy (and for policy-makers) was given explicit recognition by Keynes in his first important economic work, the *A Tract on Monetary Reform* (1923). Qualitative influences are exceptionally powerful, i.e., they exercise a strong impact on the beliefs and anticipations of those involved in the making of business and economic decisions, while themselves being incommensurable. The presence of 'unknowns' impinging on the system from without, although non-seriable (they can in fact be characterized as 'surprise' components of the Shackelian variety) and so beyond explicit incorporation into the entrepreneurial decision calculus, must nevertheless be recognized as playing an undeniably critical role in the structure of beliefs. The difficulty of accounting for such factors as may affect subjective calculation and so discounting their effects in any objective manner Keynes recognized as a serious problem for the entrepreneur and the economic observer, much as did von Thünen and Knight and others before. Because of the indeterminable influence of these systemic factors, and the epistemic uncertainty engendered, it may be impossible for the entrepreneur to arrive at any calculation of mathematical expectation upon which economic and business decisions regarding risk are based; it may be impossible to reduce uncertainty to even a measure of epistemic risk. As Keynes wrote on the subject of international capital flows:

> The possibility of financial trouble or political disturbance, and the quite appreciable probability of a moratorium in the event of any difficulties arising, or of the sudden introduction of exchange regulations which would interfere with the movement of balances out of the country, and even sometimes the contingency of a drastic demonetisation – all these factors deter bankers, even when the exchange risk proper is eliminated, from maintaining large floating balances at certain foreign centres. Such risks prevent the business from being based, as it should be, on a mathematical calculation of interest rates; they obliterate by their possible magnitude the small 'turns' which can be earned out of differences between interest rates plus a normal banker's commission; and, being incalculable, they may even deter conservative bankers from doing the business on a substantial scale at any reasonable rate at all.
>
> (Keynes, 1923, p. 105)

Account needs to be taken and can indeed be taken of quantifiable and seriable risk (both aleatory and epistemic) in those instances in which it is possible (and feasible) to identify a suitable reference class. We recognize an element of a known series, the constitution of which we are relatively certain. We also have a ready means of calculating summary measures, this being mathematical expectation. That which had been 'bothersome' because previously deemed incomprehensible is now understandable because it is subsumed within a specific and well-defined class of events and can be represented by a numerical value. The true anomalies, the unforeseen, non-seriable, incalculable, qualitative 'risks' (systemic and epistemic uncertainty) may, however, pose an even greater burden on decision-making, for they are not so easily disposed.

It was in the *Tract* that Keynes first expressed a regard for the role of expectations in the determination of economic magnitudes, stressing, e.g., the relationship between the stability of the price level and the level of investment expenditure as uncertainty in the apprehension of market signals enters the calculus of decision making. It is 'instability of the standard of value' which is responsible for producing an environment in which investment decisions are often disappointed (ibid., p. xiv). Signals upon which expectations are founded are frequently misapprehended because we are unable to discern any underlying generating mechanism. We are unaware as to the class of which they are part. The solution must be to define a series or otherwise construct a proxy, to reconstitute the environment so as to mitigate the effects of systemic instability on belief formation. It is therefore incumbent upon the designated political authorities to establish stability so as to foster a climate conducive to investors and businessmen. This is accomplished by in effect serializing anomalous phenomena in such a manner as to 'make sense of the world.' The responsibility of the monetary authority, to take an example, is to reduce anomalies by creating a climate within which decisions can be made with a high degree of certainty as to result.[194]

Although carried out within an equilibrium framework, the analysis in the *Tract* suggests a nascent keynesianism (as the term has come to be regarded). Expectations play an especially critical role in determining certain nominal values. For example, expectations affect the level of nominal rates of interest through their effects on the desire on the part of entrepreneurs to borrow funds, given the degree of probability which the borrower attaches to each and every imaginable contingency, i.e., in those possibilities reducible to quantifiable risk. Here Keynes explained the change in the nominal rate of interest in a period of inflationary expectations by reference to mathematical expectation:

> For it is not the *fact* of a given rise of prices, but the *expectation* of a rise compounded of the various possible price movements and the estimated probability of each, which affects money rates.
>
> (ibid., p. 20)

Price expectation is defined as mathematical expectation of price movement, i.e., the sum of the possible prices multiplied by their estimated probabilities. The borrower makes a decision based upon his expected value of the future outcomes. This expectation is not entirely objectively ascertained, since it is itself based upon a (subjective) quantitative measure of influential parameters. Thus Keynes, while arguing in favor of a position whereby expectations (perceptions of the future consequences of current actions) are not amenable to the rigors demanded by mathematical probability analysis, nonetheless accepted that some such programmed valuation (serialization) does take place, even if the values derived are personal ones.

TREATISE ON MONEY

The emphasis on measurement presented once again a problem for Keynes to which much space in the *Treatise on Money* (1930) is devoted.[195] A crucial part of this argument centers on the feasibility of constructing an objective measure of purchasing power, i.e., an index number. The attempts of economic researchers to arrive at such a measure, which would allow interpersonal comparisons between individuals possessed of different income levels Keynes did not believe possible. While incomes are measurable, and individuals can be separated into reference classes based upon this measure, it is not at all reasonable to accept as an *a priori* position that comparisons can be made either within or between the groups so designated. One cannot simply define arbitrarily the classes (income groups) as homogeneous, which would be a requirement for making statements within the groups. The difficulties become compounded when intergroup comparisons are made, which of course is the entire point of the exercise. Keynes in the *Treatise on Money* based his skepticism on the calculation of index numbers on the argument from the *Treatise on Probability* dealing with the indeterminacy of numerical comparisons and the problem of aggregation of dissimilar magnitudes:

> Any attempt to strike an average for the amount by which purchasing power has changed for a community as a whole necessarily involves equating the purchasing power of money for one class to its purchasing power for a different class, which cannot be done except by an arbitrary assumption.

> (Keynes, 1930, p. 87)

> This difficulty in making precise quantitative comparisons is the same as arises in the case of many other famous concepts, namely all of those which are complex or manifold in the sense that they are capable of variations of degree in more than one mutually incommensurable direction at the same time.... The same difficulty arises whenever we ask whether one thing is superior in degree to another *on the whole*, the superiority depending on the resultant of several attributes which are each variable in degree but in ways not commensurable with one another.

> (ibid., p. 88)

Even weighted averaging cannot 'solve' the aggregation problem, since the weights themselves are arbitrary and contingent; they depend as much on a multitude of external systemic influences as they do on the capriciousness and subjectivity of the human mind.

It is the costliness of information, the difficulties involved in its collection, the problem of contradictory signals, and the limitations on human information-processing abilities that restricts the entrepreneur to reliance on current information and experience, and on models 'relating to the probable consequences of changes in bank rate, the supply of credit and the state of the foreign exchanges' (ibid., p. 144). The entrepreneur as decision-maker must view as indeterminate and probabilistic the signals generated by the environment within which he operates; these signals are simply too confused and confusing, the actor's decision-making process too constrained, and time too fleeting and precious a commodity to allow for more than a contingent forecast. Yet since action must occur which has future repercussions, and which perforce requires taking stock of relevant alternatives, *a* forecast, however conditional, must be attempted; the most complete data available as to the consequences (the outcomes) of any action are required for this. [196] All available information, *within reasonable limitations*, these being limitations on the abilities of the actor in information collection and processing, must be accounted for and included in the decision-making calculus. The Keynesan entrepreneur is not one to ignore relevant data; the additional information will, after all, increase the weight [197] attributed to any decision. But we must accept that he needs to act. In other words, the need to decide means that h_1, an imperfect (in the sense that information is available but may be neglected) information set, is the relevant one upon which actions are predicated, not h, the complete information set which, while of course desirable, is generally unknown. [198]

Still, it must be acknowledged that the imperfections, inaccuracies, and inadequacies of the signals, of the system generating the signals, of the processing abilities of those using the signals, all have an impact on the anticipation of the final outcome. The most that can be asked of the actor is apprehension, not full comprehension. [199] All the individual can aspire to is to benefit from errors. Since prescience and omniscience are denied, and the necessity to decide in the absence of full and complete information pushes the individual to action, error is virtually ensured; more strongly, error is manifest in any decision. [200] Epistemic error is an irremediable element in the choice process, which being the case necessitates the employment of a device for its accounting and handling. A learning mechanism provides the actor the opportunity to at least rebound from these errors, and perhaps even profit by them. So, given his talents and abilities, including a limited measure of foresight, coupled with a form of Bayesian error-correction (the 'learning mechanism' which is readily seen as derivable from Keynes's own axiomatization of probability in the *Treatise on Probability*), Keynes's entrepreneur is driven to action.

The *Treatise on Money* not only expanded the discussion in economics of the effects of expectations on economic decision-making, but also marked Keynes's first explicit attempt at distinguishing long-term from short-term effects, a distinction (perhaps representing the influence of Marshall) which was to be of great importance in the *General Theory*. [201] The long-run and short-run determinations of securities values, e.g., differ as to the significance of discounting. Over the long-run, uncertainty can be (somewhat) discounted to an acceptable measure of risk, allowing a present value calculation; here mathematical expectation, an application of the probability calculus, is appropriate. In the short-run, there is no calculation possible, caprice being the dominant factor in our decisions; one must rely on opinion and other subjective factors in explaining the determination of securities prices over the short-run.

> In the long run the value of securities is entirely derivative from the value of consumption goods. It depends on the expectation as to the value of the amount of liquid consumption goods which the securities will, directly or indirectly, yield, modified by reference to the risk and uncertainty of this expectation, and multiplied by the number of years' purchase corresponding to the current rate of interest for capital of the duration in question.
>
> (ibid., p. 228)

> But in the very short run, it depends on opinion largely uncontrolled by any present monetary factors....
>
> Accordingly *opinion* has a dominating influence on the position to a degree which does not apply in the case of the quantity of money required to look after a given wages bill. If everyone agrees that securities are worth more, and if everyone is a 'bull' in the sense of preferring securities at a rising price to increasing his savings deposits, there is no limit to the rise in price of securities and no effective check arises from a shortage of money.
>
> (ibid., p. 228–9)

THE GENERAL THEORY

In the *General Theory of Employment, Interest, and Money* (1936), Keynes continued in the manner of the *Treatise on Probability* and the *Treatise on Money* in regard to his emphasis on the non-measurability and non-comparability of various and disparate economic magnitudes. Specifically, he continued in his insistence that a single basis of comparison between dissimilar magnitudes and objects simply does not exist. To assume the existence of a single basis of comparison prior to any satisfactory determination of a consistent set of units to serve as a basis for comparison is neither valid conceptually nor in fact possible as a practical matter (Keynes, 1936, p. 39). Any attempts at forcing comparability, whether concerning the calculation of the general price level or price index as a simple or weighted average of individual prices, or the calculation of investment expenditure as an aggregate of the physical output or value of disparate capital goods of inherently dissimilar composition and value (in use and trade), serve only to exacerbate the situation in regards to attempts to reach precise numerical valuations of qualitative measures and may involve one in a fallacy of composition.[202]

Keynes's short-term, long-term distinction from the *Treatise on Money* appears in a reinvigorated form in the *General Theory*, applying not to securities but to capital assets. Short-term expectations pertain to cost-revenue considerations; they reflect that expectation on the part of entrepreneurs of proceeds from the sale of final goods produced from the existing capital stock, the expectation being made at the beginning of the production process (ibid., pp. 46, 148). These expectations are based on a known stock of capital and a given demand for the product (which may be predicted with a fairly high degree of certainty) (ibid., pp. 147–8). The *actualized* sale-proceeds do not affect output-employment levels except indirectly as they result in a re-appraisal of expectations (ibid., p. 47). The short-term expectations are modifiable according as more recent events warrant a change, i.e., as we gradually update our information; short-term changes in expectations are 'gradual and continuous' (ibid., p. 50). They are modifiable through reference to past events, i.e., by a simple inductive extension of the past to the present and future.

Expectations as to future earnings (returns on capital) necessitating changes in the production structure itself, apprehendible only uncertainly (i.e., with a low level of confidence), are long-term and so require forecasting values which are subject to potentially large errors. Everything is assumed changeable in the long-run, making forecasting difficult. More importantly, the information upon which the long-term expectations depend is not generally available. The entrepreneur cannot predict the (long-term) future level of wages, prices, demand, consumer tastes, or the state of technology (ibid., p. 147), for he has no basis upon which to found such a prediction. He may, for one thing, be unable to determine the appropriate series to which these variables belong. Where expectations are made, so as, for example, to attempt to gauge future economic activity and production and sales prospects, the expectations are prone to capricious alteration and are extremely volatile. However, some of these magnitudes may be seriable, and exhibit a trend which is discernible and analyzable. Where this is the case, long-term expectations may exhibit a degree of stationarity despite their general overall volatility, as the disparate psychological influences compensate for one another, ultimately cancelling out to achieve a smooth trend-line, a stable, stationary long-term epistemic series. [203] This is not to imply that these long-term expectations are in fact no more than a statistical run or a smooth aleatory data series; the state of long-term expectations refers to a social convention, not a numerical data set. However, economy-wide expectations, comprised of individual expectations, may be thought of as a form of epistemic reference class, to which one may apply terminology from probability theory. It is in fact in this discussion of long-term expectations that Keynes made explicit reference to his analysis in the *Treatise on Probability*. In Chapter 12 of the *General Theory* ('The State of Long-Term Expectation') he noted the difficulty inherent in any such calculation in which epistemic uncertainty plays a dominant role, but nonetheless limited the emphasis which should be placed on it:

It would be foolish, in forming our expectations, to attach great weight to matters which are very uncertain. It is reasonable, therefore, to be guided to a considerable degree by the facts about which we feel somewhat confident, even though they may be less decisively relevant to the issue than other facts about which our knowledge is vague and scanty.

(ibid., p. 148)

Keynes reminded readers, in a footnote, that 'By "very uncertain" I do not mean the same thing as "very improbable"' (ibid., p.148n) and referred back to the discussion of the Weight of Evidence presented in Chapter 6 of the *Treatise on Probability*. 'Uncertainty' is epistemic and implies essential unknowability; apprehensions of signals are confused because there is no reference point for a comparison of events. That which is perceived is recognized as unique and non-seriable. Further, 'uncertainty' presupposes a lack of knowledge of the secondary proposition, the probability relation. This in turn implies that the employment in such instances of any numerical decision calculus is unacceptable. Therefore, systemic (environmental) uncertainty manifests itself in the epistemic uncertainty of our apprehensions of the environment.

'Improbability' implies knowability, but refers to what has been here defined as probabilistically-irrelevant elements which may be internalized or not, at the discretion of the decision-maker. Systemic (aleatory) risk manifests itself as epistemic risk. It was the pragmatic need to actually 'decide' that led Keynes to maintain that 'very uncertain' propositions (those of low weight, possibly even paucity of information, but not necessarily low probability; the probability is simply unknown and unknowable) need not be considered as relevant in the decision process; in other words, one could ignore the 'very uncertain.' One may, for the sake of convenience, dismiss also the 'very improbable' as irrelevant as a justification for belief and motivation to action. There is little to be gained in the sense of forecasting accuracy by expending a great deal of time and effort on matters which are either irrelevant (from the standpoint of short-term forecasting) or for which the computational requirements are too extreme. (One may note shades of Ramsey, von Neumann and Morgenstern, and Savage in this conclusion.) A stochastic probability calculus can then be applied (although Keynes did not give any explicit reference to this assertion) to the new constrained, relevant set of possibilities (this partition now considered as being a 'risk' series), keeping in mind that any forecast is limited in significance by this fact.[204]

For reasons of practicality (i.e., in order to decide) Keynes retreated to some degree in the *General Theory* from his position in the *Treatise on Probability* while never completely abandoning it. In the *General Theory* Keynes accepted that it is at times proper to assume that conventions develop and will persist absent some motivation for thinking otherwise. Conventions are convenient and useful heuristic devices which assist the individual in decision making.

They serve to frame events, providing a point of reference. In the practical affairs of everyday commerce, for example, a convention develops to the effect 'that the existing state of affairs will continue indefinitely, except in so far as we have specific reasons to expect a change' (ibid., p. 152). [205] We accept the convention so long as it is assumed that extraneous components exert little or no influence, and that the market maintains the convention irrespective of the expectations of the individuals participating in the market. The whole, the accepted conventional wisdom or general state of expectation of the market, the trend, if you will, of current opinion, is *not* the sum of its parts; this trend is not a composition of the beliefs and apprehensions of the individual participants in the market. It is an aggregate measure of the 'opinion of opinion' and so may be treated in disconnection from its constituent parts, through application of a Vennian-type frequentistic probability analysis (in the present instance, analysis of a cross-sectional series). [206] To reiterate, while the 'convention' is of course a social contrivance, it is not beyond examination as a stationary, homogeneous reference class. The convention has many of the same properties as the class. The postulate of the market being a collection of a large number of individual, atomistic units each with a minimal ability to exert influence on the whole, with disparate factors cancelling out as experienced in any large empirical series, is hereby maintained and validated theoretically. Interest need only be focused on the series, the convention if you prefer, not on the individual elements within the series, i.e., the individual expectations which together form the social convention.

But for Keynes such a convention serves only for the sake of simplicity, as a means of arriving at some method for the computation of a future valuation; it is not to be taken as the 'true' state of affairs. There is no basis for the belief that the convention behaves in accordance with the classical Principle of Non-Sufficient Reason, whereby it is assumed *a priori* that the individual members of the collective fall in their beliefs on one side or the other of the convention with equal probability. On the contrary, the convention serves to constrain action so as to invite treatment as a Vennian series. It serves in effect as a rule or procedure which acts to map individual behavior into a homogeneous reference class. In point of fact, Keynes warned against the unqualified use of such a convention. He admonished readers to revert to this palliative only when numerical calculation failed. Keynes phrased such qualified acceptance of the criterion in the *Treatise on Probability*:

> For it can easily be shown that the assumption of arithmetically equal probabilities based on a state of ignorance leads to absurdities. We are assuming, in effect, that the existing market valuation, however arrived at, is uniquely *correct* in relation to our existing knowledge of the facts which will influence the yield of the investment, and that it will only change in proportion to changes in this knowledge; though, philosophically speaking, it cannot be uniquely correct, since our existing

knowledge does not provide a sufficient basis for a calculated mathematical expectation.

(ibid., p. 152)

The probability calculus and the acceptance of *a priori* conventions are useful, but should be applied cautiously. The problem is that the convention is subject to 'waves of optimistic and pessimistic sentiment' (ibid., p. 154) as 'the mass psychology of a large number of ignorant individuals is liable to change violently as the result of a sudden fluctuation of opinion due to factors which do not really make much difference...; since there will be no strong roots of conviction to hold it steady' (ibid., p. 154).[207] Factors heretofore ignored in the convention may eventually reappear with dramatic effects.

The focus on speculation at the expense of enterprise (Keynes's terms) led Keynes to consider that expectations were the result of 'animal spirits' and not a systematic calculation of mathematical expectation to derive a numerical value amenable to objective choice. 'Animal spirits' is Keynes's euphemism for caprice, surprise, whim, i.e., aspects of behavior eliminated from consideration in the mechanical calculation of expected values. 'Animal spirits' is a shorthand description of the motivation behind epistemic uncertainty. Although beyond the scope of calculation, the effects should not be ignored. It is the speculative nature of individuals that is the crucial element in the investment (and general economic) process; 'animal spirits' are a necessary if sometimes forgotten component of this valuation process.[208] The necessity to decide requires acting on the basis of something less tangible than calculated averages. More to the point, lacking these capricious impulses, there would no longer exist the vital, energetic, entrepreneurial spirit, the spirit of enterprise.[209] Thus is provided a rationale for market movements beyond the mere occurrence of a historical event or episode; opinions, the individual, subjective valuations of occurrences past, present, and future, are by themselves factors of significance in economic valuation.[210] Thus is Austrianism coextensive with Keynesanism.

Similar considerations underlie the movements in the money market, epistemic uncertainty 'as to the future of the rate of interest' being a 'necessary condition' for the existence of a liquidity-preference function (ibid., p. 168). Money serves, after all, the function of linking the future to the present; dynamic equilibrium, in which expectations are in a constant state of flux, requires the service of money as a device for allowing the transition (ibid., p. 294). However, a (more important) condition concerns the differentiation in the subjective valuations of the future market rates of interest: 'For different people will estimate the prospects differently and anyone who differs from the predominant opinion as expressed in market quotations may have a good reason for keeping liquid resources....' (ibid., p. 169). Keynes felt that the emphasis on individual subjective factors as to the degree of uncertainty was essential to the stability and effectiveness of the economic structure:

It is interesting that the stability of the system and its sensitiveness to changes in the quantity of money should be so dependent on the existence of a *variety* of opinion about what is uncertain.

(ibid., p. 172)

It is this variety and variability of opinion which is responsible for the functioning and stability of the system. Unanimity of opinion as to future values of the price level or interest rates can have no effect other than forcing a re-evaluation of current asset holdings which, by definition, would eliminate differential valuations and hence eliminate speculative profit opportunities; it would in effect result in a cessation of market activity as no one would be willing to initiate trade should gains from so doing no longer be realizable: [211]

Only, indeed, in so far as the change in the news is differently interpreted by different individuals or affects individual interests differently will there be room for any increased activity of dealing in the bond market. If the change in the news affects the judgment and the requirements of everyone in precisely the same way, the rate of interest . . . will be adjusted forthwith to the new situation without any market transactions being necessary.

(ibid., p. 198)

It is to differences of knowledge and interpretation of market signals that Keynes attributed interest rate and hence money demand changes. A world populated by the 'representative agent' possessed of perfect knowledge and perfect foresight would be one in which trade was unnecessary (in fact trade would be irrational) since there would be no epistemic uncertainty, all valuations would change simultaneously and consequently no one would feel compelled to initiate trade.

In the final analysis, expectations in the *General Theory*, as in the *Tract* and the *Treatise on Money*, are of the same form as other non-seriable, non-comparable, non-measurable aggregates: although not reducible to a single numerical value, they are potentially capable of being incorporated by proxy into an economic model if one is prepared to make certain simplifying assumptions and to keep in mind that such assumptions are limited in their usefulness and applicability. As Keynes stated:

An entrepreneur, who has to reach a practical decision as to his scale of production, does not, of course, entertain a single undoubting expectation of what the sale-proceeds of a given output will be, but several hypothetical expectations held with varying degrees of probability and definiteness. By his expectation of proceeds I mean, therefore, that expectation of proceeds which, if it were held with certainty, would lead to the same behaviour as does the bundle of vague and more various possibilities which actually makes up his state of expectation when he reaches his decision.

(ibid., p. 24n3)

Keynes seems here to have 'solved' the problem of the incorporation of an epistemic uncertainty 'variable' into economic models by invoking a form of certainty-equivalence[212] as a simplifying assumption for the actual situation which obtains (this situation being the existence of a continuum of weighted expectations). He could thereby eliminate explicit consideration of probabilistic expectation in favor of an acceptance of expectations as a datum.[213] Keynes realized (as noted above) the unrealistic nature of such a simplification, but felt the objections to be of minor consequence given the advantages it allowed in terms of giving operational recognition to the concepts of expectations and uncertainty in economic models.[214]

'THE GENERAL THEORY OF EMPLOYMENT'

Keynes's method is important and in some respects unique in that he provided so much weight in his writings to his and the classical economists' twin central concerns of uncertainty and expectations. As he reiterated in his 1937 *Quarterly Journal of Economics* article, uncertainty is absolutely crucial to any analysis of a theory of investment and economic valuation, where the prime interest lay not in immediate gratification but in the remoter consequences of action (Keynes, 1937, p. 213). To outline further the economic position of the *General Theory*, Keynes found it necessary once again to define the term 'uncertain' as he had originally done in the *Treatise on Probability* and had reiterated in Chapter 12 of the *General Theory*:

> By "uncertain" knowledge, let me explain, I do not mean merely to distinguish what is known for certain from what is only probable. The game of roulette is not subject, in this sense, to uncertainty. . . . The sense in which I am using the term is that in which the prospect of a European war is uncertain, or the price of copper and the rate of interest twenty years hence . . . . About these matters there is no scientific basis on which to form any calculable probability whatever. We simply do not know.
>
> (ibid., pp. 213–14)

Keynes's consistency is remarkable. Once again, he defined uncertainty with respect to the lack of knowledge on the part of decision-makers of the probability relation and not merely a lack of enough information upon which to found a numerical value. In other words, he persevered in his insistence that uncertainty is fundamentally an epistemic concept. Perceptual difficulties prevent the agent from intuiting a probability relation. This is not a result of information deficiency; it is rather solely a result of lack of acuity. This lack of knowledge (broadly defined) means there is no means of calculating a degree of belief. The probability is not merely numerically indeterminate, it is fundamentally unknown.

The classical economists had, according to Keynes, considered only an economic system of complete certainty and perfect information, in which expectations were a datum. The economy was taken to be closed and determinate (i.e., Newtonian). True uncertainty (in the sense of Keynes and Knight) was assumed away; all risk (aleatory and epistemic) was asserted to be numerically-calculable. 'The calculus of probability, tho mention of it was kept in the background, was supposed to be capable of reducing uncertainty to the same calculable status as that of certainty itself.' (ibid., p. 213). For Keynes, decision is prone to violent, sudden shocks as unpredictable changes impinge on the system from without (ibid., pp. 214–15).[215] It is for this reason, as a means for the mitigation of such erratic movements, that money has value (is a Store of Value); money serves its function as 'a barometer of the degree of our distrust of our own calculations and conventions concerning the future' (ibid., p. 216).

OTHER WRITINGS

Keynes's 1939 critique of Jan Tinbergen's procedure for the statistical analysis of business cycles again afforded him a forum with which to reiterate his views on measurability. Noting that Tinbergen had restricted his analytical techniques to (supposedly) measurable quantities, but then appended a caveat to the effect that qualitative phenomena may exert an influence and so require supplemental analysis, Keynes suggested that the method employed by Tinbergen would itself not accept the incorporation of any supplemental factors. The parametric values of the regression equations are calculated on the assumptions of comprehensiveness and exhaustiveness, i.e., completeness in the specification of the explanatory equations, the error term postulated as taking up any residual influences. The Tinbergen procedure in its pretense to comprehensiveness then left no room for consideration of additional parameters, whether quantitative or qualitative. The equations of the model were complete as stated. What is more, the procedure could not in any event account for qualitative influences since there does not exist a definable series of qualitative variables. As Keynes wrote:

> If it is necessary that *all* the significant factors should be measurable, this
> is very important. For it withdraws from the operation of the method all
> those economic problems where political, social and psychological
> factors . . . may be significant. In particular, it is inapplicable to the
> problem of the Business Cycle.
>
> (Keynes, 1939, p. 561)

Tinbergen's insistence on measurability limited the significance and usefulness of his method, the method of linear least squares regression, in his analysis of the business cycle, for the reason that the cycle itself is composed in part of psychic components, viz., uncertainty, political factors, social trends, and the like. These extraneous factors cannot all be subsumed in the error term, since the error term is not a comprehensive residual. Neither can the measurable components of the series be considered as independent, as they must for Tinbergen's method to have any validity in empirical studies. [216]

REMARKS

Epistemic uncertainty emerges as a critical component in decision-making throughout Keynes's analysis, and something which had been only mentioned casually or neglected altogether in most other economic work of the time (excepting of course its integral importance in the work of the Austrians and its acknowledgement by classical writers). Keynes's constant and consistent reaffirmation of his stance on the matter shows the importance he felt it held for economic theory. Economics had been concerned previously (in the more simplified interpretations) with analyzing an ordered society in which knowledge, information, and expectations were held with certainty, the process culminating in a long-run equilibrium; the system was postulated to be closed, stable and orderly. Keynes was more concerned with analysis of open systems, with instability and disorder, situations in which information was not complete, expectations of the future were unclear or subject to caprice, and, in the world of the 1930s, depression and unemployment seemed to be without end. [217] Equilibrium was viewed as an idealized concept of the modeler, not a viable construct for the 'practical theorist' such as Keynes. [218]

The importance of the individual for Keynes is evident from his continued stress on the problem of the aggregation of dissimilar, non-comparable magnitudes, especially in the realm of expectations. Keynes's belief in the subjectivity of rational belief and the inability to make (ordinally or cardinally) interpersonal utility and probability comparisons again reflects a philosophical acceptance of individualism in regard to rules and ethics the usefulness or practicality of which are at the time in question (the 'religion' of Cambridge philosopher G. E. Moore (1903), which Keynes accepted), while ignoring the broader ramifications for the society as a whole (the 'morals' of Moore, which he rejected). This acceptance of individualism in the area of rules and ethics, and rejection of general rules, led ultimately to Keynes's rejection of Benthamite utilitarianism. It did not, however, prevent him from occasionally finding it necessary actually to employ just such a principle. [219]

VI

RATIONAL EXPECTATIONS AND THE NEW NEOCLASSICISTS

One legacy of Keynes to modern economics has been taken to be the explosive growth of econometric model estimation. This is of course ironic given his critique of econometric modeling in his debate with Tinbergen. To verify empirically the conclusions derived from 'keynesian' models purported to have been developed on Keynesan foundations, conclusions with respect to consumption, investment, liquidity, and the role of government intervention, keynesians were driven to employ ever more powerful econometric techniques (two-stage least squares, three-stage least squares, Probit and Tobit models, to name but a few).

Econometric models developed in the spirit of keynesianism, while providing a reasonably good 'fit' to the data and delivering tolerably good predictive performance from their inception until the early 1970s, failed to deliver and failed miserably in the period following.[220] These models proved particularly inadequate regarding recognition of the simultaneous problems of high inflation and high unemployment which characterized these later years; specifically, their *predictive* performance was especially dismal over this period. Theoretical advances in economics and econometrics also outpaced the ability of even the most sophisticated of these early (some may contend naive) models to be adapted so as to account for alternative solutions to and characterizations of the economic problem.

It was in this milieu that an alternative to the more simplistic of these formulations, simplistic as regards the incorporation of expectations, was proposed. It became clear that a novel approach to econometric modeling was necessary. This challenge to provide a better modeling paradigm led to the birth of rational expectations and to its eventual supplanting of keynesian theory as the accepted economic paradigm.

ARROW-DEBREU AS PROGENITOR

The Rational Expectations revolution initiated by John Muth and extended by Robert Lucas, Thomas Sargent, Robert Barro, Edward Prescott, and others has as its genesis the pioneering efforts in the axiomatic analyses of general

108

economic equilibrium of Kenneth Arrow and Gerard Debreu. Both of these presentations as statements of deductive theory aimed initially at the derivation of a general equilibrium model under conditions of certainty through the imposition of severe constraints on the agents in the model environment. Uncertainty, so far as it is deemed a problem, is incorporated into these axiomatic models by the use of contingent securities and commodities, which have the effect of transforming uncertainty into certainty, allowing it to be effectively ignored. Arrow's seminal 1953 article, 'The Role of Securities in the Allocation of Risk-Bearing,'[221] introduced into the argument the concept of state-contingent commodities. The employment of this concept extended the conventional meaning of 'commodity' to account for the occurrence of an event or 'state of the world,' a procedure having derived from the utility and probability theory of von Neumann and Morgenstern and central to the probabilism of Savage.[222] The 'event' or 'state of the world' becomes one of the defining characteristics of the commodity, so that not only are commodities distinguishable by virtue of their physical characteristics, but the same physical commodity at two different dates and even at different locations is in effect two different commodities.[223] A 'contract' or 'agreement' stipulates the delivery of the 'commodity' at a given date and location, contingent on the occurrence of the particular event or on our being in a particular state of the world. With S possible states and C commodities, the individual's utility function will then be a vector in SC-space, clearly of much greater magnitude than under the conventional definition in which the vector exists in C-space only.

Although Arrow's theory is purported to address the concerns inherent in an environment characterized as unpredictable, the contingent-commodity model is probability-free and uncertainty-free, at least insofar as the model is expressed in an objective guise. The individual (subjective) probabilities are irrelevant (although implicit in the model) because all contingencies are assumed known and accountable by way of the redefined commodity; the SC-space includes each and every different commodity as well as the states defining each. The model is constructed under the assumption of the existence of markets for goods defined over all possible future contingencies, foreseeable or not. Recontracting is not permitted nor can it occur because all contracts are finalized at the beginning of the market process (the market day), removing any incentive to renegotiate. There is then no need for a specific reference to probability since no contingency is unrecognized; all states and consequences of actions are presumed identifiable and discountable. The environment is so characterized as to ensure that it is perceived with complete certainty. As Debreu stated, 'This new definition of a commodity allows one to obtain a theory of uncertainty free from any probability concept and formally identical with the theory of certainty....' (Debreu, 1959, p. 98). Uncertainty then emerges in a different guise, since it now 'originates in the choice that Nature makes among a finite number of alternatives' (ibid., p. 98).

While valid theoretically as a means for handling within a static general equilibrium framework the problem of uncertainty, where uncertainty is systemic (aleatory), the computational problems of such an undertaking even within this closed system are immense. The complexities are too great to allow computational possibility. To limit the complexity, Arrow also presented (as part of the same article) an extended model in which the subjective probabilities regain operational status. In this variant of the model Arrow allowed that under the condition that money-claims replace commodity-claims, i.e., that a contingent-securities market exists for which claims are payable in money, there exists for each individual a utility function and an explicit subjective probability set for the occurrence of each state, where the utility function itself contains C elements (the C commodities). There need then be only S markets in contingent securities. The set of states is a partition of non-empty subsets of these future contingencies. The individual decision-maker is assumed to form subjective probabilities as to the occurrence of each state (as in Savage), and to act on the basis of those probabilities (Arrow, 1964, p. 91). This provision for subjective probabilities allows for uncertainty *provided* all agents have equal access to and identical apprehensions of environmental signals and subjective probability values. Yet the specification that the set of states are mutually-exclusive, complete, and exhaustive means that epistemic uncertainty is eliminable from reflection. Even the 'true' systemic uncertainty of Knight has no role. Every state imaginable has attached to it for each individual a value designating its subjective probability of occurrence. This equality between the state-commodity space and securities, designed as a hedge against uncertainty, effectively reduces uncertainty to identity with measurable risk.

Debreu, in his 1959 *Theory of Value*, followed Arrow's 'solution' to the problem of handling uncertainty by the use of contingent commodities in his axiomatic approach to the study of general equilibrium models. In Debreu's reinterpretation of general economic equilibrium, delivery of the 'uncertain commodity' is contingent upon the occurrence of an event. From here the theory of economic equilibrium proceeds in exactly the form as that under conditions of certainty, with the certainty of the deterministic models being replaced by a restrictive form of uncertainty for which commodities markets exist (or can be readily created) to deal with each contingency. The model is essentially a perfect insurance program, providing a policy to cover any and all contingencies. All states of nature are known in advance and there can be said to exist probability distributions (albeit implicit in the presentation of Debreu) covering each and every state. [224] The result is a general economic equilibrium application of the decision theory of Savage without explicit reference to probability: the preference ordering is all that is required. [225]

The Arrow-Debreu framework is an axiomatic extension of Walrasian general equilibrium theory, restated so as ostensibly to incorporate intertemporal (and interspatial) effects. Uncertainty is, after all, only valid conceptually in a temporal environment. Such a model is, however, essentially static since the only difference between commodities is in their position in time and space, state-contingent prices being specified in advance of trading, and states of nature treated *as though* all have been assigned specific probabilities of occurrence at the outset. Agents have no need of forging expectations of prices, since in such a model prices will have been pre-selected or determined within the model. The theory is deductive, and the system is closed.

RATIONAL EXPECTATIONS

John Muth presented a theory of expectations-formation which was to change the focus of macroeconomic thinking. His seminal 1961 *Econometrica* article, 'Rational Expectations and the Theory of Price Movements,' maintained a 'purely descriptive' (Muth, 1961, p. 4) hypothesis of 'rational expectations,' developed from a desire to specify a function which could relate the individual's decision rule to the environment faced by the decision-maker. The rationale behind the effort was to define a mapping so as not to limit the theory of expectations to *ad hoc* specifications of the decision function (as Muth maintained had been the case with adaptive expectations). Rationality, as Muth conceived it, becomes that which the model builder imposes upon the decision-maker from without; the rationality of the actor himself is inconsequential.

The economic modeler (the new role which the theorist must assume) in an effort to account for this imposed rationality must designate an objective probability distribution function defined over all time and space. From this it follows that subjective distribution functions central to personalist theories of utility lose content. Given this stipulation Muth was able to reorient the discussion of individual rational behavior to conclude that the individual's subjective probability distribution is distributed (or 'tends to be distributed, for the same information set' (ibid., p. 4)) as the objective probability distribution of the economic theory.[226] The subjective distribution has the same expected value and variance as the theoretical, objective distribution – the expected value of the residual is zero. Any deviation from trend is entirely random, and so can be subsumed under an appended normally-distributed error term. The individual actor as decision-maker *must* on this specification form expectations in the same manner as the economic theorist and econometrician, using the same information as efficiently, and employing essentially the same forecasting model as do the policy makers.[227] There is no need for the elucidation of a theory to explain the procedure behind the processing of information by economic agents, nor is there any need for a theory to interpret the learning or error-correction process. The entire conception is external to the decision-making process and the environment in which decisions are to be made; the probability distribution is simply imposed on the model from without. It must be asserted *a priori* that a given distribution has and will continue to serve as a description of the environment from which the signals were generated. The rational expectations environment is ergodic.

A few definitions and refinements should serve to clarify. The defining aspect of rational expectations models, and the related models of real business cycles, is that, following Savage, and von Neumann and Morgenstern, the underlying probability space has been so restricted as to include only measurable elements; this restriction alone denies altogether any role for 'true (epistemic) uncertainty' in the sense of Keynes, and even 'true (aleatory) uncertainty' in the sense of Knight. In fact, these models are usually constructed under the assumption that there exists a triple $(\Omega, \mathfrak{I}, P)$, where Ω is a state-space, $\mathfrak{I}$ is a Borel algebra (or σ-algebra) of subsets of Ω, and P is a probability measure defined on $\mathfrak{I}$.[228] This triple defines completely the character of the rational expectations model, as it identifies the restrictive domain within which the model is specified. Define a random variable as a function $\theta: \Omega \rightarrow \mathbb{R}$. By definition, then, the random variable is measurable. To be more specific, θ is measurable if, when $B \in \mathfrak{I}$, $\theta^{-1}(B) \in \mathfrak{I}$. Define a *stationary stochastic process*[229] as a collection of random variables θ indexed over time:

$$\Theta = \{\theta_1, \theta_2, \ldots, \theta_t\}$$

with the following properties:

(1) $E(\theta_t) = \mu \; \forall \, t$
(2) $\sigma(\theta_t, \theta_{t+r}) = E[(\theta_t - \mu)(\theta_{t+r} - \mu)] \; \forall \, t, \, r$
(3) $\text{var}(\theta_t) = \sigma_\theta^2 \; \forall \, t$

where E is the expected-value operator.

The process is time-independent, and may be characterized completely by the first and second moments.
Now, if

$$P[\theta_{t+1} \,|\, \theta_0, \theta_1, \ldots, \theta_t] = P[\theta_{t+1} \,|\, \theta_t] \text{ for all } t$$

then $\{\theta_t\}$ is said to be *Markovian*, and the variable is said to follow a *Markov process*. The rational expectations paradigm is constructed upon this foundation.

The implication gathered from the use of Markov processes for economic modeling is that one need only focus attention on the present; the past may be completely discounted since the probabilities do not vary temporally. Economic signals (e.g., prices) are information-laden; the present manifestation of the variables accommodates all the information contained in previous outcomes of the process. The probability of any future event, given the entire historical record of the process, depends only on the present state of the process.

To complete the model, we need to stipulate a means by which to generate an equilibrium solution so as to guarantee stability. This is achieved by the assertion of ergodicity. Ergodicity may be defined with respect to the above-mentioned stationary stochastic process. If the stochastic process is such that the average over the entire process (the spatial average) is equivalent to the time-averages of the individual components, then the process is said to be *ergodic.*[230] Given the stipulation made in rational expectations models that Θ is a stationary stochastic process confined to the ergodic set, the convergence properties of these models are pre-established. Equilibrium is guaranteed. The inductive hypothesis regains validity. As Robert Lucas and Edward Prescott (1971) noted, the ergodic set is one for which entry presupposes conformity; from the ergodic path there is no escape.[231]

That supposedly random processes exhibit regularities amenable to statistical treatment has been known since at least the time of Venn.[232] Both time series and cross-sectional series, over lengthy spans, evince some form of stationary trend or statistical regularity which is discernible. Not only are these secular regularities evident, but cyclical components are recurrent and can be, over a significant period of time, identified and so removed or at the least discounted. This feature of a long statistical series is a critical component in the viability of Muthian rational expectations theory. Only insofar as these series exist, and are analyzable as Markov processes, can one evolve a theory of information efficiencies which exploits these peculiarities of the series. In effect, Muth's theory asserts axiomatically that the individual as an agent in the economy not only utilizes the totality of information at his disposal, but that he does so efficiently, performing much as the econometric modeler expects he will.

The classical paradigm is reinvigorated by the Muthian hypothesis: markets clear fully and instantaneously under the new neoclassical paradigm.[233] The result is a forced equilibrium: the formulation of the model itself ensures at the outset that equilibrium will obtain, and be restored in the presence of potentially destabilizing external shocks (although this 'restoration' is somewhat illusory, since the system cannot deviate from the *path* towards equilibrium). As a consequence, rational expectations models and the theory underlying them are entirely pragmatic. Behavior is irrelevant; process is irrelevant. By examining the behavior of series averages, human behavior is reduced to a quantity, a mathematical expectation, and economics is reduced to a mechanistic science.[234]

Muth's theory and all other true representations of rational expectations for which the theory of stationary stochastic processes provides a foundation must then be merely predictive, corresponding to Herbert Simon's (1982) definition of objective rationality. Muthian rationality implies simply the consistency of the behavior of the decision-makers with the predictions of economic theory. All reference to the individual as a cognitive being, of 'subjective rationality', is of no relevance, as he may be replaced by the 'rational representative agent'[235] possessed of an additively-separable utility function. Rational behavior can then be defined as per Savage in terms of outcomes, devoid of process. The rationale for decision-making becomes of no consequence; the motivation behind the behavior of the individual is deemed irrelevant.[236]

Muth assumed at the outset normally-distributed disturbances, linear equations, and certainty-equivalents (Muth, 1961, p. 5), so as to facilitate econometric estimation (a rather Keynesan thing to do). The normality assumption is especially crucial in this regard: 'As long as the variates have a finite variance, a linear regression function exists if and only if the variates are normally distributed.' (ibid., p. 5n). Rational expectations models can then be constructed under the supposition of a closed system in which complete contingent markets of the Arrow-Debreu variety are conformable to the workings of actual markets.

So, at its foundation, the Muthian rational expectations hypothesis defines rationality as a consistency postulate and not as an attribute of the individual:[237] the individual's subjective probability distribution is identical with the economy's objective probability distribution. Forecasts (expectations) are 'rational' as rationality is defined, viz., as utilizing efficiently *all* available information affecting the time path of the variables of interest (e.g., prices, interest rates, etc.). Such a postulate simply ensures that errors are consistent among the participants in the market process; it serves to generate a stationary, homogeneous set of signals, but in no way postulates a theory of behavior in the face of uncertainty.[238] This attempt by Muth to force rationality by requiring that economic actors behave in a manner consistent with the underlying model of the economy is then similar in form to Savage's (and Raiffa's) expressed desire that decision-makers re-evaluate their decisions on the basis of a consistent set of axioms and thereby act accordingly. In so doing, actors *must* be rational since they *must* act in accordance with a set of rational decision axioms. But Muth requires much stronger assumptions than those considered by Savage. Muth's probabilities are imposed objectively, not derived in any subjective manner. Muthian rational expectations is programmed decision-making.

The focus in rational expectations on model building and a form of Friedmanian pragmatism necessitated a redefinition of equilibrium, away from the classical economic conception (as perceived somewhat erroneously by neoclassical writers in their quest for precursors) derived from classical mechanics of a system either at rest or approaching in the limit a given, fixed value or path and hence not receptive to internal change which would allow deviations from such a path (the 'stationary state' in Marshall's terms). The new definition of equilibrium proposed by Lucas, for example, whose work resurrected the intuitions of Muth, emphasizes the clarification and explication of objectives and environmental parameters, consistency, and feasibility (Lucas, 1987, p. 16). It follows from the econometric specifications of Muth and so implies nothing more or less than a system 'following a multivariate stochastic process' characterized 'at each point in time' by market-clearing and populated by agents acting 'in their own self-interest' (Lucas and Sargent, 1981, pp. 304–5).[239] Disequilibrium becomes a vacuous concept. Any validity the term had disappears by definition; all supposed disequilibrium phenomena are defined out of existence as the focus shifts from explanation and understanding to modeling.[240] The constitutions of time-series data simply *are* as they are. Time series are inherently expressive neither of equilibrium nor disequilibrium; if

114

anything the redefinition by the rational expectationists amounts to an anequilibrium theory.

Lucas's decision maker is situated in a dynamic environment. Faced not with prices but rather with time paths of prices at which present and future trading will occur, he is capable of dealing with systemic uncertainty through the creation of Arrow-Debreu contingency plans. Formally, he 'must formulate a subjective joint probability distribution over all unknown random variables which impinge on his present and future market opportunities' (Lucas, 1981, p. 223).[241] The Bayesian decision process (central to Savage's probability interpretation and derivable from Keynes's and the frequency interpretations as well) has no role in Lucasian rational expectations theory, as there is in effect no learning process; all is established in advance.[242]

> Unfortunately, the general hypothesis that economic agents are Bayesian decision makers has, in many applications, little empirical content: without some way of inferring what an agent's subjective view of the future is, this hypothesis is of no help in understanding his behavior. Even psychotic behavior can be (and today, is) understood as "rational", given a sufficiently abnormal view of relevant probabilities. To practice economics, we need *some* way (short of psycho-analysis, one hopes) of understanding *which* decision problem agents are solving.
>
> (ibid., p. 223)

Rationality, as it relates to the process behind the actions of individual decision-makers in an uncertain environment, is of no relevance; the entire structure of the utility optimization process of the individual under conditions of systemic uncertainty, the microfoundations of economics, is irrelevant, in contrast to the position explicitly enunciated by those advocating the rational expectations hypothesis. The result is a microeconomic-based macroeconomic theory without the need to account for the cumbersome processes involved in decision-making.[243]

But rational expectations does not claim to deal with agents operating in an *epistemically-uncertain* environment; the claim is to allow an analysis of decision within a *stochastic* (aleatory risk) environment,[244] with this environment not necessarily constrained by relation to the empirical data. The artificiality of this paradigm is readily conceded. State replaces process; construct replaces cognition. Although relying on a subjective probability distribution to provide the basis for his theory of expectations (following the lead of Muth), Lucas must have considered that the acknowledgement was sufficient; it could then be dispensed with since the rational actor himself is no longer necessary. As Lucas and Prescott announced in their study of investment under uncertainty, 'Thus we surrender, in advance, any hope of shedding light on the *process* by which firms translate correct information into price forecasts.' (Lucas and Prescott, 1971, p. 660).

Yet at the operational level, account must be taken of the decision process.

One need account not merely for Savage's consistency of preference rankings, but also his subjectivism and Keynes's insistence on non-comparability and unknowability. In other words, we need to account for the *epistemic* environment as well as the *systemic*. Under the rational expectations approach, the theories of Muth and Lucas equate the subjective probabilities to the true objective probabilities of the occurrence of events. In conditions where this in fact obtains, we have the definition of a calculable aleatory risk; this is undeniable. The existence of a known, objectively-valid distribution function descriptive of an objectively stochastic environment makes it so. In those instances where a probability distribution is incalculable, for reasons of non-comparability or unknowability or non-measurability, the case of true uncertainty obtains. For his part, Lucas acknowledged that the rational expectations hypothesis was not of relevance to situations involving uncertainty, but applied only to those cases reducible to risk:[245]

> It will *most* likely be useful in situations in which the probabilities of interest concern a fairly well defined recurrent event, situations of "risk" in Knight's terminology. In situations of risk, the hypothesis of rational behavior on the part of agents will have usable content, so that behavior may be explainable in terms of economic theory. In such situations, expectations are rational in Muth's sense. In cases of uncertainty, economic reasoning will be of no value.
>
> (Lucas, 1981, pp. 223–4)

Non-comparability, non-measurability, and unknowability, while attractive from an epistemic standpoint, are irrelevant by assumption. Consequently, pure epistemic uncertainty as described by Keynes and Shackle as of integral importance to their economics does not enter into the rational expectations calculus, because it has been assumed either not to exist or, if acknowledged, not to apply. The economy is stationary, i.e., the equilibrium of the system is the steady-state; the system is balanced in that competing forces generate outcomes tending to a specific time-path. This is Marshall's stationary state, his 'evenly rotating economy.'[246] Uncertainty has been completely reduced to risk, and the deviations of actual values from their expectations are assumed to be distributed as a normal random variable, with constant mean and finite variance. The result is that, under the rational expectations paradigm, an equilibrium is guaranteed; it is established by definition, the use of the ergodic theorems ensuring that this will be the case.

REINTERPRETATIONS OF RATIONAL EXPECTATIONS

That rational expectations models are flawed in this respect has been accepted by among others Kenneth Arrow. Arrow accepted the bounded rationality hypothesis of Simon, arguing that the subsidiary postulates of the homogeneity of agents' utility functions and complete information are necessary conditions for the existence of a rational expectations equilibrium. Since rationality in these models requires agents to have knowledge of the conditional probability distributions, there is no longer any cost involved in the acquisition of information or its processing. Once these assumptions are relaxed, e.g., if the states of the world exceed the number of contingent securities, there can no longer exist a unique equilibrium solution; one is left instead with a continuum of possible equilibria (Arrow, 1987, p. 212).[247]

Even when modifications were made to the rational expectations models, these were nothing more than extensions of the existing models, indistinguishable in form and substance from the originals. Douglas Gale (1983), for instance, pondered a case of imperfect information on the part of agents, leading to the possibility of 'surprises.' This Gale claimed to be consistent with rational expectations, while exhibiting a degree of empirical validity. But this concession to reality, to the procedural aspects of economic decision, was short-lived. The 'limiting case' (fashioned to serve as a counter to the 'straw man' of perfect foresight) assumed policy variables stipulated *ad hoc*, independently and identically distributed (Gale, 1983, p. 11). Where is the surprise? The model in all its essentials is identical to the stock rational expectations model. Randomness is, as in the prototypical rational expectations model, incorporated as a necessary condition. The environment is thus *asserted* to be patterned, stationary, and homogeneous; the qualitative, non-distributional constituents are still excluded from attention.

At the individual level, Gale allowed a role for epistemic risk and uncertainty, distinguishing 'reasonable' from 'unreasonable' expectations (ibid., p. 184). Individuals are reasonable in their anticipations, e.g., of the government's fiscal policy, if they have completely internalized the requisite function, e.g., the government's policy function. Individuals are unreasonable, by contrast, when they are not so able to internalize; they are not able to accurately 'forecast' since they 'unreasonably' fail to make the connection. This is a mere rephrasing of Muth's definition of rational expectations as the identity of objective and subjective distribution functions. The actor is reasonable if the identity holds, unreasonable if not. A reasonable actor is therefore not 'fooled' by efforts at stabilization, for instance, since he 'knows' the model being used and it is further internalized as his own.

Reasonableness and unreasonableness are not defined, however, with respect to the individual; they are rather stipulated with respect to the equilibrium properties of the economic model. Thus was Gale able to reduce epistemic risk and uncertainty to aleatory risk and uncertainty. Risk is removable, uncertainty implies unreasonableness and therefore irrational behavior. As in Muth they are not Simonian procedural terms, but rather substantive definitions.

The new neoclassical methodology, the new orthodoxy, of which these reinterpretations are part, seems to consider any model viable so long as it 'fits the data' or allows the researcher to 'generate' like (or consistent) data. Using restrictive modeling assumptions, including *ad hoc* probability distributions, it is easy to construct economic models which generate data exhibiting 'cycles,' similar in form to empirical business cycles. As Thomas Sargent (1979, p. 218) has observed, it is possible to generate data series from high-order non-stochastic linear difference equations that mimic empirical economic data (time) series. It is just as possible to generate like-data from low-order stochastic difference equations. The viability of this procedure lies in its usefulness in providing a reasonable description of the time-series data. Typically time series are of a nature conducive to such techniques.

To achieve more for rational expectations requires extensive modification and redefinition. The choice process previously ignored must regain supremacy, taking precedent over the emphasis on data-generating techniques. Bayesian learning, although feasible, is generally considered by the rational expectationists as being inappropriate for empirical reasons, these being (1) the difficulty of modeling non-stationary processes, and (2) the difficulty of obtaining the prior probability values required for the use of Bayes' theorem (Lucas and Sargent, 1981, p. 315).[248] Attempts have been made to reconcile Muthian rationality with individual decision-making, but these too require restrictions on uncertainty. Richard Cyert and Morris DeGroot (1974) extended Muth's hypothesis through recourse to a Bayesian learning procedure to account for the process to equilibrium. Since rational expectations as originally stipulated is simply a consistency postulate specifying no underlying model of the process of expectations formation, such a restatement results not so much in a modification as in a virtual abandonment of the hypothesis.[249]

Cyert and DeGroot began their restatement of the new neoclassical economics with three assumptions: (1) agents possess identical prior distributions; (2) 'true (epistemic and systemic) uncertainty' is non-existent (since Bayesian decision models require measurable subjective probability); and (3) there exists a 'correct' model which agents 'discover' through the Bayesian learning process. They then considered two approaches to the process of adjustment of expectations.[250] In the first, the underlying model of the economy is unknown, i.e., the specific learning process and the data-generating model of the system itself are unknown to the agents in the economy. The economic actor 'chooses' a learning model and a prior probability value with which to initiate the process.[251] Of course, the initial choices are invariably mistaken. Such an approach ('inconsistent' in the Cyert-DeGroot terminology because the actor is 'incorrect' in his choice) is dependent for convergence on the value of the initial prior probability and the specific form of the chosen learning model. As this requires the actor to formulate a 'guess' as to the correct process and initial prior probability value, a rational expectations equilibrium is not guaranteed, since 'irrational' (erroneous) solutions are allowed; it may be the case that the learning model adopted is one allowing consistent errors to proliferate. Since the outcome is process-specific, the stability of the model and its convergence to a rational expectations equilibrium is by no means assured.

The second ('consistent') approach assumes at the outset that agents 'know'

118

the 'true' expectation-generating model, but not necessarily the parameter values of the model. The model parameters are 'correctly' determined via the use of a Bayesian learning procedure. While unknowledgeable about certain aspects of the environment, agents compensate by knowing the correct method of learning. The decision-maker need only choose parameter values, e.g., price expectations, and the model thereafter signifies whether these parameters are correct or not. If so, the process ends; if not, a new value is derived. A rational expectations solution is guaranteed (asymptotically) as the outcome of a Bayesian process under the additional assumption of extreme computational and information-gathering abilities.

Although this model (in both variants) is purported by advocates to incorporate learning into rational expectations models of the Muthian type, it succeeds instead, by centering attention on process, in replacing Muthian rationality with an entirely different concept. Muthian proceduralism defines rationality so as to make learning irrelevant; the equation of objective and subjective distributions leaves no substantive role for learning. The Cyert-DeGroot model requires that rationality be redefined so as to incorporate a learning procedure, specifically Bayesian learning, and thus does not require the equation of subjective with objective probability distributions. It requires only knowledge of an explicit learning procedure (any procedure in variant one, the correct one in variant two) and a well-defined prior probability. Consistent expectations replace rational expectations. In point of fact, Muthian rationality is for Cyert-DeGroot only a necessary condition for consistency (Cyert and DeGroot, 1974, p. 531), a requirement for the existence of a unique equilibrium. [252] It is not sufficient for a complete elucidation of the process towards equilibrium. The model is therefore more correctly representative of a restrictive form of Simonian satisficing, of bounded rationality, than it is of Muthian rationality.

Robert Townsend (1978) arrived at essentially the same conclusion as Cyert and DeGroot in attempting to incorporate within a rational expectations framework some form of learning procedure, i.e., to develop a 'psychological' theory which, when incorporated into a rational expectations model, is capable of leading to rational expectations-type solutions. To this end Townsend concluded that a Nash equilibrium is equivalent to and may be considered as a type of rational expectations equilibrium. It is to the Nash solution that Bayesian learning is applicable, not to the Muthian-Lucasian rational expectations formulation. But Townsend amended his conclusion to advance a more conciliatory attitude, noting that 'in a larger sense, questions concerning the stability of the more general notion of rational expectations equilibria may be ill-posed,' since 'if the extended model is well defined its equilibria will necessarily be rational' (Townsend, 1978, p. 493).

In terms of the present approach, the unrestricted models (those labelled 'inconsistent' by Cyert and DeGroot) of rational expectations wherein the individual is allowed to err in his choice of procedures are not inconsistent with and may in fact lead to results in accord with those of the Austrian and Keynesan positions. The point is not whether the environment is objectively stable or unstable, predictable or unpredictable. It is rather the manner in which the actors can perceive the signals generated, and whether they can ever really 'know' the underlying model of the economy, that is important. The best they can be expected to do is to formulate a subjective idea, a 'guess', as to which of a possible infinity of processes is at work. If in error, there remains the opportunity to reformulate next period; if correct, they stand to gain, to reap rewards (although even if in error, there may be rewards if everyone else is correct). Those models restricted to consistency, even though allowing for a type of Bayesian learning, serve no purpose other than to facilitate the re-emergence of the mechanical apparatus alleged of the classical economists. Decision is inconsequential; there is in essence no reward to be gathered from making a prediction 'against the grain' for all are assumed equally well-informed. The playing field has been leveled, but the game has lost its appeal. Inconsistency at least allows a place for imagination and choice.

Finally, mention must be made of another variant within the rational expectations framework which shows more promise than any of the above in its ability to allow for true uncertainty to enter into the economic model. This is the model of 'sunspot activity' investigated by, among others, Costas Azariadis (1981) and David Cass and Karl Shell (1983).

According to this procedure, the distinguishing characteristic of sunspot models is the inclusion of a parameter which accounts for 'extrinsic (or "extraneous") uncertainty', denoted as sunspot activity, which is defined as uncertainty which does not affect the 'fundamentals' (technology, preferences, endowments) of the economy. In the Cass-Shell model, two cases were presented. In case one, individuals are assumed to have identical beliefs as to the nature of the extrinsic uncertainty, so that the objective and subjective probabilities are equal. The result is consistent with a Muthian rational expectations solution. Markets are complete and continually in equilibrium. In this Arrow-Debreu economy, sunspots do not matter. The true uncertainty of Keynes, Knight, and Shackle is irrelevant.

In case two, an overlapping-generations model is assumed, with restricted access in markets and subjectively-held probability distributions. These assumptions supply the crucial ingredients which lead to the conclusion that this variant is more process-dependent. Objective and subjective distributions need not necessarily coincide; extraneous components may enter into the probability distribution function of the economic agent. In this model, sunspots, not terribly inconsistent with 'surprise' phenomena, matter. Equilibrium and market clearing are by no means ensured. A variant of Keynes-Knight-Shackle uncertainty gains significance.

Although 'true uncertainty' is allowed a place in the overlapping-generations framework, this uncertainty is extrinsic (or systemic): it is not psychological (epistemic) uncertainty, i.e., it is not defined with respect to the perceptual abilities of the individual actors. It is more in the form of an external shock, an objective discordance, which is *perceived* and *apprehended* subjectively. The subjective perception is the reason for terming this a 'Keynes-Shackle type' of uncertainty, and not 'true' Keynes-Shackle uncertainty. A 'true' Keynes-Shackle uncertainty would of course be epistemic, an attribute of the actors themselves, not a parameter imposed on the model. It would be intrinsic. However, these models come a long way toward acceptance of a form of epistemic uncertainty as a critical factor absent from the rational expectations models of Muth and Lucas (among others). They represent at least attempts at traveling beyond the restricted domain of Muthian-Lucasian models, with their stipulations as to identity of objective and subjective probabilities. In effect, they represent, as do the Bayesian reformulations, not rational expectations models, but post-rational expectations models, or, for lack of a better term, non-classical rational expectations approaches. They represent at least a flirtation with process, a nascent realization that the world is not determinate.

REMARKS

The philosophy of rational expectations is, at least in the mainstream, unabashed instrumentalism. Although in some variants consistent with Friedmanian positivism, it is not quite accurate to assert that this naive and primitive methodological stance is descriptive of everyone practicing within the paradigm.

Lucas, for one, defined his method of theorizing as one of Ideal Types. As defined by Ernest Nagel (1963), Ideal Types are statements of strict construction applying to no actual or realized phenomena, and are therefore neither non-exhaustive nor descriptively true or false. 'Economic man' is an example of such a hypothetical construct, a simplification that allows one to derive conclusions from an abstract model which have an application to empirical problems. This contrasts with Friedman's (1953) methodology in that the distillation from the model of its 'essence' to the point of creating an abstraction devoid of any connection to or semblance of reality is rejected. The 'unreality' of the Lucasian economic model is a result solely of its abstractness and simplicity, not the falsity of its assumptions.

> Any model that is well enough articulated to give clear answers to the questions we put to it will necessarily be artificial, abstract, patently "unreal."
>
> (Lucas, 1981, p. 271)

> The more dimensions on which the model mimics the answers actual economies give to simple questions, the more we trust its answers to harder questions. This is the sense in which more "realism" is clearly preferred to less.
>
> (ibid., p. 272)

121

Lucas's achievement lay in attempting to advance more realistic criteria for the acceptance of theoretical models through the use of advanced mathematical and statistical computational procedures. The demand for essence as opposed to goodness-of-fit places Lucas is a somewhat unique position among the rational expectationists. Abstraction and simplicity, an appeal to Occam's Razor, is preferred to descriptively false theories which may fit the facts but otherwise are useless as descriptions of process and behavior. To his credit Lucas is (apparently) the sole adherent to this view, in fact one of the few to express any position on methodology.

His economics is another matter. As pointed out above, even Lucas's models are too highly abstract to appeal to the realists among us. Acceptance of the Muthian approach (although it has been modified since its inception) is enough to place one in the pantheon of Friedmanians for its dismissal of individual subjective motives (the probability distributions of such) as coextensive with the objective probability distribution belies an appeal to realistic albeit abstract models. The thesis that an appeal to reality, that description of the actual economic situation taking into account the decision processes and individual interactions, is a desired and desirable aim of economics is laudable; its realization is even more so.

VII

CONCLUSION

Since its incarnation as a 'science' (taken to be with the publication in 1776 of Adam Smith's *Wealth of Nations*), economic theoreticians and other practitioners of the 'dismal science' have acknowledged that a great many of those variables essential to an understanding of the actual workings of an economy are immeasurable of being measured. Among those variables for which measurement and calculation are impractical if not impossible are many, such as utility, uncertainty, and intensity of preferences, which are so subjective but which are nonetheless (or at any rate should be) among the primary concerns of the discipline.

The realization that much of the domain of study in economics is comprehensible only by description has not swayed economists from continuing their crusades for better methods of measurement and the elaboration of more elegant quantitative models. Economists have delighted in their ability to demarcate the general domain of social science into scientific and non-scientific (rigorous and non-rigorous) specialties. Under the rubric, 'The more mathematical the discipline, the more scientific and, *ipso facto*, the greater the validity of, its pronouncements,' positive economists have driven economics further into the scientific realm. Quantitative measurement and calculation are certainly distinguishing characteristics of economics as a social science discipline, giving it a unique position vis-à-vis political science and sociology, for example, where the emphasis remains on descriptions of patterns and tendencies, and on variables devoid of and resistant to precise numerical characterization. Published series of prices, output, unemployment, interest rates, exchange rates, and even an index of consumer confidence serve as reminders that economics is, in terms of quantification, far in advance of the traditional 'social' sciences. Despite this fact, the data sets cited as evidence of economics as a quantitative discipline represent but a small subset of the domain of economics; economics remains for the most part a qualitative, behavioral discipline, indistinct in many respects from political science and sociology, so that for many interesting problems broadly defined as economic, measures are simply not applicable. Tendencies and patterns are noted where measures are lacking; surrogate measures are applied when and where a correspondence is distinguished (and often times inappropriately so). The demarcation is illusory.

This was abundantly clear to the Classical economists. The individual was the focal point of exposition of many of the early classical theories, the macroeconomy assumed composed of and so analyzable through reference to such atomic units, viz., through a process of aggregation. The reason for this individualist orientation centered again on measurement problems, not unique to social disciplines but rather of concern to all science. It may be possible to 'measure' some aspects of individual behavior. Questioning an individual with respect to his preferences, for instance, may yield a fairly accurate representation of his overall preference map. But the applicability of this procedure is limited to the time period and over the consumption bundles examined, and so extrapolation to other time periods and consumption bundles cannot be made (since preferences for other goods may not exist).

The problem is that measures, while applicable to single units, are not comparable across the individual units absent a clear description of the units themselves and the series of which they are a part. Refinement is required to produce the desired homogeneity. Only when the field is so refined, when the units of study are so manipulated as to be made more readily assimilable as consistent and viable statistical series, can the techniques of mathematical analysis be applied. Here is the situation of the macro-series as the basis of analysis, individual behavior being cloaked in the guise of the 'representative agent.'

Yet even this sleight-of-hand did not prove powerful enough. For even when calculation was attempted, so as to at least approach to some degree of accuracy a consistent and viable measure applicable to macroeconomic conditions, and to give to economics an air of scientific respectability, problems came immediately to the fore. Primary among these problems was the realization that determinism is not viable as a description of the social environment, that uncertainties epistemic and systemic play a major role. To be more specific, it became apparent that the requisite underlying probability distribution functions, added to primarily deterministic models so as to give an air of stochasticity, and hence take care of the chance element in behavior, need not be smooth and differentiable; they may instead be discontinuous or even singularities. Smooth distribution functions such as the standard normal exhibit known and well-defined properties; moment generating functions are for these distributions known and established. Singularities and discontinuous functions are not so well represented. The assumption of the existence of the one when the other is in fact relevant may allow theoretical simplicity, but will lead in the end to incorrect, counterfactual outcomes of the process being described. In other words, assumptions based on a particular shape of the underlying probability density function, accepted as a valid representation of the underlying empirical environment, when the environment is instead indeterminate, lead to erroneous theoretical conclusions and additional problems, the solutions of which are not readily apparent.[253]

In the economy of indeterminism, the economy of Keynes and the Austrians, process is paramount; the interactions among the agents in the economy are of the utmost importance. Where equilibrium is discussed at all, it is a manifestation of the process. Equilibrium is not stipulated as being a feature of the economic environment; it is not imposed upon the model from without. The interactions among individuals in the theoretical economy, *absent external influences*, tend toward an equilibrium solution. But Austrian and Keynes's economics view these external influences as crucial in that they affect and are affected by the individual economic interactions. In these 'models' (rather one should say 'characterizations of the economic process'), the primary requirement is a divergence, or incompatibility, of expectation and outcome; events do not always follow as expected or willed, even under the most favorable conditions. Equilibrium *per se* never obtains. Something invariably intercedes to upset the return to the path towards equilibrium, to hamper the movement towards the expected goal. But it is precisely this divergence of outcome from expectation that is responsible for a re-equilibration once the tendency toward equilibrium is disturbed. True epistemic uncertainty acquires crucial import since its presence ensures that expectations, derived subjectively, will at times be incompatible among the agents in the economic system. Institutional considerations then become more important as institutions acquire the role of interactive mechanisms.

Formally, those economic theories wherein explicit recognition is granted to uncertainty and risk (whether aleatory or epistemic) as separate components deny the existence of a unique solution, while those which reduce all uncertainty to risk (in addition to other simplifications) have guaranteed the existence of an equilibrium solution. Even advocates of dynamic stochastic models designed to incorporate uncertainty parametrically must resort invariably to a measure which corresponds to some specific distribution function, and therefore impose a distribution or pattern artificially upon a generally patternless environment.

Certain aspects of individual behavior simply cannot be calculated or even approximated with any acceptable degree of certainty. Reactions to uncertain and unique situations, decision-making over an incomplete set of alternatives or in the face of incomplete or insufficient information, the inherent subjectivity of the decision process, are but some of the problem areas. There is no *a priori* rationale for attributing to the individual actor in his economic role traits analogous to an automaton in a mechanical system. [254]

This realization, to the extent that it has been accepted, has led theorists to adopt one of two tacks, based on their perceptions of uncertainty. Those economic theories which explicitly accept the presence of epistemic uncertainty and risk as separate components, the Keynes-Shackle theories of economics, deny the existence of a unique equilibrium solution, while those which reduce all uncertainty to aleatory risk, the neoclassical and new neoclassical theories, have guaranteed the existence of equilibrium through reliance on the use of mathematical convergence theorems. Events are by nature of a unique variety; numerical measurement and the use of statistical frequencies required to give credence to the ergodic theorems depend for their existence on a series of repetitive events (or at the least repeatable events). While the unique instances are not amenable to the probability calculus, events seen as part of a discernible random series are so describable. The paradigm one follows must then be a result of how one views single events in their relation to the economic whole.

Uncertainty has been and continues to be of vital importance for theoretical economics. It would not be much of an exaggeration to suggest that this is *the* most important aspect of economic theory, and one about which agreement as to its importance is universal. Nonetheless, beyond the acceptance of its importance, the concept of epistemic uncertainty is not so universally understood as evidenced by its place in formal theoretical constructions, viz., formal mathematical models. The assertion made here is that it is especially not, despite protestations to the contrary, well formulated in current new neoclassical, i.e., rational expectations, models of economic behavior, in part due to some fundamental tenets of this approach: the concentration on measurability and numerical probability, the inability to deal with (or even accept as relevant) indeterminate solutions, the closed nature of the universe, and the pragmatic concerns of adherents. Individuals in the new neoclassical view are important, but only so far as they represent a part of a definable and necessarily stationary and homogeneous aleatory series. All alternatives (i.e., utility choices) are comparable; rationality is consistency. Because of this focus, even the Knightian distinction between aleatory risk and true aleatory uncertainty has been and is being neglected in favor of purely pragmatic results. Pragmatism is being practiced at the expense of explanation and understanding, since these concerns are, after all, deemed of practical irrelevance: the answer to the question 'Why?' is 'Who cares? Just do it.'

Yet at the same time the theories articulated by the Austrian economists and Keynes's own formulation clearly take account of this distinction and, because of the centrality ascribed to motivation, are more firmly grounded theoretically at the microeconomic level than those of the neoclassical variety. [255] Individuals are important in and of themselves; economics is, after all, the study of individual *behavior*, not the study of statistical time series. It is also not the study of behavior deemed constrained by arbitrarily-specified postulates. It is the study of actual economizing behavior, of real decision processes undertaken with respect to real constraints and under real conditions. Some alternatives are not comparable; rationality is behavior. [256]

At a methodological level, the debate centers around a general theme as identified by Martin Hollis, this being the distinction between Humean and Kantian rationality. While similar in many respects to Simon's procedural-substantive rationality dichotomy, or any other programmed–non-programmed decision-making distinction, it is more general in attacking the problem at the philosophical level. For the Humean, the individual is a choice-maximizer (and

126

a maximum will always exist). Any action on his part is preceded by an internal motivation, be it 'passion', 'feeling', 'desire', or whatever. 'Reason' may lead to an action, but reason itself is caused (initiated) by an internal motivation; it is not itself a contributory factor to decision, since the choice process is external to reason. 'Reason is, and ought only to be the slave of the passions, and can never pretend to any other office than to serve and obey them.'(Hume, 1740, Bk.II, Pt.III, sec.III, p. 462).

Humean rationality requires a consistency calculus; it is in a fashion determinate. Its adoption essentially minimizes the role of the human actor in the choice process as motivation is replaced by result. As Hollis noted, 'Given preferences, then, are a requirement of a theory of rational action which regards rational choice as the use of instrumental reason in the service of the passions.' (Hollis, 1987, p. 65). Humean rationality is ends-oriented. Conduct is judged by the results engendered; utilitarianism prevails. Preferences drive rationality so that outcome is all that matters. 'Rationality' in the Humean context is taken as the primitive concept from which may be derived neoclassical optimization principles. Experience impresses upon the mind of the actor forms from which analysis proceeds. It is the ultimate empiricist methodology.

Kantian rationality, by contrast, does not restrict the actor to consistency; reason alone becomes a motivating factor. The individual is a choice-optimizer (since a maximum may not exist when the actor alone defines what constitutes an optimum); he does the best he can given his desires and the restrictions in place. He is not forced to consistency in his choices since his full range of choices is unknown in any eventuality, and reason may at times dictate irrationality. The human actor is allowed to realize his potential, unconstrained by external factors. 'Rational agents act from objectively good reasons, whose merits are conceptually independent of their current desires.' (ibid., p. 74). Many situations faced by the decision-maker are inconclusive; they are conditional on environmental factors which may act to preclude a maximum, allowing instead only for a second-best, satisficing solution. It is perfectly reasonable under these circumstances for a conclusion to be reached at one point in time that is less-than-optimal at another time. Kantian rationality is means-oriented. The means themselves are seen as correct or incorrect, valid or invalid, as perceived by the individual, regardless of the results. Forms are innate; forms precede external impressions. Rationality drives preferences and the concern is with process. The actor frames his environment instead of having his environment frame his choices. As the individual is supreme, utility then is the primitive concept; rationality is simply the effort to maximize utility, and behavior may therefore be irrational as defined neoclassically. This is the realization, the affirmation, of the philosophical (as opposed to the economic) meaning of rationality.

Applied to economic theories, it can be seen that models of the rational expectations school and those considered as 'keynesian' (but not 'Keynesan') are within the Humean sphere.[257] Insofar as these models are either determinate or rely on a consistency calculus of the sort envisaged by Savage and the personalists (there is here more than a passing interest in a law of the uniformity of nature), they espouse a notion of human behavior constrained to internal consistency; the demand is for a Benthamite calculus. The decision process is pre-programmed. The results suggest a deductive theory based on a series of tautologies. Epistemic uncertainty and hence probability really have no part to play; it is enough to mention their importance, so that they may then be dispensed with. The probability relation is in any event believed to exist solely as an empirical construct; probability values, always possible, are but manifestations of empirical events. The values themselves are objectively valid; there is no question as to what the values should be.

Austrian articulations, Keynes's own models, and Simon's conception of rationality are very much of a Kantian type. Rationality need only be 'bounded' to be valid. Since the list of possibilities facing the actor is non-exhaustive and the actor is always in a position of at least partial ignorance about the constitution of his environment, he can only be said to be irrational in the sense of Hume, and so his actions are those of someone uneducated in the use of the rational decision postulates. It is not irrational in the Kantian sense for the individual to behave against the dictates of any set of decision axioms, and against even his own perceived self-interest; he need only have *some* reason behind his actions for the actions to be for him rational. Subjective factors thereby assume a much greater importance. The probability relation itself, being of a logical form, is solely a mental construct, hence *a priori* and unique to the individual. The probability relation cannot exist apart from the human actor asserting a probability judgment. Shackle becomes the leading contemporary spokesman in economics for such a theory, as the indeterminacy of his decision calculus formalizes many aspects of the approach in an economic context. Even Smith of the classical school falls into this category.[258] The theory is individualistic and inductive, with special emphasis placed on delving into the motivation behind the decision-process. Rationality *qua* consistency is redefined as rationality *qua* rationality, i.e., reason.

As John Hicks proclaimed in *Value and Capital*: 'Pure economics has a remarkable way of producing rabbits out of a hat – apparently *a priori* propositions which apparently refer to reality. It is fascinating to try to discover how the rabbits got in; for those of us who do not believe in magic must be convinced that they got in somehow.' (Hicks, 1946, p. 23). Hicks's admonition that economists pay attention to the propositions of their science, to explaining 'how the rabbits got in,' has in the main been neglected in favor of pragmatism. Certainly, in the argument presented herein, it is clear that classical economists were so concerned with process and motivation, with the individual actor as a cognitive, rational being, interacting with other rational beings in a social environment, that they eschewed quantitative modeling for qualitative reasoning and explanation. Just as clear is the treatment by Keynes and the

Austrians of the behavior of the 'rabbits' themselves; the desire to know not merely how they got into the hat, but what prompted them to desire to get in. It is only in neoclassical and new neoclassical economics that the question has changed, from 'how did they get in?' to 'O.K., they're in there. So what do we do about it?' and even 'How does the hat behave?' To say that a 'rabbit,' the economic actor, behaves in accordance with a stationary stochastic process tells us nothing substantive about his *behavior*; it notes only that this particular 'rabbit' is one of a number of representative 'rabbits' whose behavior is predictable and can, indeed, if placed in the proper context, be characterized with certainty. It tells us only that he is in the hat, which we know already, and presumably that he must stay in the hat.

NOTES

CHAPTER I: INTRODUCTION

1 Although many physicists would perhaps disagree with this assertion.
2 Emil Kauder (1957) noted that Menger, in correspondence with Walras, defined 'exact laws' as 'statements about invariable sequences which are not influenced by time and place' (Kauder, 1957, p. 416).
3 'Strict (exact) laws of phenomena can never be the result of the realistic school of thought in theoretical research even if this were the most perfect conceivable and its fundamental observation the most comprehensive and most critical.' (Menger, 1883, p. 57). 'If, therefore, exact laws are at all attainable, it is clear that these cannot be obtained from the point of view of empirical realism . . . .' (ibid., p. 60).
4 Some, perhaps most, may argue that Menger's ideal laws are synthetic *a priori*, not analytic. However, Menger insisted they are not empirically derived but rather of the nature of mathematical truths. They are then redefinable as tautologies, and hence analytic. Barry Smith (1986) argued that Menger, writing under the influence of Aristotelianism, actually presented a theory utilizing the synthetic *a priori*, the outline of which does not appear explicitly in his works, but is rather dealt with in the philosophical works of Edmund Husserl. Despite Menger's Aristotelianism, his ideal laws still seem analytic if for no other reason than their being necessary and redefinable as tautologies.
5 For Menger, the inductive method is 'only able to increase the guarantees of the absoluteness of the laws' but can never 'offer absolute guarantee of it.' (Menger, 1883, p. 57).
6 On this see the work of the philosopher Alexander Rosenberg, especially (1976).
7 The definition of classical economists used here is consistent with that given by John Maynard Keynes in the *General Theory* (1936), encompassing writers from Adam Smith to A. C. Pigou.
8 Mill never accepted that an objective measure of *value* was possible. He did, however, acknowledge that such a measure may be forthcoming for *cost of production*. 'But if there existed such a commodity, we should derive this advantage from it, that whenever any other thing varied permanently in relation to it, we should know that the cause of variation was not in it, but in the other thing. It would thus be suited to serve as a measure, not indeed of the value of other things, but of their cost of production.' (Mill, 1871, Bk.III, Ch.XV, p. 566).
9 An excellent reference on the subject of equilibrium in economic models is Robert Kuenne (1963). For the historical development of the general equilibrium concept, see E. Roy Weintraub (1985).

10 This definition is key to G. L. S. Shackle's elucidation of a 'scheme' of economic theory. See esp. Shackle (1965).

11 'For a society then we *can* speak of a *state* of equilibrium at a point in time – but it means only that compatibility exists between the different plans which the individuals composing it have made for action in time.' (Hayek, 1937, p. 41).

12 General equilibrium as used here refers to a more expansive concept than that of the formal axiomatic presentations of modern usage, viz., Arrow-Debreu-type models. The definition here is of classical vintage. This older definition is of particular relevance to the theories of the Austrians and Keynes.

13 The terms 'static' and 'dynamic' are not equivalent to the terms 'stationary' and 'non-stationary'. A stationary system is characterized by a non-changing, equilibrium solution, while a non-stationary system is one of disequilibrium and continual change. Thus a static model is necessarily stationary, while a dynamic model need not be.

14 Self-contained models are 'those in which a lagged interdependence of all variables could explain an unending and genuinely cyclical fluctuation.' It is 'a "business cycle machine" complete in itself, to which regular and therefore predictable oscillation is as natural as the tides or the seasons.' (Shackle, 1965, p. 5). A non-self-contained model is one 'receptive of any kind of stimulus from outside itself and responding in an appropriate and broadly reliable manner to each different kind, but not containing any *perpetuum mobile* of its own.' (ibid., p. 5). This type of model 'deliberately leaves out some of the linkages which would be needed in order to calculate the future from the past.' (ibid., p. 98).

15 It should be noted that the partial equilibrium model may be considered as a special case of the general model, wherein the economy collapses to a single market in which is produced a single good, and the solution vector is then shifted through successive iterations along a time axis, so that time becomes incorporated explicitly into the analysis. Cobweb models of the 1920s represented early efforts to dynamize the static demand-supply analysis of classical microeconomic theory.

16 'Probabilistic' does not have the same meaning as Tony Lawson's (1988) 'probabilistic knowledge,' which refers to an uncertainty representable by a probability distribution. Lawson's 'probabilistic knowledge' more closely corresponds to 'stochastic' in the present case.

17 It should be noted that the terms 'probabilistic' and 'stochastic' do not reference probability types. They reflect merely two ways of representing uncertainty. Probability is a different matter entirely.

18 Although recent literature on sunspot models, to be discussed later, provides an exception.

19 This is not really a contentious point. Samuel Hollander (1973, p. 13) and Roger Backhouse (1985, p. 23) both maintained that Smith advocated a form of general equilibrium.

20 On the various uses of the term 'tendency' in classical economics, see Thomas Sowell (1974).

21 For Cournot, the problem with a practical application of a general equilibrium solution was in the empirical calculation: 'But this would surpass the powers of mathematical analysis and of our practical methods of calculation, even if the values of all the constants could be assigned to them numerically.' (Cournot, 1838, p. 127).

22 'Therefore, while it is understandable that partial analysis has been and is being widely used, it is equally understandable that it has been condemned from the first by theorists of the sterner type, especially by Walras and Pareto.' (Schumpeter, 1954, p. 991).

23 This will be more fully developed in Chapter II.

24 Statistics are useful 'provided that careful attention be paid not only to their liability to error; but to the even greater dangers that arise from their inability to take account of some of the most important influences that bear on almost every economic issue.' (Marshall, 1929, p. 309).

25 'We cannot indeed measure motives of any kind, whether high or low, as they are in themselves: we can measure only their moving force.... [M]oney affords a fairly good measure of the moving force of a great part of the motives by which men's lives are fashioned.' (Marshall, 1920, Bk.I, Ch.IV, p. 39).

As a motivation for this contention, Marshall elaborated two fundamental assumptions of economics: (1) economics deals with measurable quantities; and (2) problems of economics 'are found to make a fairly homogeneous group.... [T]here is a fundamental unity of form underlying all the chief of them.' (ibid., Bk.I, Ch.II, p. 27).

26 Frank H. Knight, commenting on the economic writings of the late 1920s, asserted that:

> no science of economic dynamic exists.... At best it may be said that the statistical economics now being prosecuted with so much zeal in various quarters might yield data for some of these definitions.... In actual usage economic dynamics, or dynamic economics, has become merely a critical and negative term to refer to the limitations of 'static' analysis.... Its least vague usage is that of a sort of catch-all for stressing changes in given conditions in contrast with adjustments to given conditions. In practice it suggests an insistence that there are no given conditions, which view if consistently maintained would mean that there are no predictable reactions and that science is impossible.... Economic literature includes no treatment of the relations between measured force, resistance, and movement. What it calls dynamics should be called evolutionary or historical economics.
>
> (Knight, 1935, pp. 166–7)

27 The opinion of Sanford Grossman (1981) that the classical economists equated uncertainty with certainty is, given this interpretation, an invalid characterization.

28 Even Irving Fisher's approach, characteristic of the 'classical' American school, although more mathematical than the early British presentations, was still not entirely deterministic.

29 See especially Burns and Mitchell (1947). But note the following from Mark Perlman: '...if Mitchell's principal concern was to make measurements, like all sophisticated scholars he was acutely alert to the qualitative (perhaps subjective) bases in any measuring process.' (Perlman, 1986, p. 272).

30 Cf. John R. Commons: 'If the concept of purpose is omitted then the social scientist falls into either physics or metaphysics.' (Commons, 1924, p. 127). See Perlman (1986) for the view that Commons is the American Institutionalist link to Austrian economic thought.

31 Milton Friedman (1955) wrote that Walras' system was not the solution of a specific empirical problem, but rather an elegant formal statement of an idealized economic system. He further suggested that advances in input–output analysis have not been in the spirit of Walras, but rather extensions of the analysis of Cournot, whose system consisted of a detailed examination of economic interrelations founded on an empirical basis and which, as Cournot felt and Friedman concurred, was incapable of solution due to the extreme complexity and magnitude of the calculations involved. Thus, according to Friedman, Walras was concerned with form, while Cournot was more concerned with substance.

32 Including but not limited to Anna Carabelli, Bradley Bateman, Rod O'Donnell, Tony Lawson, and Jochen Runde, but excluding such Post-keynesians as Paul Davidson.

33 Note that when discussing interpretations of Keynes, the term 'keynesian' will be used, while when discussing Keynes' own views, the term 'Keynesan' will be used. With regard to Keynes' probability theory, the term 'Keynesian' will still be used.

34 As for instance do certain applications in game theory.

CHAPTER II: THEORIES OF PROBABILITY

35 Although admittedly this is not true of the 'growth of knowledge' literature.

36 See A. J. Ayer (1952), especially pp. 79–80, 85–7.

37 This is not to be confused with John Maynard Keynes' 'weight of argument' which will be discussed below.

38 Consider the comment by Bertrand Russell: 'The man who has fed the chicken every day throughout its life at last wrings its neck instead, showing that more refined views as to the uniformity of nature would have been useful to the chicken.' (Russell, 1912, p. 63).

39 Ayer's justification for induction did not rest on theoretical grounds, but rather on practicality: the fact that a procedure works is enough to confirm its validity. 'We are entitled to have faith in our procedure just so long as it does the work which it is designed to do.' (Ayer, 1952, p. 50).

40 As Hume stated: '. . . all our reasonings concerning causes and effects are deriv'd from nothing but custom; and that belief is more properly an act of the sensitive, than of the cogitative part of our natures.' (Hume, 1740, Bk.I, Pt.IV, sec.I, p. 234). Further, '. . . it evidently follows, that many of our impressions have no external model or archetype.' (ibid., sec.IV, p. 276).

41 In addition, Todhunter, Keynes, and Savage all include lengthy bibliographies of the literature on probability.

42 'Thus our empirical knowledge does not constitute a part of the content of the Probability$_1$ statement (which would make this statement empirical) but rather of the sentence e [the evidence] which is dealt with in the Probability$_1$ statement.' (Carnap, 1950, p. 32). Note that this is the empirical element of Probability$_1$; the empirical knowledge enters through the evidence or evidentiary propositions.

43 While some may contend that this applies to *all* subjectivists, it is not at all certain that this is so.

44 Included here would be the economic and probability theories of Savage and Keynes.

45 Included here would be the economic theories of Frank H. Knight and Robert E. Lucas, Jr.

46 Later in the same article referenced above, Lawson reconsidered his classificatory scheme, dividing the field into 'interactionist realists' (Keynes and Knight) and 'subjectivist idealists' (Savage and Lucas), thereby introducing a degree of overlap which aids in the categorization of uncertainty and probability to be discussed later.

47 P(a) may be more restrictively defined as the Lebesque measure $\forall\ a \in A$.

48 See especially Debreu, 1959, pp. 7–8; A. N. Kolmogorov and S. V. Fomin, 1970, pp. 20–1; Savage, 1972, pp. 18, 21. John Chipman (1960) termed the partial order a 'proper order.' The corresponding total order he termed a 'simple order.'

49 Most authors use the term 'complete', but this implies that the relation is connected *and* antisymmetric. Arrow (1963) used connection, taking the term from the field of logic.

50 Arrow (1951) in his survey took the total order as being a generally accepted axiom of the theory of choice.
51 Consider as in Halmos the sets of the σ-algebra to be rectangles and P(*a*) (where *a* is any given set) to be the area of *a*. Then it is obvious that P(*a*) > 0 since the area of a rectangle of any given size is positive. If, however, *a* is a single point, then P(*a*) is zero since a point (and even more extensively a line segment) has no area. The point (and the line) are then said to be of measure zero. (Halmos, 1944, pp. 498–9).
52 On this see especially Salmon (1967, sec.VII).
53 It should be noted that the classical theory is not to be equated with the frequency theory. Classical probability theory has more in common with, and may be considered as progenitor of, the necessarian and personalist theories, in that these theories posit the existence of a prior probability (to allow for the use of Bayesian learning) based on some form of Principle of Non-Sufficient Reason. The frequency theory, on the other hand, asserts no such principle, but consider that any prior probability is empirically established. Bayes's theorem is then applicable based on this value.
54 The *a priori* assumption has led some (e.g., Martin Hollis and Edward Nell, 1975, pp. 75–9) to insist that the classical and frequency interpretations are analytic and hence tautologous.
55 The Principle of Non-Sufficient Reason, although of dubious value from a philosophical standpoint (except insofar as it provides a prior probability for use in Bayesian theory), has been of service to various game-theoretic bargaining models. See Alvin Roth, 1979, p. 27. Also, the Principle of Non-Sufficient Reason is not synonymous with non-comparability. In fact, the Principle assumes comparability, so that for instance, if one cannot decide whether P(*a*) > P(*b*) or P(*b*) > P(*a*), one can say that P(*a*) = P(*b*).
56 An excellent reference on the history of classical probability is Hacking (1990).
57 According to Hacking (1990), Laplace (and A. A. Cournot and S.-D. Poisson) distinguished between objective probability ('facilité') and subjective probability ('probabilité'). See especially pages 96–7. This dichotomy is similar to the physical/psychological classification of I. J. Good (1965) and the aleatory/epistemic classification of Hacking (1975).
58 This is but one means of expressing the law of large numbers. It may also be expressed as the limit of the probability of the deviation of the relative frequency of attributes in a single series of given length from the true but unknown probability value. On different 'laws' of large numbers, see Richard von Mises (1957).
59 Bernoulli's theorem applies to drawings from a single event-space, an example being balls drawn from a single urn. A similar theorem, another 'law of large numbers,' was proposed by S.-D. Poisson, and applied to single drawings from a number of different event-spaces, such as a multitude of urns each containing a number of balls, a choice being made at random among both urns and balls. The 'Poisson trials' show less variance and hence converge more rapidly than do the 'Bernoulli trials.' In fact, the Bernoulli distribution (or Binomial distribution) leads in the limit to the Poisson distribution. See Hacking (1990), pp. 102–4.
60 See, e.g., Venn, 1888, p. 16.
61 According to Venn, a series is 'the ultimate basis upon which all the rules of Probability must be based.' (Venn, 1888, p. 12). Richard von Mises (1941, 1957) advocated a limiting-frequency theory, using the term 'kollektiv' (later 'collective') to refer to the Vennian concept of 'series.' Specifically, a collective is 'a sequence of uniform events or processes which differ by certain observable attributes, say colours, numbers, or anything else.' (R. von Mises, 1957, p. 12).

62 Cf. R. von Mises: '... in no case is a probability value attached to a single event by itself, but only to an event as much as it is an element of a well-defined sequence.' (Mises, 1941, p. 192). Also Ayer: 'The best that can be said for the frequency theory is that, unlike the logical theory, it does not seriously attempt to deal with the individual case.' (Ayer, 1961, p. 371).

63 'The limiting value of the relative frequency of a given attribute, assumed to be independent of any place selection, will be called "the probability of that attribute within the given collective."' (R. von Mises, 1957, p. 29).

64 Although, as Jochen Runde has suggested to me, the idea of the uniformity of nature may be viewed as the aleatory counterpart to the epistemic Principle of Insufficient Reason. Both give credence to the idea of equiprobability.

65 Cf. Laplace of the classical school: '... in a series of events indefinitely prolonged the actions of regular and constant causes ought to prevail in the long run over that of irregular causes.' (Laplace, 1820, p. 62).

66 Venn described three stages which an empirical series may exhibit: (1) irregularity caused by too few observations; (2) uniformity as the series is extended (although the extension must not be of such a length as to exhibit fluctuations); and (3) irregularity as the smooth series fluctuates. These stages may be termed the short, intermediate, and long runs.

67 Even so, Venn believed that it may be possible to modify belief through recourse to experience so as to allow the use of the calculus of probability in its analysis: 'If we refuse to be controlled by experience, but confine our attention to the laws according to which belief is naturally or instinctively compounded and distributed in our minds, we have no right then to appeal to experience afterwards even for illustrations, unless under the express understanding that we do not guarantee its accuracy.' (Venn, 1888, pp. 131–2).

68 Cf. F. Y. Edgeworth: 'There is only one class of practical problems to which the subjective view is exclusively applicable; those actions which cannot be regarded as forming part of a 'series' in Mr. Venn's sense; a class which with the increase of providence and sympathy is likely to disappear.' (Edgeworth, 1884, p. 224).

69 Ayer expressed a difficulty with the frequency theory in specifying the reference class to which a given occurrence will belong. His solution involves narrowing the reference class by conjunction: taking into consideration the number of A who are B who do C, etc. (Ayer, 1961, pp. 369–70). Salmon (1967) desired the broadest homogeneous reference class.

70 Other treatments of probability from a necessarian perspective include those of Ludwig Wittgenstein (in the *Tractatus Logico-Philosophicus* (1921)) and Rudolf Carnap (*Logical Foundations of Probability* (1950)).

71 Keynes's first attempt in 1907 at securing a fellowship with the dissertation was unsuccessful. He subsequently overcame any negative opinion and was awarded a prize fellowship in 1909. This is the date used here. See Robert Skidelsky, 1982, pp. 182, 204.

72 Distinctions between Keynes and Venn are three: (1) Keynes does not regard probability as identical with statistical frequency (as does Venn); (2) propositions, not events, are the subject matter of probability; and (3) probability includes induction as a means for logical preference under conditions of uncertainty. (Keynes, 1921, p. 110). Keynes also noted certain advantages of the frequency interpretation: it involved no new indefinables, presented no intuitive problems, and presented no measurement problems (since frequencies are simple 'ordinary numbers') (ibid., p. 103).

73 Keynes distinguished what he termed 'rational belief' from 'mere belief' based on the degree of knowledge held concerning any proposition:

> If a man believes something for a reason which is preposterous or for no reason at all, and what he believes turns out to be true for some reason not known to him, he cannot be said to believe it *rationally*, although he believes it and it is in fact true. On the other hand, a man may rationally believe a proposition to be *probable*, when it is in fact false. The distinction between rational belief and mere belief, therefore, is not the same as the distinction between true beliefs and false beliefs. The highest degree of rational belief, which is termed *certain* rational belief, corresponds to *knowledge*. We may be said to know a thing when we have a certain rational belief in it, and *vice versa*.
>
> (Keynes, 1921, p. 10)

Bradley Bateman (1988) is mistaken when he argues that the 'rational' degree of belief is equivalent in Keynes to the 'correct' degree of belief: the 'correct' belief cannot be false, but the 'rational' may be.

74 Keynes noted that he was unclear as to whether certainty or probability should be the fundamental proposition. If certainty is accepted, probability becomes that which possesses a 'lower degree of rational belief than certainty,' while if probability is fundamental, certainty is definable as 'maximum probability.' (Keynes, 1921, p. 16).

Alan Coddington (1982, 1983) disagreed as to the basis of belief, preferring ignorance as a basis as opposed to Keynes's certainty: 'The appropriate base line for assessing beliefs is ignorance, not omniscience . . . . The state of certainty is in any case itself an ambiguous idea . . . . Perfect confidence in a belief is perhaps far better sustained by ignorance than by understanding.' (Coddington, 1983, p. 55). Yet there is nothing gained by such a change in emphasis. Basing a belief on certainty (which Coddington believed unattainable) is in fact superior to basing belief on ignorance (which is also, in its perfect state, unattainable), for although a person may express a degree of certainty about a proposition given the evidence at his disposal, once he possesses *any* evidence whatsoever, ignorance is no longer possible. How is anyone to know whether he has enough evidence to make an assertion, if he is in fact ignorant as to the composition of certainty? How can he know when there is enough non-ignorance? Certainty provides a convenient end-point; ignorance is limitless.

75 Although Keynes's probabilities are thought by some to have been defined in Platonic terms by Keynes himself, the term 'constructs' is nonetheless considered acceptable.

76 Compare the following statements: 'A man may rationally believe a proposition to be probable when it is in fact false, if the secondary proposition on which he depends is true and certain . . . .' (Keynes, 1921, p. 11). 'Knowledge . . . of a secondary proposition involving a degree of probability lower than certainty, together with knowledge of the premis of the secondary proposition, leads only to a *rational belief of the appropriate degree* in the primary proposition.' (ibid., pp. 15–16). Throughout much of the *Treatise*, Keynes *assumes* direct (certain) knowledge of the secondary proposition.

77 Notationally, in Keynes's system $a \mid h$ = P, i.e., the conclusion a stands in the relation of probability to the premise h; this is the fundamental relation. If $a \mid h$ is redefined to refer to an argument from h to a, then the probability of the argument is $P(a \mid h)$. The two are to be construed as equivalent, although the latter is more generally accepted in the literature on probability.

78 Keynes himself viewed his work as fundamentally subjective: 'The method of this treatise has been to regard subjective probability as fundamental and to treat all other relevant conceptions as derivative from this.' (Keynes, 1921, p. 312). Hence the conclusion of Bateman (1987, 1988) that Keynes in the *Treatise* held a fundamentally objective view of probability is mistaken. The *relation* is objective and knowable in each and every instance by all possessed of a keen enough intellect. The primary proposition, however, is known only through the evidentiary propositions, and the degree of belief in this proposition is determined subjectively. This is the reason for the subjective aspect of Keynesian probability being termed fundamental. Also, cf. Weatherford (1982): 'Keynes explicitly denies that probability-relations are objective in the sense that any rational being would agree to them . . . . The validity of P depends, therefore, in a very Kantian sense, on the constitution of the human mind.' (pp. 112–13). The presentation by Rod O'Donnell (1989) clarifies the distinction between subjective and objective probability in Keynes' work, but still errs in considering subjective elements as secondary. (See especially pp. 24–5). The Logical Positivist R. von Mises categorized Keynes as a subjectivist, although obviously not of the personalist stripe of Ramsey and Savage, whose interpretations will be discussed below (R. von Mises, 1957, pp. 78, 94).

79 Since Keynes was interested in a 'general theory of arguments from premises leading to conclusions which are reasonable but not certain' (Keynes, 1921, p. 106), his theory is not an alternative to that of Venn and the frequentists but instead in some ways subsumes it.

80 Cf. Edgeworth: 'Probability, as Mr. Keynes rightly insists, is ever relative to some assumed premises. A premiss may be subjective such as the belief in one's own existence. But the relation between the premiss and what may with more or less probability be inferred from it is "rational" or "objective".' (Edgeworth, 1922, p. 260).

81 In contrast to the strict necessarianism of the early Wittgenstein (of the *Tractatus*). The truth-function is fundamental to Wittgenstein, as to Laplace and to an extent even Keynes. Events occur or not, objectively; relations of certainty may then be extended to relations of probability. Wittgenstein later changed his views on probability, to embrace those of the frequentists.

82 Keynes: '[L]ogic can never be made purely mechanical. All it can do is so to arrange the reasoning that the logical relations, which have to be perceived directly, are made explicit and are of a simple kind.' (Keynes, 1921, p. 15). Thus it may be the case that aPh is replaceable by aP_ih, where i = 1, . . ., n represents the n individuals under consideration. Then P_i is still the logical relation of probability, relating premises to conclusion, and is objective, but is, as are the premises, unique to the individual. This interpretation would seem to remove Shackle's (1972) objection to Keynes's theory for it provides an explanation of rational subjective judgments. This is also consistent with the position of de Finetti (1985).

83 Keynes no more completely denied the ability to calculate numerical probability than did Whitehead and Russell the existence of numerical arithmetic. What Keynes did, following Whitehead and Russell, was to provide a logical foundation for the theory of probability; in fact, Keynes's Chapter 15 (of the *Treatise*) is devoted to the exposition of a method allowing for the calculation of numerical probability (albeit a rather primitive presentation). What Keynes contended was that numerical probability is not the sole subset of probability theory. Cf. also the more recent expression of such a view by D. G. Champernowne (1969).

84 Hacking referred to necessarian probability as epistemic and qualitative in nature: 'There is nothing logically defective in mere comparisons of probability. But as a

matter of historical fact epistemic probability did not emerge as a significant concept for logic until people thought of measuring it.' (Hacking, 1975, p. 73).

85 Keynes gave four reasons as to why a numerical comparison may be indeterminate: (1) there may be no probability value assignable; (2) no common unit of measure exists; (3) measures exist, but are unknown; (4) probability may be theoretically, but not practically, determinable (Keynes, 1921, p. 33).

86 Despite holding such a view, the *distinction* for Keynes between measurable and non-measurable probability as applied in the then-fashionable classical theories was 'not fundamental.' 'Common usage . . . does not *consistently* exclude those probabilities which are incapable of [measurement].' (Keynes, 1921, p. 36). The popular conception of probability had been confined to its use in games of chance and betting situations. The question of measurement, however, concerns the necessity of incorporating non-measurable elements which had hitherto been ignored into a general, comprehensive theory of probability for which a theoretical basis had not previously been constructed. This was the task Keynes set for himself.

87 Although cf. Keynes's position in his 1938 correspondence with Hugh Townshend: 'One arrives presumably at the numerical estimations by some system of arranging alternative decisions in order of preference, some of which will provide a norm by being numerical. But that still leaves millions of cases over where one cannot even arrange an order of preference.' (Keynes, 1979, p. 289). Parenthetically, one must wonder how, if alternatives are essentially unknowable, can Keynes know that there are millions of cases still to be reckoned with.

88 ' . . .it is not always possible to say that the degree of our rational belief in one conclusion is either equal to, greater than, or less than the degree of our belief in another.' (Keynes, 1921, p. 37).

89 Venn as well recognized this point: 'It is obvious that every individual thing or event has an indefinite number of properties or attributes observable in it, and might therefore be considered as belonging to an indefinite number of different classes of things.' (Venn, 1888, p. 213). Cf. also Richard von Mises: 'It happens often that one and the same fact can be considered as an element of different kollektivs. It may then be that different probability values can be ascribed to the same event.' (R. von Mises, 1941, p. 192).

90 The lack of a suitable homogeneous reference class was a key objection by Keynes to the Parental Alcoholism study of Ethel Elderton and Karl Pearson in 1910. See Keynes (July and December 1910; 1911) for an early explication of this aspect of his probability theory.

91 'Many probabilities . . . are numerically measurable in the sense that there is *some* other probability with which they are comparable . . . . But they are not numerically measurable in the most usual sense, unless the probability with which they are thus comparable is the relation of certainty.' (Keynes, 1921, p. 175–6).

92 'Inasmuch as relations of probability cannot be assumed to possess the properties of numbers, the terms *addition* and *multiplication* of probabilities have to be given appropriate meaning by definition.' (Keynes, 1921, p. 130).

93 'The possibility of numerical measurement . . . arises out of the addition theorem.' (Keynes, 1921, p. 174).

94 Accounts of Keynes's concept of weight include Mark Stohs (1980), Anna Carabelli (1988), O'Donnell (1989), and Jochen Runde, (1990). Runde in particular argues (rather convincingly) that Keynes was not consistent throughout the *Treatise on Probability* in his definition of weight.

95 As Ayer expressed it, the statement 'an observation increases the probability of a hypothesis' is 'equivalent to saying that the observation increases the degree of confidence with which it is rational to entertain the hypothesis.' (Ayer, 1952, p. 101).

96 Ayer seems to have missed this point. His problem with the 'logical' theory was that it allowed different judgments of probability based on different evidence, each of which could be true. What he failed to consider was that additional evidence does not lead just to a new 'logical truth,' but instead the new probability value replaces completely the old; the old value becomes irrelevant. Far from Ayer's contention ('But this would mean that there was never any point in looking for further evidence; for all that could result would be an addition to our stock of logical truths.' (Ayer, 1961, p. 366)), the additional evidence is not irrelevant, nor does it present any paradoxical result; it increases the weight of the argument and leads to a new value for probability, with the old no longer 'true' based on the new evidence.

97 I. J. Good termed this the Keynes-Russell Principle of Cogent Reason (Good, 1962, p. 140).

98 Cf. Laplace: 'Analogy is based upon the probability that similar things have causes of the same kind and produce the same effects. This probability increases as the similitude becomes more perfect.' (Laplace, 1820, p. 180).

99 Positive and negative analogies may be either 'total' or 'known' as the analogy involves complete or only partial knowledge, respectively.

100 Subjective probability is not synonymous with psychological probability. I. J. Good defined *psychological* probability as 'a degree of belief or intensity of conviction that is used for betting purposes, for making decisions, or for any other purpose, not necessarily after mature consideration and not necessarily with any attempt at "consistency" with one's other opinions.' (Good, 1965, p. 6). A *subjective* probability is a psychological probability that is consistent (so that a Dutch book is not possible). It is maintained in the present work that necessarian probability is as well a special case of psychological probability, but is broader in scope than the personalist or subjective theory since it allows the incorporation of partial orderings.

101 The work of Bruno de Finetti is also of great importance. However, the basic arguments are well-represented in the views of those here presented.

102 Borel dismissed Part II of the *Treatise on Probability*, stating that it was 'written under the direct influence of Bertrand Russell.' (Borel, 1924, p. 48). Keynes for his part freely admitted this (Keynes, 1921, p. 125).

103 Borel and Ramsey were not the first to advocate the use of betting procedures in eliciting quantitative measures of essentially qualitative belief. Hacking noted that 'gaming' was used as early as the Port Royal Logic (1662) to 'represent epistemic probability on a numerical scale.' (Hacking, 1975, p. 85).

104 Ramsey later (in 1929) admitted a defect in his probability theory, i.e., 'that it took partial belief as a psychological phenomenon to be defined and measured by a psychologist. But this sort of psychology goes a very little way and would be quite unacceptable in a developed science.' (Ramsey, 1929a, p. 95).

105 Ramsey continually emphasized in his essay the correspondence between the measurement of psychological belief and the use of measurement techniques in theoretical physics. Also cf. Edgeworth: 'We may be content with the conception of measurement which satisfies the physicists.' (Edgeworth, 1922, p. 258). And cf. R. von Mises: '... repeated observations and frequency determinations are the thermometers of probability theory.' (R. von Mises, 1957, p. 76).

106 Edgeworth, in expressing disagreement with Venn as to the measurability of degrees of belief, presented a very similar argument.

It is finally objected that the phenomenon of a fraction being assigned to belief may be accounted for otherwise than on the supposition that the quantity of belief is measurable. The fraction is the measure of the quantity of advantage which Laplace calls esperance .... Still it may be observed that, upon theories which are current that belief is of the nature of volition and that all volition is determined by the prospect of pleasure, the explanation propounded does not so much destroy as fulfil the theory that the fraction in question is the measure of quantity of belief. If belief cannot be identified with volition, then indeed those who dissent from Mr. Venn will have to postulate a sort of pre-established harmony between the distinct processes of volition and intellect. Yet this postulate cannot be regarded as very extravagant.

(Edgeworth, 1884, p. 226)

107 Ramsey: '. . . for the beliefs which we hold most strongly are often accompanied by practically no feeling at all.' (Ramsey, 1926, p. 65).
108 For this reason the term 'betting' should perhaps be replaced with the term 'behavioristic experimentation.'
109 This is not the place for an exhaustive discussion of utility theory. Excellent surveys include George Stigler (1950), Daniel Ellsberg (1954), Savage (1972), and Mark Machina (1987).
110 Note the following from Ellsberg: The von Neumann-Morgenstern utility index

is not "measurable" in the sense that it is correlated with any significant economic quantity such as quantity of feeling or satisfaction, or intensity, such as intensity of liking or preference. It is derived from *choices*, and describes only *preferences*. It would be "cardinal" ("measurable") only to the extent that the numerical operation of forming mathematical expectations on the basis of these numbers would be related to observable behavior, so as to be empirically meaningful.

(Ellsberg, 1954, p. 538)

This is in contrast to the classical Marshallian or Jevonsian desire to measure pleasure and satisfaction, i.e., to make a Benthamite calculation.
111 Cardinal utility requires (1) the existence of a suitable transformation function, and (2) additively-separable utility functions. The ordinalist view is that this is infeasible if not impossible since alternatives are generally not independent. But cf. Simon: 'If a utility scale can be defined, the additional assumption that it can be defined for choices among uncertain prospects guarantees its cardinality.' (Simon, 1982, p. 324).
112 The linear transformation is order-preserving, sign-preserving, and marginal utility-preserving, unlike the ordinal measure which is only order- and sign-preserving.
113 As Shackle observed, the design of the problem corresponding to the definition of utility had as much to do with outcome as any other element:

. . . if von Neumann and Morgenstern's operation, by which they seek to define utility, refers to a *unique* lottery drawing, the resulting observed behaviour will spring from the *combined* effect of two subjective judgments, one concerned with degrees of belief in outcomes and the other concerned with degrees of satisfaction arising from given face-values of outcomes, and that it will be impossible, by observation alone . . . to disentangle the effects of these two elements. If, on the other hand, von Neumann and Morgenstern have in mind an indefinitely long series of drawings of the same lottery, then risk and uncertainty are eliminated and the proposed method breaks down.

(Shackle, 1956, p. 216)

But cf. R. Duncan Luce and Howard Raiffa (1957), who accept that the frequency interpretation of probability is valid in attaching probability values to the occurrence of events, but, since the experiment (lottery) itself is a one-time event, subjective considerations come into play which necessitate recourse to another approach.

114 Cardinality in Savage is evident from his insistence that, if U is a utility function, then U' (= αU + β) is also; and if U and U' are utility functions, then there exists α, β such that U' = αU + β (Savage, 1972, p. 74). Cardinal utility requires definition up to a linear transformation; ordinal utility requires only a monotonic transformation. Also note the statement: 'If utility is regarded as controlling only consequences, rather than acts, it is not true . . . that utility is determined except for a linear transformation. . . . Under these circumstances there is little, if any, value in talking about utility at all . . . .' (ibid., p. 96).

115 When Keynes claimed that probability is not measurable, he may have meant that, for some events or propositions, the probability measure equals zero or that the measure does not exist. Measurability is defined through the axioms of probability and so is established as a fact. What is non-measurable may be given a measure of zero. The distinction between Keynes and Savage then occurs in the handling of zero measures: Keynes included them as relevant, Savage excluded them as irrelevant.

116 One interesting aspect of Savage's theory is its relation to Keynes's in the consideration of the probability relation itself. Keynes's probability relation P is indefinable; a P h is asserted to mean that the conclusion a stands in a relation of probability to the premise h. Savage simply reinterpreted P to refer to the personal judgment of the individual making the probability estimate. These are both epistemic theories since they are in Hacking's words 'concerned with the credibility of propositions in the light of judgement or evidence' (Hacking, 1975, p. 14).

117 Duncan Luce found Savage's theory tantamount to an objective probability theory: 'Savage's aim was to construct a foundation for probability theory and so he postulated sufficiently strong axioms to arrive at a subjective probability function possessing all of the formal properties of objective probability.' (Luce, 1958, p. 205).

118 Once again 'probabilistic' and 'probability' as defined herein are distinct concepts.

119 This classification has been suggested to me by Jochen Runde, but derives from Lawson (1988). It can also readily be seen to derive from the epistemic/aleatory categorization of Hacking (1975) and the earlier subjective/objective or form of/object of knowledge classifications noted above.

120 See Salmon (1985) for the idea that the key question of empiricism concerns the nature of unobservables: acceptance implies a positivistic temperament, rejection a realist one.

CHAPTER III: PROBABILITY AS A FUNDAMENTAL CONCEPT IN ECONOMICS

121 One of the problems addressed by Smith was that of the impossibility of aggregating over incommensurable units to arrive at summary statistical measures, such as the mean. Units of capital, for instance, are not comparable with those of labor and land. There are no objective measures which can be applied to these variables to force comparability. The most that can be expected is a modal value, a restrictive measure of central tendency. Even this second-best valuation is not completely acceptable, for the dispersion in most economic data is so great as to deny to the economist any aggregate measure whatsoever.

It is not easy ... to ascertain what are the average wages of labour even in a particular place, and at a particular time. We can, even in this case, seldom determine more than what are the most usual wages. But even this can seldom be done with regard to the profits of stock. Profit is so very fluctu-ating that the person who carries on a particular trade cannot always tell you himself what is the average of his annual profit. It is affected not only by every variation of price in the commodities which he deals in, but by the good or bad fortune both of his rivals and of his customers, and by a thou-sand other accidents to which goods when carried either by sea or by land, or even when stored in a warehouse, are liable. It varies, therefore, not only from year to year, but from day to day, and almost from hour to hour. To ascertain what is the average profit of all the different trades carried on in a great kingdom must be much more difficult; and to judge of what it may have been formerly, or in remote periods of time, with any degree of precision, must be altogether impossible.

(Smith, 1789, Bk.I, Ch.IX, p. 191)

122 As J. R. Hicks commented: 'At the very least, that work [of Knight's] has laid securely the first foundation on which any future theory of profits must rest – the dependence of profits on uncertainty.' (Hicks, 1931, p. 170).
123 The description of uncertainty developed by Knight had been expressed early by Keynes in the *Treatise on Probability*, but was done so in terms of the logic of prob-ability and not in regard to economic theory. However, both the *Treatise on Probability* and *Risk, Uncertainty and Profit* were published in the same year, 1921, and so it is highly unlikely that Knight was familiar with Keynes's work.
124 The debt here to Hume is obvious.
125 Marshall defined 'uncertainty' as an '*objective* property which all well-informed persons would estimate in the same way' (Marshall, 1899, p. 77, n.1); the differen-tial between present and future values he termed 'a *subjective* property which different people would estimate in different ways according to their individual characters, and their circumstances at the time.' (ibid., p. 77, n.2). Thus Marshall's risk-uncertainty categories are epistemic. Marshall later downgraded the import-ance of uncertainty in practical matters: ' ... in most cases the evils of uncertainty count for something, though not very much ....' (Marshall, 1920, Bk.V, Ch.VII, p. 400).
126 With the incorporation into the discipline of a specific reference to risk and uncer-tainty, Marshall established a basis for the inclusion of interest. Gross interest included not only a 'reward for waiting', but also an allowance for risk, and thus 'a great part of what appears to the borrowers as interest, is, from the point of view of the lender, earnings of management of a troublesome business.' (Marshall, 1899, p. 285).
127 Hicks disagreed with the risk–uncertainty dichotomy, arguing that such was tanta-mount to basing an economic theory on 'metaphysics and psychology' (Hicks, 1931, p. 171). Marschak (1950) equated Knight's true uncertainty with incomplete information. Hicks later (1979) recognized that Knight's distinction is similar to the distinction between aleatory and epistemic probability which Hicks judged to be of great importance to economics.
128 'The practical difference between the two categories, risk and uncertainty, is that in the former the distribution of the outcome in a group of instances is known ... while in the case of uncertainty this is not true, the reason being in general that it is impossible to form a group of instances, because the situation dealt with is in a high degree unique.' (Knight, 1921, p. 233).

129 Knight discussed the need for two types of foresight in business dealings: (1) the final outcome of a deal needs to be predicted at the beginning; and (2) 'wants' to be satisfied by the goods produced need to be predicted also at that time.

130 Cf. the classification system of Charles Hardy (1923): here probabilities are defined as: (1) objective, wherein a specific mathematical probability point value is derived; (2) 'statistical basis for action', wherein inductions are made on the basis of a uniform empirical series; and (3) subjective, wherein no probability value is discernible, nor is extrapolation from a series possible. This last class includes unique events. In opposition to Knight, Hardy insisted that class (3) can be handled by the use of 'a very crude application of the statistical method' (Hardy, 1923, p. 46). For Hardy, 'true uncertainty' and 'statistical probability' are alike, with information-differentials, constraints as to the length of the appropriate series, and stipulations as to the classification all acting to cause perceived differences (ibid., pp. 54–5).

131 'The doctrine of real probability, if it is to be valid, must, it seems, rest upon inherent unknowability in the factors, not merely the fact of ignorance.' (Knight, 1921, p. 219).

132 See also Stephen LeRoy and Larry Singell (1987), especially sec.III.

133 This is a sufficient, but not a necessary, condition.

134 LeRoy and Singell (1987) regard the insurance market itself as an indicator of the existence of true uncertainty: where insurance markets exist, the situation is one of risk; where they are absent, true uncertainty obtains. In commenting on Knight's work, they argued that he rejected the idea 'that in some situations the probabilistic calculus is inapplicable' (p. 401). This is simply wrong. Their rationale behind this conclusion is that Knight considered subjective probability 'universally applicable in situations of uncertainty' (ibid., p. 402). The passages cited, however, do not support their conclusion that uncertainty for Knight was the result of moral hazard or adverse selection; even they seem to contradict themselves, e.g., in footnote 5, when they cite Hicks as one writer with whom they are in agreement. Hicks is quoted: 'Risks, according to Knight, arise from random sequences; so they can be covered, if there are enough of them, by insurance. True uncertainties, which he recognizes to be of greater importance in economics, cannot.' This is the contention made here in the present essay: that the risk–uncertainty dichotomy is the correct reading of Knight, irrespective of whether subjective probabilities are held. Seriable events are insurable because the insurer can determine a pattern and thereby classify risks; non-seriable events are beyond our means to classify, and so are uninsurable because of this.

135 'It is evident that a great many hazards can be reduced to a fair degree of certainty by statistical grouping – also that an equally important category cannot.' (Knight, 1921, p. 215).

136 This is of course not the case with more modern dynamic models.

137 See I. N. Herstein and John Milnor (1953) for a re-statement of von Neumann-Morgenstern utility theory that is more elementary mathematically than the original; see Jacob Marschak (1950) for a somewhat different axiomatization; see Arrow (1971) for a re-statement of the Ramsey-Savage axiomatization. Luce (1958) presented a probabilistic version of the von Neumann-Morgenstern theory. See also Luce and Raiffa (1957, App.I). For a technical comparison of the axiomatizations of von Neumann-Morgenstern, Savage, Marschak, and Arrow, see Kenneth MacCrimmon and Stig Larsson (1979).

138 See Paul Anand (1991) for a survey of the subject and a non-technical presentation of an alternative to standard subjective expected utility theories consistent with Keynes's probability treatment. Cf. the presentation of Isaac Levi (1986).

139 Cf. Arrow: 'Abstention from a decision cannot exist; some social state will prevail.' (Arrow, 1963, p. 118) Also R. G. D. Allen: 'The concept of preference or utility... is an ordered but non-measurable one.' (Allen, 1938, p. 290).

140 Continuity implies that, for all a, b, $c \in A$, and for some τ, δ, $(0 \leqslant \tau \leqslant 1$; $0 \leqslant \delta \leqslant 1)$, $\tau a + (1 - \tau) \, c \leqslant b \leqslant \delta a + (1 - \delta)c$. This is the form appearing in Peter Fishburn (1989). Chipman (1960) has shown that if the continuity axiom (the Axiom of Substitution or the Axiom of Archimedes) is weakened or violated, the result is a lexicographic utility scale. It should be noted that Ramsey also relied on the Axiom of Archimedes and an Axiom of Continuity in his probability theory (Ramsey, 1926, p. 75).

141 Samuelson (1952) argued that the independence axiom was implicit in the von Neumann-Morgenstern axiomatization and crucial to Savage as well. See also the note by Edmond Malinvaud (1952).

142 Of course, the same holds true for the strong ordering.

143 See, e.g., Donald Davidson and Patrick Suppes (1956), Mark Machina (1982), Peter Fishburn (1983), and Eddie Dekel (1986), each of which remove separability in favor of non-linearity in probability.

144 In the case where the individual was deemed 'indifferent to the dispersion of psychological values' (Allais, 1952, p. 77), the Allais and von Neumann-Morgenstern theories would coincide.

145 Allais considered probability to be of the classical (Laplacian) form. The index of cardinal utility was then based on reference to the Weber-Fechner law, a law in experimental psychology stressing a mathematical relation between stimulus and sensation. See G. Stigler (1950, pt.II) for a discussion of the Weber-Fechner law and its applications to utility theory.

146 Thus the postulates either: (1) 'failed to be acceptable in those circumstances as normative rules'; (2) failed as predictive tools; or (3) were not sufficiently drilled into the decision-makers to allow them to appreciate the need for adherence (Ellsberg, 1961, p. 646).

147 This problem is from Ellsberg (1961). A similar example is presented in MacCrimmon and Larsson (1979), Decision Problem IV, pp. 376-80. Levi (1986) presented a reconsideration of the Allais-Ellsberg paradoxes, with a similar example. Keynes (1921) and Knight (1921) also have somewhat similar examples.

148 See also Ellsberg (1954) for the argument that von Neumann-Morgenstern utility is valid only for situations involving risk.

149 'Inevitable and important though this vagueness of preference is, not everyone is agreed that a normative theory of the *homo economicus* can be improved by incorporating vagueness...' (Savage, 1977, p. 7).

150 Laplace expressed much the same idea: 'One of the great advantages of the calculus of probabilities is to teach us to distrust first opinions.' (Laplace, 1820, p. 164).

151 As mentioned previously, Savage accepted the *possibility* of a partial order, but rejected it as not *feasible* in the derivation (and application) of his decision theory.

152 See Levi (1986) for the view that the problem with 'strict Bayesianism' is its failure to accept the indeterminateness of rankings. For Levi, decision-making under conditions of risk implies that utility maximization (whereby definite numerical values are assigned to available options) is the appropriate criterion for selecting from available options, while decision-making under conditions of uncertainty implies that it is not possible (certainly not 'legitimate') to make such numerical valuations. See Robert Aumann (1962, 1964) for a presentation of utility theory without the total order (completeness) requirement.

153 One may also consider the restructured probability axioms of Good (1962) and Henry Kyburg (1992).

154 'Risk' may be more formally defined as a quantifiable (i.e., measurable) subset of uncertainty, composed of elements of a minimal σ-algebra reduced by identification according to sets of measure zero for which a probability measure is defined. It is not necessarily a quantity objectively known (especially in its epistemic variant), since each individual decision-maker will arrive at his own subjective valuation based upon his apprehension of signals generated in the economy. It is, however, numerically valued and so insurable.

155 'True uncertainty' may be more formally defined as a non-quantifiable subset of uncertainty composed of elements of a σ-algebra which are either non-measurable or of measure zero and therefore not subsumed under the minimal σ-algebra. This is the epistemic uncertainty of Keynes and the aleatory uncertainty of Knight. It will also be shown to be the epistemic uncertainty of Shackle.

156 In a similar manner, Gerald P. O'Driscoll and Mario J. Rizzo distinguished between 'process economics' and 'dynamic-state economics', the former referring to the activity of individuals engaged in error-correcting behavior with a specific goal in view, in an environment devoid of coordinating mechanisms (so that the result is a non-deterministic system); the latter concentrated on the necessary existence of equilibrium states and their concomitant equilibrium end-values, so that uncertainty corresponds to a strictly deterministic system, any exogenous shocks leading the system back toward a calculable (or at least knowable) end-value. 'Process economics' is then time-dependent and allows the explicit incorporation of uncertainty; the focus is on the individual decision process as it involves the restructuring of the desired choice set as external factors disrupt initial choices and so force a reconsideration. 'Dynamic-state economics' is time-independent, and may be thought of as involving a backward calculation from chosen ends to the means of arriving at those ends (O'Driscoll and Rizzo, 1985, p. 5). Paul Davidson's (1988) distinction between ergodic and non-ergodic theory, although seemingly similar to that of O'Driscoll and Rizzo, is fundamentally different. Davidson concocts a binary environment of certainty (1) and uncertainty (0) (for those existentially inclined, this may be termed Being and Nothingness). He can then deny by definition the existence of a continuum of probability values. I am indebted to Jochen Runde for pointing out this flaw in Davidson's Post Keynesian theory of uncertainty. (See also Runde, forthcoming.)

157 Of course, this implies reliance on the simplistic, pedagogical classical model, and not the models advanced by the classical economists.

158 Simon carefully avoided confusing this with the possibility of limited information about consequences.

CHAPTER IV: AUSTRIAN ECONOMICS

159 This is not to imply that all Austrians are Kantians. Mises was a neo-Kantian, while Menger adhered to Aristotelian philosophy. Hayek and Shackle may best be described as Kantians.

160 Of course, Wittgenstein himself denied that these 'pictures' were true *a priori*. See especially Proposition 2.225.

161 Not that others did not also hold similar positions and argue just as forcefully; it is just that these figures appear to be the most prominent spokesmen, advancing ideas directly related to the topic at hand. That three of the four happen to also be the most rationalist of the Austrians is probably not a coincidence.

162 Shackle is, it must be acknowledged, a figure in the Post-keynesian movement. However, his work antedates this variant of keynesianism. As a student of F. A. Hayek, his Austrian credentials are well-established, while characterization as a

Post-keynesian does a general disservice to his work. His views on uncertainty, for instance, are very much in the Austrian spirit. Perhaps those Post Keynesians sympathetic to Shackle's views should re-label themselves as Shackelians.

163 Smith's objective labor value is thus an anachronism since obviously labor, land, capital, and entrepreneurial ability add significantly to any measure of objective cost.

164 For a fuller expression of this view, see Friedrich Wieser (1891).

165 'Men are especially prone to let themselves be misled into overestimating the importance of satisfactions that give intense momentary pleasure but contribute only fleetingly to their well-being, and so into underestimating the importance of satisfactions on which a less intensive but longer enduring well-being depends.' (Menger, 1871, p. 148).

166 A recent expositor of this view is Israel M. Kirzner. See especially Kirzner, 1979.

167 The foremost current expositor of the Mises position is Murray Rothbard. See especially his (1957) and (1976).

168 'If man knew the future, he would not have to choose and would not act. He would be like an automaton, reacting to stimuli without any will of his own.' (Mises, 1966, p. 105).

169 'Apodictic certainty is only within the orbit of the deductive system of aprioristic theory. The most that can be attained with regard to reality is probability.' (Mises, 1966, p. 105.

170 Mises expressed disdain for the frequency concept: 'Only preoccupation with the mathematical treatment [of probability] could result in the prejudice that probability always means frequency.' (Mises, 1966, p. 107).

171 'The characteristic mark of insurance is that it deals with the whole class of events. As we pretend to know everything about the behavior of the whole class, there seems to be no specific risk involved in the conduct of the business.' (Mises, 1966, p. 109).
   Cf. the statement of Fisher: 'While it is possible to calculate mathematically risks of a certain type like those in games of chance or in property and life insurance where the chances are capable of accurate measurement, most economic risks are not so readily measured.' (Fisher, 1930, p. 316).

172 'Such an estimate of relative values in no way involves the idea of measurement.' (Mises, 1953, p. 39).

173 Hayek did consider a second case beyond mutual compatibility, in which objective and subjective data sets could coincide. This was the case where the *expectations* based upon the data sets in fact obtain. Hayek rejected this, since 'it would never be possible to decide otherwise than *ex post*, at the end of the period for which people have planned, whether at the beginning the society has been in equilibrium.' (Hayek, 1937, p. 40).

174 Economists have been slow to recognize that order may be the result of chaos. Hayek termed economics 'the *last* remnant of that primitive attitude which made us invest with a human mind everything that moved and changed in a way adapted to perpetuate itself or its kind.' We as economists must 'recognise that the spontaneous interplay of the actions of individuals may produce something which is not the deliberate object of their actions but an organism in which every part performs a necessary function for the continuance of the whole, without any human mind having devised it.' (Hayek, 1933, p. 130).

175 It is not clear that Shackle accepted the Keynesian trichotomy of probabilistic, stochastic, and unknown (as defined here). The probabilistic and unknown categories may be combined in the Shackelian non-distributional class.

176 'The essential condition for the use of a distributional uncertainty variable is that the list of suggested answers should be complete without a residual hypothesis.' (Shackle, 1969, p. 49).

177 'They can, for example, all be zero, and thus express the individual's feeling, which cannot be expressed by frequency-ratio probability, that every one of the rival hypotheses has "nothing known against it".' (Shackle, 1949–50, p. 70). So Shackle does not accept that sets of measure zero are identical to the null set; it is possible that $P(A) = 0$, where $A = \{a_1, a_2, \ldots\}$.

178 Arrow (1951) equated Shackle's theory with the statistical theory of Jerzy Neyman and Egon Pearson.

179 As Erich Streissler stated Shackle's position: 'Shackle sees the inapplicability of probability in the uniqueness of situation and result; as we are faced with a single occurrence we cannot apply frequency-ratio probability for lack of a universe.' (Streissler, 1959, p. 219). Again, note that Streissler did not deny the validity of the frequency theory applied in this respect. Streissler's statement must be qualified.

180 '. . . the possible outcomes of any act do not, in general, constitute a limited and finite set such as would exist if we were concerned with a game with stated rules.' (Shackle, 1969, p. 7).

181 This of course does not apply to more modern statements, including theories incorporating asymmetric information.

182 Shackle considered game theory to also be within the rational-decision framework of the classicists since it involves situations (games) played under a set of given and completely known rules. While not being completely knowledgeable of the final outcome, the decision-maker knows all possible outcomes that can occur and their respective pay-offs as well (Shackle, 1972, p. 161).

183 See Roy Radner (1968) for a proof that money (liquidity demand) results from limitations on foresight and computational ability.

184 'Money is precisely that which enables choice to be deferred. But equilibrium is that model in which no aspect of choice can be deferred.' (Shackle, 1965, p. 23).

185 This is explained in more depth in Shackle, 1979, Ch.13.

186 'Economic choice . . . consists in first creating, by conjecture and reasoned imagination on the basis of mere suggestions offered by visible or recorded circumstance, the things on which hope can be fixed. . . . It is only in the timeless fiction of general equilibrium that reason can prevail alone.' (Shackle, 1972, p. 96).

187 'By the kaleidic theory I mean the view that the expectations . . . are at all times so insubstantially founded upon data and so mutably suggested by the stream of "news" . . . that they can undergo complete transformation in an hour or even a moment . . .' (Shackle, 1974, p. 42). Compare the kaleidic world of Shackle with the definition of rationality advanced by A. G. Hart (1951). Hart defined rationality as operating on four distinct but interconnected levels: (in descending order of occurrence) acts, plans, estimates, and the assembly of information (Hart, 1951, p. 4). Each level need not fulfill the condition of classical rationality as a precondition for the rationality of the higher levels. It may be that the estimates made (e.g., by the entrepreneur) are irrational while based on rationally collected evidence, and still lead to rationally calculated plans (ibid., p. 5). Although the levels of rationality are interconnected, they do not and need not form a logical chain of inference. This states, somewhat more clearly than Shackle, the kaleidic nature of the decision process. A clearly defined chain of reasoning is not required as a precondition of rational decision-making; nor is it even possible.

188 I am indebted to Mark Perlman for pointing out to me this facet of Shackle's kaleidic world.

189 Cf. the Principle of Equipossibility and the Principle of Non-Sufficient Reason (classical probability) and the Principle of Indifference (Keynes).

190 Cf. David Hume: 'Nothing is more dangerous to reason than the flights of the imagination.' (Hume, 1740, Bk.I, Pt.IV, sec.VII, p. 314). Also: '... the understanding, when it acts alone, and according to its most general principles, entirely subverts itself, and leaves not the lowest degree of evidence in any proposition.' (ibid., sec.VII, p. 315).

191 Cf. the position of the American Institutionalists, especially that of Commons. For Commons, 'purpose is the choice of probabilities' (Commons, 1924, p. 127); this purposive action is the basis of economics as a behavioral (volitional) discipline.

192 Ludwig Lachmann (1976) (among others) noted these similarities between Mises and Shackle, and noted differences as well. Unlike Mises, Shackle: (1) extended the Austrian subjectivism by explicitly incorporating expectations; (2) gave expectations center stage; and (3) allowed for divergent expectations. These have been discussed in the previous presentation of the views of Shackle and are abundantly clear from his writings.

CHAPTER V: KEYNESAN ECONOMICS

193 Two excellent book-length studies of the philosophical foundations of Keynes's economics are Anna Carabelli (1988) and Rod O'Donnell (1989), both extended versions of earlier doctoral dissertations at Cambridge. Also of importance is the biography of Keynes by Robert Skidelsky (vol. I: 1983; vol. II: 1992). These accounts draw not only on Keynes's published work, but on unpublished archival material at Kings College. The presentation here draws only on published material and is not meant to be as rigorous or comprehensive in this area as these studies, although anyone writing in this area will have a large degree of overlap.

194 Note the similarity of the Keynesan position to the position of Hayek discussed above.

195 The stated purpose of the *Treatise on Money* is the discovery of the process of moving from one equilibrium position to the next, in essence to discover the laws of passage of the system (Keynes, 1930, p. xvii).

196 'There seems ... a good deal to be said for the conclusion that, other things being equal, that course of action is preferable, which involves least risk and about the results of which we have the most complete knowledge.' (Keynes, 1921, p. 347).

197 It is the increased weight which is most important to decision-making, since it leads to greater confidence in any decision. But one can never be certain that one has even sufficient data upon which to act.

198 'The statistical result is so attractive in its definiteness that it leads us to forget the more vague though more important considerations which must be, in a given particular case, within our knowledge.' (Keynes, 1921, p. 356).

199 Cf. the commentary on Shackle.

200 This is similar to the Austrian (Mengerian) discussion of error.

201 Keynes in the *Tract* also presented a long-run, short-run theoretical distinction, but not in the explicit terminology of the *Treatise on Money*.

202 The difficulty with the measurement of economic magnitudes left Keynes in the position of limiting his analysis of the macroeconomy to the consideration of only two 'units', money and labor, both of which he considered of a measurable nature in that each was assumed to be of the nature of a homogeneous commodity.

203 In the *General Theory*, Keynes concluded his digression on long-term expectations by noting: 'We should not conclude from this that everything depends on waves of irrational psychology. On the contrary, the state of long-term expectation is

often steady, and, even when it is not, the other factors exert their compensating effects.' (Keynes, 1936, p. 162). In the *Tract*, Keynes viewed the long-run as unaffected by expectations, while the short-run was akin to the ocean in 'tempestuous seasons' (Keynes, 1923, p. 65). The short-run is unstable as subjective expectations influence the movements of prices; the long-run, by contrast, is the classical situation of order and stability.

204 In his discussion of uncertainty in Keynes's *General Theory*, Mark Stohs (1980) erred on several points:

   (1) 'uncertainty' in Keynes is not simply 'lack of knowledge about the future' (p. 374). It is more fundamentally a lack of any mechanism allowing us to gain such knowledge to any significant degree.
   (2) Keynes did not believe that 'the probabilities about prospective yields can be calculated' (pp. 377–8). Keynes quite obviously believed the opposite. Stohs's argument that these probabilities need not be numerical denies that they can be calculated at all, for certainly numericality is part and parcel of calculation, even if that calculation is a subjective degree of belief.
   (3) uncertainty most definitely does not solely arise 'in conjunction with the weight of those calculations' (p. 378). Uncertainty for Keynes underlies his dissatisfaction with a numerical probability calculus; it is a focal point for his probability theory.
   (4) it is evident from the above that 'uncertain' and 'improbable' are not synonymous.

   Points (2) and (3) have been made by O'Donnell (1989, p. 373).
   Alan Garner (1983) pointed out that a problem with Stohs's treatment was his use of a misprinted version of Keynes's 1937 *QJE* article. See also the rejoinder by Stohs (1983).

205 Compare the *Tract*: ' . . . stability of the exchange from day to day cannot be maintained merely by the *fact* of stability in these underlying conditions. It is necessary also that bankers should have a sufficiently certain *expectation* of such stability to induce them to look after the daily and seasonal fluctuations of the market in return for a moderate commission.' (Keynes, 1923, pp. 92–3). One may also compare to the Principle of Non-Sufficient Reason from the *Treatise on Probability*.

206 Cf. Mill: ' . . . an approximate generalisation is, in social inquiries, for most practical purposes equivalent to an exact one; that which is only probable when asserted of individual human beings indiscriminately selected, being certain when affirmed of the character and collective conduct of masses.' (Mill, 1872, p. 34).

207 Cf. Arthur Ellis: ' . . . the swaying of opinion from wrong to right and beyond – from excessive pessimism to immoderate optimism – is the usual and immediate cause of fluctuations.' (Ellis, 1892, p. 110).

208 It is for this reason that Keynes suggested the State exercise some control over the process of investment, thus mitigating the vagaries of the market and the fluctuations caused by such unpredictable waves of investor behavior (Keynes, 1936, p. 164).

209 'Thus if the animal spirits are dimmed and the spontaneous optimism falters, leaving us to depend on nothing but a mathematical expectation, enterprise will fade and die.' (Keynes, 1936, p. 162).

210 Cf. Ellis: 'It is often noticed . . . that a diffused or strong opinion that a given event will have a certain effect on a market is more potent in the way of influencing prices than the event itself.' (Ellis, 1892, p. 114).

211 Cf. the discussion in the *Tract* (Keynes, 1923, p. 132) on the re-establishment of monetary equilibrium without involving exchange or changes in the money supply or velocity of circulation.
212 Axel Leijonhufvud noted this simplification on the part of Keynes (Leijonhufvud, 1968, p. 41).
213 Marschak considered the use of two parameters: the mathematical expectation and the coefficient of variation, i.e., both first and second moments, citing the *Treatise on Probability* as rationale (Marschak, 1938, p. 320). Hart defined uncertainty as simply 'a high dispersion of anticipations around the expectation' (Hart, 1951, p. 65).
214 David Begg (1982) considered this as evidence of Keynes's development of an early form of rational expectations. But this conclusion relies on reading in Keynes a misapprehension of the distinction between expectations and *changes* in expectations. It remains to be shown here that the rational expectations view is *fundamentally* different from the view of Keynes (although admittedly there are aspects which may lead to the same or similar *conclusions*).
215 'New fears and hopes will, without warning, take charge of human conduct.' (Keynes, 1937, p. 215).
216 See also Tinbergen's (1940) reply to Keynes's review.
217 Keynesians as a group (differentiated from Post Keynesians and new Keynesians) err in not attributing to the *General Theory* its essential feature: the insufficiency of knowledge of the environment and the circumstances or consequences of actions. This may be due to their reliance on the simplification of the *General Theory* by J. R. Hicks. Hicks's (1937) restatement of the *General Theory* neglected the role of expectations and uncertainty, both of which Keynes greatly emphasized. Samuelson (1947) also contributed to the perpetuation of the misstatement in his construction of a non-stochastic keynesian economic model. The misinterpretations continue, e.g., in Thomas Sargent (1979).
218 This is not to say that Keynes was therefore a disequilibrium theorist. The concept simply does not apply.
219 For clarification of Moore's influence on Keynes, see Keynes (1938), Skidelsky (1986), Carabelli (1988), and O'Donnell (1989). Bateman's (1988) account of a reverse influence (from Keynes to Moore) is flawed by a misinterpretation of Moore's *Principia Ethica* and its relation to his later *Ethics* of 1912.

CHAPTER VI: RATIONAL EXPECTATIONS AND THE NEW NEOCLASSICISTS

220 See, e.g., Robert E. Lucas, Jr. (1976), and Lucas and Thomas Sargent (1981).
221 Published originally in French. The citation is to the 1964 English-language reprint.
222 Henry Thornton (1802) also followed a state-contingent approach to the problem of uncertainty, predicated on a notion of the indeterminacy of events. Our view of the future is contingent on the occurrence of a given state; allowance must be made for other possible contingencies, each of which may affect our outlook on the future. What is said to be unique to Arrow and Debreu is the idea of a security that allowed reduction of uncertainty to risk. Although cf. Hart: 'By making futures contracts, and by insurance, uncertainties may be eliminated for the individual entrepreneur, and this quite aside from the question whether the thing insured is strictly an "insurable risk."' (Hart, 1937, p. 286n4).

223 The use of the convention of treating commodities at different dates as different commodities Arrow credited to Hicks (Arrow, 1978, p. 159).

224 As Debreu did not extend his analysis to include securities markets, there was no need to take explicit account of subjective probabilities.

225 It is interesting to note that Savage referred to this as the 'Look Before You Leap' Principle, but had reservations about its unqualified use:

> Carried to its logical extreme, the 'Look before you leap' principle demands that one envisage every conceivable policy for the government of his whole life (at least from now on) in its most minute details, in the light of the vast number of unknown states of the world, and decide here and now on one policy. This is utterly ridiculous, not – as some might think – because there might later be cause for regret, if things did not turn out as had been anticipated, but because the task implied in making such a decision is not even remotely resembled by human possibility. It is even utterly beyond our power to plan a picnic or to play a game of chess in accordance with the principle, even when the world of states and the set of available acts to be envisaged are artificially reduced to the narrowest reasonable limits.
>
> (Savage, 1972, p. 16)

But Savage considered it as being desirable as a principle for decision-making 'in so far as the looking is not unreasonably time-consuming and otherwise expensive....' (ibid., p. 16). Thus Savage seemed to have anticipated Simon's (1982) rationale for satisficing as an alternative to maximizing behavior.

226 Cf. the earlier theory of Hart, itself an early form of rational expectations. Hart listed three properties of market anticipations: (1) the decision-maker forms a (subjective) 'expectations schedule,' wherein is given price expectations for each future date; (2) these expectations are not point-values, but rather constitute ranges (numerically-valued) with increasing variability (dispersion) over longer time-periods; and (3) as the future approaches, the dispersion is expected to narrow. (Hart, 1937, pp. 285–6). See also A. A. Walters (1971) for a theory of 'consistent' as opposed to 'rational' expectations.

227 This problem was discussed very early on by Hayek in his 1937 'Economics and Knowledge.' As Hayek stated the distinction between objective and subjective data:

> There seems to be no possible doubt that these two concepts of 'data', on the one hand in the sense of the objective real facts, as the observing economist is supposed to know them, and on the other in the subjective sense, as things known to the persons whose behaviour we try to explain, are really fundamentally different and ought to be kept carefully apart. And, as we shall see, the question why the data in the subjective sense of the term should ever come to correspond to the objective data is one of the main problems we have to answer.
>
> (Hayek, 1937, p. 39)

228 See e.g., Edward Prescott and Robert Lucas (1972), Douglas Gale (1982, 1983), and others writing in the rational expectations paradigm who explicitly (or implicitly) restrict the underlying state-space in this manner.

229 See Thomas Sargent (1979), especially Chapter XI, sec.2, for a rigorous explanation of the use of stationary stochastic processes in economic models.

230 Note that not all stationary processes are ergodic. For instance, a 'limit cycle' is stationary but not ergodic.

NOTES

231 Ergodicity does not imply perfect knowledge, nor does non-ergodicity imply ignorance. Ergodicity is merely a (sufficient) condition for convergence to equilibrium; it makes no claims as to restrictions on knowledge. Perfect knowledge would need to be defined and specified by an additional postulate. The view of Davidson (1988, 1991) wherein knowledge is defined as contingent on the environment being ergodic, while uncertainty is by default the antithesis, characterized by non-ergodicity, is misguided.

232 Cf. Jevons:

> The use of an average, or, what is the same, an aggregate result, depends upon the high probability that accidental and disturbing causes will operate, in the long run, as often in one direction as the other, so as to neutralize each other. Provided that we have a sufficient number of independent cases, we may then detect the effect of any *tendency*, however slight. Accordingly, questions which appear, and perhaps are, quite indeterminate as regards individuals, may be capable of exact investigation and solution in regard to great masses and wide averages.
>
> (Jevons, 1911, pp. 15–16)

Given a large enough sample size, over the long run (consistent with a Bernoullian classical probability analysis), the tendencies (i.e., the secular components of the series) become demonstrably evident. It is after all these tendencies which form the data of interest to economists. The findings of N. D. Kondratieff (1935) and Eugen Slutsky (1937) are simply empirical manifestations of this Jevonsian hypothesis.

233 See Samuelson (1968) for the opinion that the classical economists were at heart ergodic theorists. Davidson has gone so far as to insist that Samuelson made the hypothesis 'the sine qua non of the scientific method in economics.' (Davidson, 1991, p. 133). As pointed out above, this position is untenable.

234 This is undoubtedly not the outcome foreseen by Armen Alchian (1950) when he suggested a 'marriage' of stochastic processes and economic theory.

235 As Ian Hacking (1990) has shown, the 'average man' emerged initially as a statistical artifact in the work of Adolph Quetelet, but eventually took on a 'real' meaning. As the frequency theory of probability makes clear, the statistical average is but a shorthand construct based on a random series. It is meaningless outside of the series from which it is derived. Quetelet re-interpreted this average to apply to a real attribute of the series, so giving it validity beyond the domain of the series. This desire to breathe life into a statistical artifact Hacking deemed 'a crucial step in the taming of change. It began to turn statistical laws that were merely descriptive of large-scale regularities into laws of nature and society that dealt in underlying truths and causes.' (Hacking, 1990, p. 108). That which had been conceived initially as an objective measure of a given group became a measure of the archetypical group representative.

236 Consider the following from Begg: '...the great strength of the [rational expectations] hypothesis is that it is not *ad hoc*, but is based instead on the sound optimising principle that individuals do the best they can.' (Begg, 1982, p. 259). As the theory is a modeling principle, disconnected from process, it has precious little to do with individual optimizing behavior (at least in its Muthian form).

237 Even Lucas is of this opinion: 'The term "rational expectations", as Muth used it, refers to a consistency axiom for economic models, so it can be given precise meaning only in the context of specific models.' (Lucas, 1987, p. 13n.4).

238 That is, unless Muth considered he was describing a *situation* and not a *process*.

239 Lucas recognized the limitations of the rational expectations hypothesis as regards anything other than econometric modeling: 'John Muth's hypothesis of rational

152

expectations is a technical model-building principle, not a distinct, comprehensive macroeconomic theory.' (Lucas, 1981, p. 1).

240 Cf. Mill:

> The remark, however, must here be once more repeated, that knowledge insufficient for prediction may be most valuable for guidance. It is not necessary for the wise conduct of the affairs of society, no more than of any one's private concerns, that we should be able to foresee infallibly the results of what we do. We must seek our objects by means which may perhaps be defeated, and take precautions against dangers which possibly may never be realised . . . . A knowledge of the tendencies only, though without the power of accurately predicting their conjunct result, gives us to a considerable extent this power.
>
> (Mill, 1872, p. 86)

241 This view of the rational expectations hypothesis led Arrow to the conclusion that 'in the rational expectations hypothesis, economic agents are required to be superior statisticians, capable of analyzing the future general equilibria of the economy.' (Arrow, 1978, p. 160). Also cf. Knight: 'We do not perceive the present as it is and in its totality, nor do we infer the future from the present with any high degree of dependability, nor yet do we accurately know the consequences of our own actions.' (Knight, 1921, p. 202).

242 The distinguishing feature of a Bayesian is his 'readiness to incorporate intuitive probability into statistical theory and practice.' (Good, 1965, p. 8).

243 By denying the usefulness (or even the validity) of the Bayesian learning process, Lucas cannot be sympathetic to the microfoundations since at the operational level account must be taken of the decision process through its explicit incorporation in the economic model.

244 'In particular, any distinction between *types* of randomness (such as Knight's (1921) distinction between "risk" and "uncertainty") is, at this level [the level of the individual decision-maker] meaningless.' (Lucas, 1981, p. 223).

Cf. Fisher who asserted that 'Risk is synonymous with uncertainty – lack of knowledge'. (Fisher, 1930, p. 222). Unlike Lucas, Fisher did not think uncertainty meaningless conceptually; it was simply removed from consideration in an effort to construct a viable theory. Hicks (1931), however, is much more in sympathy with Lucas.

245 The reasoning behind Lucas's decision is obvious: he wished to investigate business cycles as recurrent phenomena. 'Insofar as business cycles can be viewed as repeated instances of essentially similar events, it will be reasonable to treat agents as reacting to cyclical changes as "risk," or to assume their expectations are *rational* . . . .' (Lucas, 1981, p. 224). The position is indeed similar to that of Venn (1888) in his statement of the rationale for the frequency view of probability, although Venn is nowhere mentioned by Lucas as a source for his views.

246 See Marshall, 1920, Bk.V, Ch.V, pp. 366–7.

247 See also Radner (1968) for the thesis that Arrow-Debreu-type models rely on a superabundance of markets and extreme computational ability.

248 But cf. Radner (1968, esp. p. 40) whose theoretical model allows prior information to enter.

249 This view is not accepted by Grossman (1981).

250 A third model, the control model, is excluded here from consideration.

251 Cyert and DeGroot assume that this choice is erroneous.

252 Cf. the similar findings by Lawrence Blume and David Easley (1982). See also Margaret Bray (1982). For a survey of the rational expectations literature as it relates to the stability problem, see Blume, Bray, and Easley (1982).

CHAPTER VII: CONCLUSION

253 For Levi (1986), indeterminacy, i.e., the inability to arrive at precise numerical probability values, leads to a collapse of Bayesian decision theory. Where definite numerical values cannot be had, a secondary criterion replaces the primary criterion of utility maximization. The single, defined probability distribution is a requirement for expected utility maximization; under conditions of uncertainty, all possible distributions are valid. It should be noted that Levi distinguished indeterminateness from measurability: the existence of a measure does not preclude an indeterminate outcome.

254 Although perhaps the neoclassical writers can provide plausible reasons.

255 Allan Meltzer accepted the proposition that the Keynes-Knight distinction is an important but neglected concept in economics (Meltzer, 1988, pp. 145–6).

256 In his *Causality in Economics*, Hicks judged that since economists do not deal with the results of randomized experimentation, use of the frequency theory of probability in economics, and indeed in social science in general, is invalid; an epistemic theory is more applicable to economic problems: 'I have myself come to the view that the frequency theory, though it is thoroughly at home in many of the natural sciences, is not wide enough for economics.' (Hicks, 1979, p. 105).

257 This is despite the protestation of some that the *Treatise on Probability* is an empirical work, and so may reflect a Humean tradition. See Lawson (1987) and O'Donnell (1989, p. 350).

258 That this is so is evident from his position in the *Theory of Moral Sentiments*. Here Smith advocated the primacy of reason over passion; such was not to be unqualified, however, since empirical elements need be accounted for at times to initiate the process. To quote Smith:

> It is by reason that we discover those general rules of justice by which we ought to regulate our actions: and it is by the same faculty that we form those more vague and indeterminate ideas of what is prudent, of what is descent, of what is generous or noble, which we carry constantly about with us, and according to which we endeavour, as well as we can, to model the tenor of our conduct. The general maxims of morality are formed, like all other general maxims, from experience and induction . . . . But induction is always regarded as one of the operations of reason. From reason, therefore, we are very properly said to derive all those general maxims and ideas. It is by these, however, that we regulate the greater part of our moral judgments, which would be extremely uncertain and precarious if they depended altogether upon what is liable to so many variations as immediate sentiment and feeling.

> (Smith, 1790, p. 319)

BIBLIOGRAPHY

Alchian, Armen A. 'Uncertainty, Evolution, and Economic Theory,' *Journal of Political Economy*, vol. 58, no. 3 (June 1950), pp. 211–21.

Allais, Maurice. 'The Foundations of a Positive Theory of Choice Involving Risk and a Criticism of the Postulates of the American School,' in Maurice Allais and Ole Hagen, eds., *Expected Utility Hypotheses and the Allais Paradox*. Boston: D. Reidel, 1979 [1952].

Allen, R. G. D. *Mathematical Analysis for Economists*. New York: St. Martin's Press, 1938.

Anand, Paul. 'The Nature of Rational Choice and *The Foundations of Statistics*,' *Oxford Economic Papers*, vol. 43, no. 2 (April 1991), pp. 199–216.

Arrow, Kenneth J. 'Alternative Approaches to the Theory of Choice in Risk-Taking Situations,' *Econometrica*, vol. 19, no. 4 (October 1951), pp. 404–37.

——. *Social Choice and Individual Values*. 2nd. ed. New Haven: Yale University Press, 1963.

——. 'The Role of Securities in the Allocation of Risk- Bearing,' *Review of Economic Studies*, vol. XXXI (1964), pp. 91–6.

——. 'Exposition of the Theory of Choice Under Uncertainty,' in K. J. Arrow, ed. *Essays in the Theory of Risk-Bearing*. Chicago: Markham, 1971.

——. 'The Future and the Present in Economic Life,' *Economic Inquiry*, vol. 16, no. 2 (April 1978), pp. 157–69.

——. 'Risk Perception in Psychology and Economics,' *Economic Inquiry*, vol. XX, no. 1 (January 1982), pp. 1–9.

——. 'Rationality of Self and Others in an Economic System,' in Robin M. Hogarth and Melvin W. Reder, eds. *Rational Choice: The Contrast Between Economics and Psychology*. Chicago: University of Chicago Press, 1987.

Aumann, Robert. 'Utility Theory Without the Completeness Axiom,' *Econometrica*, vol. 30, no. 3 (July 1962), pp. 445–62.

——. 'Utility Theory Without the Completeness Axiom: A Correction,' *Econometrica*, vol. 32, no. 1 (January 1964), pp. 210–12.

Ayer, Alfred Jules. *Language, Truth, and Logic*. New York: Dover, 1952.

——. 'On the Probability of Particular Events,' *Revue Internationale de Philosophie*, vol. XV, no. 58 (1961), pp. 366–75.

Azariadis, Costas. 'Self-Fulfilling Prophecies,' *Journal of Economic Theory*, vol. 25, no. 3 (December 1981), pp. 380–96.

Backhouse, Roger. *A History of Modern Economic Analysis*. Oxford: Basil Blackwell, 1985.

Barro, Robert, and Herschel Grossman. 'A General Disequilibrium Model of Income and Employment,' *American Economic Review*, vol.61 (March 1971), pp. 82–93.

———. *Money, Employment, and Inflation*. Cambridge: Cambridge University Press, 1976.

Bateman, Bradley W. 'Keynes's Changing Conception of Probability,' *Economics and Philosophy*, vol. 3 (April 1987), pp. 97–119.

———. 'G. E. Moore and J. M. Keynes: A Missing Chapter in the History of the Expected Utility Model,' *American Economic Review*, vol. 78, no. 5 (December 1988), pp. 1098–106.

Begg, David K. H. *The Rational Expectations Revolution in Macroeconomics*. Baltimore: Johns Hopkins University Press, 1982.

Bernoulli, Daniel. 'Exposition of a New Theory of Risk Evaluation,' in William J. Baumol and Stephen M. Goldfeld, eds., *Precursors in Mathematical Economics*. London: London School of Economics and Political Science, 1968 [1738].

Blume, Lawrence E., Margaret M. Bray, and David Easley. 'Introduction to the Stability of Rational Expectations Equilibria,' *Journal of Economic Theory*, vol. 26, no. 2 (April 1982), pp. 313–17.

Blume, Lawrence E., and David Easley. 'Learning to Be Rational,' *Journal of Economic Theory*, vol. 26, no. 2 (April 1982), pp. 340–51.

Borel, Emile. 'Apropos of a Treatise on Probability,' in Henry E. Kyburg, Jr. and Howard E. Smokler, eds., *Studies in Subjective Probability*. New York: John Wiley and Sons, 1964 [1924].

Braithwaite, R. B. Editorial Foreward to J. M. Keynes, *Treatise on Probability*. *The Collected Writings of John Maynard Keynes*, vol. VIII. London: St. Martin's, 1973.

Bray, Margaret. 'Learning, Estimation, and the Stability of Rational Expectations,' *Journal of Economic Theory*, vol. 26, no. 2 (April 1982), pp. 318–39.

Burns, Arthur, and Wesley C. Mitchell. *Measuring Business Cycles*. New York: National Bureau of Economic Research, 1947.

Cantillon, Richard. *Essai sur la nature du commerce en general*. New York: Augustus M. Kelley, 1964 [1755].

Carabelli, Anna. *On Keynes's Method*. New York: St. Martin's Press, 1988.

Carnap, Rudolf. *Logical Foundations of Probability*. Chicago: University of Chicago Press, 1950.

Cass, David, and Karl Shell. 'Do Sunspots Matter?,' *Journal of Political Economy*, vol. 91, no. 2 (April 1983), pp. 193–227.

Champernowne, D. G. *Uncertainty and Estimation in Economics*. San Francisco: Holden Day, 1969.

Chipman John S. 'The Foundations of Utility,' *Econometrica*, vol. 28, no. 2 (April 1960), pp. 193–224.

Clark, John Bates. 'Insurance and Business Profit,' *Quarterly Journal of Economics*, vol. VII, (October 1892), pp. 40–54.

Clower, Robert. 'The Keynesian Counterrevolution: A Theoretical Appraisal,' in F. H. Hahn and F. P. R. Brechling, eds. *Theory of Interest Rates*. New York: St. Martin's Press, 1965.

Coddington, Alan. 'Deficient Foresight: A Troublesome Theme in Keynesian Economics,' *American Economic Review*, vol. 72, no. 3 (June 1982), pp. 480–7.

———. *Keynesian Economics: The Search for First Principles*. London: George Allen and Unwin, 1983.

Commons, John R. *Legal Foundations of Capitalism*. New York: Macmillan, 1924.

Cournot, Augustin. *Researches into the Mathematical Principles of the Theory of Wealth*. New York: Augustus M. Kelley, 1971 [1838].

Cyert, Richard M. and Morris H. DeGroot. 'Rational Expectations and Bayesian Analysis,' *Journal of Political Economy*, vol. 82, no. 3 (May/June 1974), pp. 521–36.

Davidson, Donald, and Patrick Suppes. 'A Finitistic Axiomatization of Subjective Probability and Utility,' *Econometrica*, vol. 24, no. 8 (July 1956), pp. 264–75.

Davidson, Paul. 'A technical definition of uncertainty and the long-run non-neutrality of money,' *Cambridge Journal of Economics*, vol. 12, no. 3 (September 1988), pp. 329–37.

——. 'Is Probability Theory Relevant for Uncertainty? A Post Keynesian Perspective,' *Journal of Economic Perspectives*, vol. 5, no. 1 (Winter 1991), pp. 129–43.

Debreu, Gerard. *Theory of Value*. New Haven: Yale University Press, 1959.

Dekel, Eddie. 'An Axiomatic Characterization of Preferences Under Uncertainty: Weakening the Independence Axiom,' *Journal of Economic Theory*, vol. 40, no. 2 (December 1986), pp. 304–18.

Dempsey, Bernard. *The Frontier Wage*. Chicago: Loyola University Press, 1960.

Dreze, Jacques, ed. *Allocation Under Uncertainty: Equilibrium and Optimality*. New York: John Wiley and Sons, 1974.

Edgeworth, Francis Y. 'The Philosophy of Chance,' *Mind*, vol. IX, (1884), pp. 223–35.

——. 'Miscellaneous applications of the Calculus of Probabilities,' *Journal of the Royal Statistical Society*, vol. LX, (Sept. 1897), pp. 681–98; vol. LXI (Sept. 1898), pp. 534–44.

——. 'Applications of Probabilities to Economics,' *Economic Journal*, vol. 20 (June 1910), pp. 284–305; 441–65.

——. 'The Philosophy of Chance,' *Mind*, vol. XXXI, no. 123 (July 1922), pp. 257–83.

Ellis, Arthur. 'Influence of Opinion on Markets,' *Economic Journal*, vol. II, no. 5 (March 1892), pp. 109–16.

Ellsberg, Daniel. 'Classic and Current Notions of "Measurable Utility",' *Economic Journal*, vol. LXIV, no. 255 (September 1954), pp. 528–56.

——. 'Risk, Ambiguity, and the Savage Axioms,' *Quarterly Journal of Economics*, vol. LXXV (November 1961), pp. 643–69.

——. 'Reply,' *Quarterly Journal of Economics*, vol. LXXVII (November 1963), pp. 336–42.

de Finetti, Bruno. 'Cambridge Probability Theorists,' *The Manchester School*, vol. 53, no. 4 (December 1985), pp. 348–63.

Fishburn, Peter C. 'Transitive Measurable Utility,' *Journal of Economic Theory*, vol. 31, no. 2 (December 1983), pp. 293–317.

——. 'Retrospective on the Utility Theory of von Neumann and Morgenstern,' *Journal of Risk and Uncertainty*, vol. 2, no. 2 (June 1989), pp. 127–56.

Fisher, Irving. *The Nature of Capital and Income*. New York: Augustus M. Kelley, 1965 [1906].

——. *Mathematical Investigations in the Theory of Value and Prices*. New Haven: Yale University Press, 1925.

——. *The Theory of Interest*. New York: Kelley and Millman Inc., 1954 [1930].

Friedman, Milton. 'The Methodology of Positive Economics,' in Milton Friedman, *Essays in Positive Economics*. Chicago: University of Chicago Press, 1953.

——. 'Leon Walras and His Economic System: A Review Article,' *American Economic Review*, vol. 45, no. 5 (December 1955), pp. 900–9.

Friedman, Milton, and Leonard J. Savage. 'The Utility Analysis of Choices Involving Risk,' *Journal of Political Economy*, vol. LVI, no. 4 (August 1948), pp. 279–304.

Gale, Douglas. *Money: In Equilibrium*. Cambridge: Nisbet/Cambridge, 1982.

——. *Money: In Disequilibrium*. Cambridge: Nisbet/Cambridge, 1983.

Garner, C. Alan. '"Uncertainty" in Keynes' *General Theory*: a Comment,' *History of Political Economy*, vol. 15, no. 1 (Spring 1983), pp. 83–6.

Good, I.J. 'Subjective Probability as the Measure of a Non-Measurable Set,' in Henry E. Kyburg, Jr. and Howard E. Smokler, eds., *Studies in Subjective Probability*. 2nd ed. Huntington, New York: Robert E. Krieger Publishing Co., 1980 [1962].

——. *The Estimation of Probability: An Essay in Modern Bayesian Methods*. Cambridge, Mass.: MIT Press, 1965.

Grossman, Sanford J. 'An Introduction to the Theory of Rational Expectations Under Asymmetric Information,' *Review of Economic Studies*, vol. XLVIII, no. 4 (1981), pp. 541–59.

Haavelmo, Trygve. 'The Probability Approach in Econometrics,' *Econometrica*, vol. 12 (supplement) (1944).

Hacking, Ian. *The Emergence of Probability*. Cambridge: Cambridge University Press, 1975.

——. *The Taming of Chance*. Cambridge: Cambridge University Press, 1990.

Halmos, Paul R. 'The Foundations of Probability,' *American Mathematical Monthly*, vol. 51 (November 1944), pp. 493–510.

Hardy, Charles O. *Risk and Risk-Bearing*. Chicago: University of Chicago Press, 1923.

Hart, Albert Gailord. 'Anticipations, Business Planning, and the Cycle,' *Quarterly Journal of Economics*, vol. 51, no. 2 (February 1937), pp. 273–97.

——. *Anticipations, Uncertainty, and Dynamic Planning*. New York: Augustus M. Kelley, 1965 [1951].

Hawley, Frederick B. 'The Risk Theory of Profit,' *Quarterly Journal of Economics*, vol. VII (July 1893), pp. 459–79.

Hayek, Friedrich A. The Trend of Economic Thinking,' *Economica*, vol. XIII, no. 40 (May 1933), pp. 121–37.

——. 'Economics and Knowledge,' *Economica* (NS), vol. IV, no. 13 (February 1937), pp. 33–54.

——. 'The Use of Knowledge in Society,' *American Economic Review*, vol. XXXV, no. 4 (September 1945), pp. 519–30. Reprinted in *Individualism and Economic Order*. London: Routledge and Kegan Paul, 1949.

——. 'The Meaning of Competition,' Stafford Little Lecture, Princeton University, May 20, 1946. Reprinted in *Individualism and Economic Order*. London: Routledge and Kegan Paul, 1949.

Haynes, John. 'Risk as an Economic Factor,' *Quarterly Journal of Economics*, vol. 9 (July 1895), pp. 409–49.

Herstein, I. N., and John Milnor, 'An Axiomatic Approach to Measurable Utility,' *Econometrica*, vol. 21, no. 2 (April 1953), pp. 291–7.

Hicks, J. R. 'The Theory of Uncertainty and Profit,' *Economica*, vol. 11, no. 32 (May 1931), pp. 170–89.

——. 'Mr. Keynes' Theory of Employment,' *Economic Journal*, vol. XLVI (June 1936), pp. 238–53.

——. 'Mr. Keynes and the "Classics": A Suggested Interpretation,' *Econometrica*, vol. 5, no. 1 (April 1937), pp. 147–59.

——. *Value and Capital*. 2nd. ed. London: Oxford University Press, 1946.

——. *Causality in Economics*. New York: Basic Books, 1979.

——. 'Rational Behavior – Observation or Assumption?' in Israel Kirzner, ed. *Subjectivism, Intelligibility and Economic Understanding*. New York: NYU Press, 1986.

Hollander, Samuel. *The Economics of Adam Smith*. Toronto: University of Toronto Press, 1973.

Hollis, Martin. *The Cunning of Reason*. Cambridge: Cambridge University Press, 1987.

Hollis, Martin, and Edward Nell. *Rational Economic Man*. Cambridge: Cambridge University Press, 1975.

Hume, David. *A Treatise of Human Nature*. London: Penguin Books, 1984 [1740].

Jevons, W. Stanley. *The Theory of Political Economy*. 4th ed. New York: Augustus M. Kelley, 1965 [1911].

Kauder, Emil. 'Intellectual and Political Roots of the Older Austrian School,' *Zeitschrift für Nationalokonomie*, vol. 17 (1957), pp. 411–25.

Keynes, John Maynard. Review of *A First Study of the Influence of Parental Alcoholism on the Physique and Ability of the Offspring*, *Journal of the Royal Statistical Society*, vol. LXXIII (July 1910), pp. 769–73.

——. 'Correspondence: Influence of Parental Alcoholism,' *Journal of the Royal Statistical Society*, vol. LXXIV (December 1910), pp. 114–21.

——. 'Correspondence: Influence of Parental Alcoholism,' *Journal of the Royal Statistical Society*, vol. LXXIV (February 1911), pp. 339–45.

——. *Treatise on Probability. The Collected Writings of John Maynard Keynes*, vol. VIII. Ed. by D. Moggridge. New York: St. Martin's Press for the Royal Economic Society, 1973 [1921].

——. *A Tract on Monetary Reform. The Collected Writings of John Maynard Keynes*, vol. IV. Ed. by D. Moggridge. London: Macmillan and St. Martin's Press for the Royal Economic Society, 1971 [1923].

——. *Treatise on Money. The Collected Writings of John Maynard Keynes*, vol. V. Ed. by D. Moggridge. London: Macmillan and St. Martin's Press for the Royal Economic Society, 1971 [1930].

——. Review of *The Foundations of Mathematics* by F. P. Ramsey, *The New Statesman and Nation*, N.S., vol 2, no. 32 (October 3, 1931), p. 407.

——. 'Two Memoirs: My Early Beliefs,' *Essays in Biography. The Collected Writings of John Maynard Keynes*, vol. X. Ed. by D. Moggridge. London: Macmillan and St. Martin's Press for the Royal Economic Society, 1972 [1938].

——. *The General Theory of Employment, Interest, and Money*. New York: Harcourt Brace Jovanovich, 1964 [1936].

——. 'The General Theory of Employment,' *Quarterly Journal of Economics*, vol. LI, no. 2 (February 1937), pp. 209–23.

——. 'Professor Tinbergen's Method,' *Economic Journal*, vol. XLIV, no. 195 (September 1939), pp. 558–68.

——. 'Comment' (on Tinbergen's reply), *Economic Journal*, vol. L, no. 197 (March 1940), pp. 154–6.

——. *The General Theory and After: A Supplement. The Collected Writings of John Maynard Keynes*, vol. XXIX. Ed. by D. Moggridge. London: Macmillan and Cambridge University Press for the Royal Economic Society, 1979.

Keynes, John Neville. *The Scope and Method of Political Economy*. 4th. ed. Clifton, N.J.: Augustus M. Kelley, 1973 [1917].

Kirzner, Israel M. *Perception, Opportunity, and Profit*. Chicago: University of Chicago Press, 1979.

Knight, Frank H. *Risk, Uncertainty, and Profit*. New York: Augustus M. Kelley, 1964 [1921].

——. *The Ethics of Competition*. New York: Harper and Brothers, 1935.

——. *On the History and Method of Economics*. Chicago: University of Chicago Press, 1956.

Kolmogorov, A. N. *Foundations of the Theory of Probability*. Trans. by Nathan Morrison. New York: Chelsea, 1950.

Kolmogorov, A. N., and S. V. Fomin. *Introductory Real Analysis*. New York: Dover, 1970.

Kondratieff, N. D. 'The Long Waves in Economic Life,' *The Review of Economic Statistics*, vol. XVII, no. 6 (November 1935), pp. 105–15.

Koopman, Bernard O. 'The Bases of Probability,' in Henry E. Kyburg, Jr. and Howard E. Smokler, eds. *Studies in Subjective Probability*. New York: John Wiley and Sons, 1964 [1940].

Kuenne, Robert E. *The Theory of General Economic Equilibrium*. Princeton: Princeton University Press, 1963.

Kyburg, Henry E., Jr. 'Getting Fancy with Probability,' *Synthese*, vol. 90, no. 2 (February 1992), pp. 189–203.

Lachmann, Ludwig. 'The Role of Expectations in Economics as a Social Science,' *Economica*, vol. X, no. 37 (February 1943), pp. 12–23.

———. 'From Mises to Shackle: An Essay on Austrian Economics and the Kaleidic Society,' *Journal of Economic Literature*, vol. XIV, no. 1 (March 1976), pp. 54–62.

Laplace, Pierre Simon. *Philosophical Essay on Probabilities*. Trans. by F. W. Truscott and F. L. Emory. New York: Dover, 1951 [1820].

Lawson, Tony. 'The Relative/Absolute Nature of Knowledge and Economic Analysis,' *Economic Journal*, vol. 97, no. 388 (December 1987), pp. 951–70.

———. 'Probability and Uncertainty in Economic Analysis,' *Journal of Post Keynesian Economics*, vol. XI, no. 1 (Fall 1988), pp. 38–65.

Leijonhufvud, Axel. *On Keynesian Economics and the Economics of Keynes*. Oxford: Oxford University Press, 1968.

LeRoy, Stephen F. and Larry D. Singell, Jr. 'Knight on Risk and Uncertainty,' *Journal of Political Economy*, vol. 95, no. 2 (April 1987), pp. 394–406.

Levi, Isaac. 'The Paradoxes of Allais and Ellsberg,' *Economics and Philosophy*, vol. 2, no. 1 (April 1986), pp. 23–53.

Lucas, Robert E., Jr. 'Econometric Policy Evaluation: A Critique,' in Karl Brunner and Allan H. Meltzer. *The Phillips Curve and Labor Markets*. Carnegie-Rochester Conference Series on Public Policy, vol. 1. Amsterdam: North-Holland, 1976.

———. 'Understanding Business Cycles,' in Robert E. Lucas, Jr. *Studies in Business-Cycle Theory*. Cambridge, Mass.: MIT Press, 1981.

———. *Models of Business Cycles*. New York: Basil Blackwell, 1987.

Lucas, Robert E., Jr. and Edward C. Prescott, 'Investment Under Uncertainty,' *Econometrica*, vol. 39, no. 5 (September 1971), pp. 659–81. Also included in Robert E. Lucas, Jr. and Thomas J. Sargent, eds. *Rational Expectations and Econometric Practice*. Minneapolis: University of Minnesota Press, 1981.

Lucas, Robert E., Jr. and Thomas J. Sargent. 'After Keynesian Macroeconomics,' in Robert E. Lucas, Jr. and Thomas J. Sargent, eds. *Rational Expectations and Econometric Practice*. Minneapolis: University of Minnesota Press, 1981.

Luce, R. Duncan. 'A Probabilistic Theory of Utility,' *Econometrica*, vol. 26, no. 2 (April 1958), pp. 193–224.

Luce, R. Duncan, and Howard Raiffa. *Games and Decisions: Introduction and Critical Survey*. New York: Dover, 1985 [1957].

MacCrimmon, Kenneth R., and Stig Larsson. 'Utility Theory: Axioms versus "Paradoxes",' in Maurice Allais and Ole Hagen, eds. *Expected Utility Hypotheses and the Allais Paradox*. Boston: D. Reidel, 1979.

Machina, Mark. '"Expected Utility" Analysis Without the Independence Axiom,' *Econometrica*, vol. 50, no. 2 (March 1982), pp. 277–323.

———. 'Choice Under Uncertainty: Problems Solved and Unsolved,' *Journal of Economic Perspectives*, vol. 1, no. 1, (Summer 1987), pp. 121–54.

Machlup, Fritz. *Knowledge: Its Creation, Distribution, and Economic Significance*. Vol. III: *The Economics of Information and Human Capital*. Princeton: Princeton University Press, 1984.

Maki, Uskali. 'Scientific realism and Austrian explanation,' *Review of Political Economy*, vol. 2, no. 3 (November 1990), pp. 310–44.

Malinvaud, Edmond. 'Note on von Neumann-Morgenstern's Strong Independence Axiom,' *Econometrica*, vol. 20, no. 4 (October 1952), p. 679.

Marschak, Jacob. 'Money and the Theory of Assets,' *Econometrica*, vol. 6, no. 4 (October 1938), pp. 311–25.

——. 'Rational Behavior, Uncertain Prospects, and Measurable Utility,' *Econometrica*, vol. 18, no. 1 (January 1950), pp. 111–41.

Marshall, Alfred. 'On the Graphic Method of Statistics,' *Journal of the Royal Statistical Society*, (Jubilee edition) (June 22–24, 1885).

——. *Economics of Industry*. 3rd ed. London: Macmillan, 1958 [1899].

——. *Principles of Economics*. 9th (Variorum) ed. New York: Macmillan, 1961 [1920].

——. *Money, Credit and Commerce*. London: Macmillan, 1929.

McCann, C. R., Jr. *Uncertainty, Expectations, and Rationality in Economic Models: An Analysis of the Foundations of Keynesian, Austrian, and Rational Expectations Models*. Ph.D. dissertation, University of Pittsburgh, 1991.

Meltzer, Allan. *Keynes's Monetary Theory: A Different Interpretation*. Cambridge: Cambridge University Press, 1988.

Menger, Carl. *Principles of Economics*. Trans. by James Dingwall and Bert F. Hotelitz. Glencoe, Ill.: The Free Press, 1950 [1871].

——. *Problems of Economics and Sociology*. Trans. by Francis J. Nock. Urbana, Ill.: University of Illinois Press, 1963 [1883].

Mill, John Stuart. *Principles of Political Economy*. 7th ed. New York: Augustus M. Kelley, 1961 [1871].

——. *The Logic of the Moral Sciences*. 8th. ed. LaSalle, Ill.: Open Court, 1988 [1872].

von Mises, Ludwig. *The Theory of Money and Credit*. New Haven: Yale University Press, 1953.

——. *Theory and History*. New Haven: Yale University Press, 1957.

——. *Epistemological Problems of Economics*. Trans. by George Reisman. Princeton, N.J.: D. Van Nostrand Co., Inc., 1960.

——. *Human Action*. 3rd. ed. Chicago: Henry Regnery Co., 1966.

von Mises, Richard. 'On the Foundations of Probability and Statistics,' *Annals of Mathematical Statistics*, vol. 12 (1941), pp. 191–205.

——. *Probability, Statistics and Truth*. 3rd. ed. Trans. by Hilda Geiringer. New York: Dover, 1957.

Mitchell, Wesley C. 'Quantitative Analysis in Economic Theory,' *American Economic Review*, vol. XV, no. 1 (March 1925), pp. 1–12.

Moore, G. E. *Principia Ethica*. Cambridge: Cambridge University Press, 1962 [1903].

Muth, John F. 'Rational Expectations and the Theory of Price Movements,' in Robert E. Lucas, Jr. and Thomas J. Sargent, eds. *Rational Expectations and Econometric Practice*. Minneapolis: University of Minnesota Press, 1981 [1961].

Nagel, Ernest. 'Assumptions in Economic Theory,' *American Economic Review*, vol. LIII, no. 2 (May 1963), pp. 211–19.

von Neumann, John, and Oskar Morgenstern. *Theory of Games and Economic Behavior*. 3rd. ed. New York: John Wiley and Sons, 1953.

O'Donnell, R. M. *Keynes: Philosophy, Economics, and Politics*. London: Macmillan, 1989.

O'Driscoll, Gerald P., Jr. and Mario J. Rizzo. *The Economics of Time and Ignorance*. New York: Basil Blackwell, 1985.

Patinkin, Don. *Money, Interest, and Prices*. 2nd. ed. New York: Harper and Row, 1965.

Perlman, Mark. 'Subjectivism and American Institutionalism,' in Israel Kirzner, ed. *Subjectivism, Intelligibility and Economic Understanding*. New York: NYU Press, 1986.

——. Review of *The Economics of Time and Ignorance* by O'Driscoll and Rizzo. *Business Economics*, vol. XXIII, no. 1 (January 1988), pp. 61-2.

Pigou, A. C. *The Economics of Welfare*. London: Macmillan, 1920.

——. 'Review of "A Treatise on Probability" by J. M. Keynes,' *Economic Journal*, vol. XXXI, no. 124 (December 1921), pp. 507-12.

——. 'Some Aspects of Welfare Economics,' *American Economic Review*, vol. XLI, no. 3 (June 1951), pp. 287-302.

Prescott, Edward C., and Robert E. Lucas, Jr. 'A Note on Price Systems in Infinite Dimensional Space,' *International Economic Review*, vol. 13, no. 2 (June 1972), pp. 416-22.

Radner, Roy. 'Competitive Equilibrium Under Uncertainty,' *Econometrica*, vol. 36, no. 1 (January 1968), pp. 31-58.

Raiffa, Howard. 'Risk, Ambiguity, and the Savage Axioms: Comment,' *Quarterly Journal of Economics*, vol. LXXV (November 1961), pp. 690-4.

Ramsey, Frank P. 'Truth and Probability,' in F. P. Ramsey, *Philosophical Papers*. Ed. by D. H. Mellor. Cambridge: Cambridge University Press, 1990 [1926].

——. 'Probability and Partial Belief,' in F. P. Ramsey, *Philosophical Papers*. Ed. by D. H. Mellor. Cambridge: Cambridge University Press, 1990 [1929a].

——. 'Knowledge,' in F. P. Ramsey, *Philosophical Papers*. Ed. by D. H. Mellor. Cambridge: Cambridge University Press, 1990 [1929b].

Roberts, Harry V. 'Risk, Ambiguity, and the Savage Axioms: Comment,' *Quarterly Journal of Economics*, vol. LXXVII (November 1963), pp. 327-36.

Rosenberg, Alexander. *Microeconomic Laws: A Philosophical Analysis*. Pittsburgh: University of Pittsburgh Press, 1976.

Roth, Alvin E. *Axiomatic Models of Bargaining*. Berlin: Springer-Verlag, 1979.

Rothbard, Murray N. 'In Defense of "Extreme Apriorism",' *Southern Economic Journal*, vol. XXIII, no. 3 (January 1957), pp. 314-20.

——. 'Praxeology: the Methodology of Austrian Economics,' in E. G. Dolan, ed. *The Foundations of Modern Austrian Economics*. Kansas City: Sheed and Ward, 1976.

Runde, Jochen. 'Keynesian Uncertainty and the Weight of Arguments,' *Economics and Philosophy*, vol. 6, no. 2 (October 1990), pp. 275-92.

——. 'Keynesian uncertainty and the instability of beliefs,' *Review of Political Economy*, vol. 3, no. 2 (April 1991), pp. 125-45.

——. 'Paul Davidson and the Austrians.' Paper presented at the History of Economics Society annual meeting, George Mason University, Fairfax, VA., May 31-June 2, 1992. Forthcoming in *Critical Review*.

Russell, Bertrand. *The Problems of Philosophy*. Oxford: Oxford University Press, 1912.

——. *Human Knowledge: Its Scope and Limits*. New York: Simon and Schuster, 1948.

Salmon, Wesley C. *The Foundations of Scientific Inference*. Pittsburgh: University of Pittsburgh Press, 1967.

——. 'Empiricism: The Key Question,' in Nicholas Rescher, ed. *The Heritage of Logical Positivism*. Lanham, MD: University Press of America, 1985.

Samuelson, Paul A. *Foundations of Economic Analysis*. Cambridge, MA: Harvard University Press, 1947.

——. 'Probability, Utility, and the Independence Axiom,' *Econometrica*, vol. 20, no. 4 (October 1952), pp. 670-8.

——. 'What Classical and Neoclassical Monetary Theory Really Was,' *Canadian Journal of Economics*, vol. I, no. 1 (February 1968), pp. 1-15.

Sargent, Thomas J. *Macroeconomic Theory*. New York: Academic Press, 1979.

Savage, Leonard J. *The Foundations of Statistics*. New York: Dover, 1972.

——. 'The Shifting Foundations of Statistics,' in Robert G. Colodny, ed. *Logic, Laws, and Life*. Pittsburgh: University of Pittsburgh Press, 1977.

Schumpeter, Joseph A. *History of Economic Analysis*. New York: Oxford University Press, 1954.

Shackle, G. L. S. 'Expectations and Employment,' *Economic Journal*, vol. LXIX (September 1939), pp. 442–52.

——. 'A Non-Additive Measure of Uncertainty,' *Review of Economic Studies*, vol. XVII (1949–50), pp. 70–4.

——. 'The Logic of Surprise,' *Economica*, vol. XX (May 1953), pp. 112–17.

——. 'Expectation and Cardinality,' *Economic Journal*, vol. LXVI, no. 262 (June 1956), pp. 211–19.

——. *A Scheme of Economic Theory*. Cambridge: Cambridge University Press, 1965.

——. *Decision, Order, and Time in Human Affairs*. 2nd. ed. Cambridge: Cambridge University Press, 1969.

——. *Expectation, Enterprise, and Profit*. London: George Allen and Unwin, Ltd., 1970.

——. *Epistemics and Economics*. Cambridge: Cambridge University Press, 1972.

——. 'Keynes and Today's Establishment in Economic Theory: A View,' *Journal of Economic Literature*, vol. XI, no. 2 (June 1973), pp. 516–19.

——. *Keynesian Kaleidics*. Chicago: Aldine, 1974.

——. *Imagination and the Nature of Choice*. Edinburgh: Edinburgh University Press, 1979.

Simon, Herbert A. 'Discussion,' *American Economic Review*, vol. 53, no. 1 (May 1963), pp. 229–31.

——. *Models of Bounded Rationality*. Vol. II. Cambridge, MA: MIT Press, 1982.

——. 'Rationality in Psychology and Economics,' in Robin M. Hogarth and Melvin W. Reder, eds. *Rational Choice: The Contrast Between Economics and Psychology*. Chicago: University of Chicago Press, 1987.

Skidelsky, Robert. *John Maynard Keynes: Hopes Betrayed, 1883–1920*. London: Macmillan, 1983.

——. *John Maynard Keynes: The Economist as Saviour, 1920–1937*. London: Macmillan, 1992.

Slutsky, Eugen. 'The Summation of Random Causes as the Source of Cyclic Processes,' *Econometrica*, vol. 5 (1937), pp. 105–46.

Smith, Adam. *The Wealth of Nations*. 5th ed. London: Penguin Books, 1986 [1789].

——. *The Theory of Moral Sentiments*. 6th. ed. Ed. by D. D. Raphael and A. L. Macfie. Indianapolis, IN: Liberty Press, 1982 [1790].

Smith, Barry. 'Austrian Economics and Austrian Philosophy,' in Wolfgang Grassl and Barry Smith, eds. *Austrian Economics: Historical and Philosophical Background*. New York: NYU Press, 1986.

Sowell, Thomas. *Classical Economics Reconsidered*. Princeton: Princeton University Press, 1974.

Stigler, George J. 'The Development of Utility Theory,' *Journal of Political Economy*, Part I: vol. LVIII, no. 3 (June 1950), pp. 307–27; Part II: vol. LVIII, no. 5 (October 1950), pp. 373–96.

Stigler, Stephen M. 'Jevons as Statistician,' *The Manchester School*, vol. 50, no. 4 (December 1982), pp. 354–65.

Stohs, Mark. '"Uncertainty" in Keynes' *General Theory*,' *History of Political Economy*, vol. 12, no. 3 (Fall 1980), pp. 372–82.

——. '"Uncertainty" in Keynes' *General Theory*: a rejoinder,' *History of Political Economy*, vol. 15, no. 1 (Spring 1983), pp. 87–91.

Streissler, Erich. 'Shackle and the Theory of Risk,' *Zeitschrift für Nationalokonomie*, vol. XVIII (1959), pp. 208–22.

Sweezy, Paul. 'Expectations and the Scope of Economics,' *Review of Economic Studies*, vol. V (1937–8), pp. 234–7.

Thornton, Henry. *The Nature and Effects of the Paper Credit of Great Britain*. New York: Farrar and Rinehart, Inc., 1939 [1802].

Tinbergen, Jan. 'On a Method of Statistical Business-Cycle Research: A Reply,' *Economic Journal*, vol. L, no. 197 (March 1940), pp. 141–54.

Todhunter, Isaac. *A History of the Mathematical Theory of Probability*. New York: Chelsea, 1949 [1865].

Townsend, Robert M. 'Market Anticipations, Rational Expectations, and Bayesian Analysis,' *International Economic Review*, vol. 19, no. 2 (June 1978), pp. 481–94.

Townshend, Hugh. Review of G. L. S. Shackle's *Expectations, Investment and Income*, *Economic Journal*, vol. XLVIII, no. 191 (September 1938), pp. 520–3.

Venn, John. *The Logic of Chance*. 4th ed. New York: Chelsea Publishing Co., 1962 [1888].

Walters, A. A. 'Consistent Expectations, Distributed Lags, and the Quantity Theory,' *Economic Journal*, vol. 81, no. 322 (June 1971), pp. 273–81.

Weatherford, Roy. *Philosophical Foundations of Probability Theory*. London: Routledge and Kegan Paul, 1982.

Weintraub, E. Roy. *General Equilibrium Analysis: Studies in Appraisal*. Cambridge: Cambridge University Press, 1985.

Whitehead, Alfred North, and Bertrand Russell. *Principia Mathematica*. 2nd. ed. Cambridge: Cambridge University Press, 1925.

Wieser, Friedrich. 'The Austrian School and the Theory of Value,' *Economic Journal*, vol. 1, no. 1 (March 1891), pp. 108–21.

Wittgenstein, Ludwig. *Tractatus Logico-Philosophicus*. Trans. by D. F. Pears and B. F. McGuinness. London: Routledge and Kegan Paul, 1963 [1921].

INDEX

Carnap, Rudolf 25–7, 38, 44, 78,
133, 135
Cass, David 120
catallactics 80–1
cause 54–5
certainty 5–6, 10, 23–4, 25, 28, 31,
37–8, 40–2, 54–6, 57, 60, 62, 64,
66, 72, 80, 90–1, 95, 96, 100, 104,
105–7, 109–10, 113–14, 129, 132,
136, 137;
apodictic 80, 146; equivalence
72, 105, 113; relation 38
Champernowne D. G. 137
chance 52–3, 54–6, 63, 66, 124
Chapman, Janet xii
Chipman, John 133, 144
Clark, John Bates 60
classical economics 4–5, 8, 10, 11,
15–16, 58–60, 63, 66, 73, 84, 89,
90, 92, 105–6, 107, 113, 114, 120,
124, 128, 130, 132
classical probability interpretation 30–2,
36, 41, 43, 61, 63, 65, 134, 135,
152
'closed' versus 'open' systems 2, 6, 9,
10–11, 12, 16, 31, 73, 86, 88–9, 91,
94, 106, 107, 110, 111, 114, 126
Clower, Robert 17
Cobweb models 131
Coddington, Alan 136
collective see reference class
Commons, John R. 132, 148
competitive equilibrium 66, 83–4
connectedness 50, 67, 71, 133
consequence 49, 50, 51, 73, 78, 80,
84, 91, 98, 141
'constant conjunction' 6, 35, 54–5
'contingent truth' 80
conventions 100–3
Cournot, Augustin Antoine 12, 16,
131, 132, 134
Cyert, Richard 21, 118–20, 153

Davidson, Donald 144
Davidson, Paul 133, 145, 152
Debreu, Gerard 16, 19, 109–10, 133,
150, 151
'deductive theory' 10, 31, 109, 111,
128
DeGroot, Morris 21, 118–20, 153
Dekel, Eddie 144

Dempsey, Bernard 61
determinism 2, 9, 10–11, 16, 17, 19,
31–2, 64, 73, 81, 88, 94, 106, 111,
124, 127–8, 132, 145
discovery 45, 90, 91
'Dutch Book' 79, 139
dynamics 7–9, 11–12, 15, 18–19,
115, 131, 132

Easley, David 154
econometric models 108, 113, 114
economic theories classification of 7–9
Edgeworth, Francis Ysidro 135, 137,
139–40
Elderton, Ethel 138
Ellis, Arthur 149
Ellsberg, Daniel 21, 68–70, 71, 73,
140, 144
'Ellsberg paradox' 69–70, 144
'emotions' 13, 33, 35–6
entrepreneurs 10, 13, 60–1, 65–6, 81,
95, 96, 97–8, 100, 103, 104
epistemic risk see risk, epistemic
epistemic uncertainty see uncertainty,
epistemic
ergodic processes 18, 72, 111–13, 116,
126, 151–2
error 13, 24, 27, 58–60, 64, 72, 78–9,
98, 100, 106–7, 111, 114, 118, 120,
132
'ethically-neutral propositions' 48
'evenly-rotating economy' 116
evidential propositions 37, 38, 39,
133, 137
'expected hypothesis' 87
'expectational vista' 91

fallacy of composition 99
de Finetti, Bruno 27, 137, 139
Fishburn, Peter 144
Fisher, Irving 61–2, 63, 132, 146, 153
Fomin, S. V. 133
frequentistic probability interpretation
20, 27, 30, 32–6, 40, 41, 43, 45, 49,
50, 51, 52, 53, 63, 65, 79, 81, 86,
87, 88, 102, 115, 135, 137, 139, 141,
152, 154
Friedman, Milton 114, 121–2, 132

Gale, Douglas 21, 117, 151
games of chance 27, 30, 31, 32, 34–5,
70, 138

Laplace, Pierre Simon 20, 28, 31, 134, 135, 137, 139, 144
Larsson, Stig 143, 144
law of large numbers 31, 134
'laws of economics' 4–6, 12–14
Lawson, Tony 27, 52–3, 131, 133, 141, 154
Leibniz, Gottfried 40
Leijonhufvud, Axel 150
LeRoy, Stephen 143
Levi, Isaac 143, 144, 154
logical interpretation of probability *see* necessarian probability interpretation
Logical Positivism 25, 57, 76, 141
'Look Before You Leap' principle 151
Lucas, Robert E., Jr. 21, 108, 113–16, 118, 119, 121–2, 133, 150, 151, 152–3
Luce, R. Duncan 141, 143

MacCrimmon, Kenneth 143, 144
Machina, Mark 140, 144
Machlup, Fritz 53–4
Malinvaud, Edmond 144
Markov process 112–13
Marschak, Jacob 142, 143, 150
Marshall, Alfred 12–15, 58, 62, 63, 98, 114, 116, 132, 140, 142, 153
Marshallian equilibrium 14–15
mathematical expectation 35, 53, 88, 95, 96, 98, 102–3, 113, 149
measurement problem 1–4, 33, 41, 47, 48, 58–60, 97, 106, 123–4, 135, 138, 139, 148
Meltzer, Allan 154
Menger, Carl xi, 4, 21, 76–9, 81, 83, 85, 93, 130, 145, 146, 148
Mengerian rationality *see* rationality, Mengerian
Mill, John Stuart 5–6, 11, 16, 58–9, 130, 149, 153
Milnor, John 143
von Mises, Ludwig xi, 21, 76, 79–83, 86, 87, 92–3, 145, 146, 148
von Mises, Richard 27, 35, 134, 135, 137, 138, 139
Mitchell, Wesley Clair 15–16, 132
modus ponens 24
money and monetary economics 2, 3, 7, 8, 10, 14, 48, 59, 82–3, 89–90, 97–9, 103, 104, 106, 110
Moore, G. E. 57, 107, 150

Morgenstern, Oskar 21, 49–50, 67–9, 71, 101, 109, 112, 140, 143, 144
Muth, John 18, 19, 21, 108, 111, 113–16, 117, 118, 119, 121–2, 152

Nagel, Ernest 121
Nash solution 119
necessarian probability interpretation 20, 30, 27, 28, 36–45, 51, 52, 65, 68, 71, 74, 115, 134, 135, 137–8
necessary connection 55
Nell, Edward J. x
von Neumann, John 21, 49–50, 67–9, 71, 101, 109, 112, 140, 143, 144
Newtonian system 89, 106
Neyman, Jerzy 147
Neyman-Pearson statistics 91
non-ampliative inferences 24–5
non-determinism 3, 11, 15, 17, 32, 55, 58, 73, 81, 90–1, 94, 98, 121, 124–5, 126, 128, 138, 154
'non-programmed' decision-making 74, 126

objective probability distribution 18, 45, 111, 114, 116, 117, 119, 120, 121, 122
Occam's Razor 122
O'Donnell, R. M. x, xii, 56, 133, 137, 138, 148, 149, 150, 154
O'Driscoll, Gerald P. xi, 145
'open' systems *see* 'closed' versus 'open' systems
order 41–3, 51–2, 68, 75, 87, 107, 110, 137;
    partial 28–9, 42, 50, 67, 71, 133, 144; proper 133; simple 133; total 28–9, 43, 49, 50, 51, 67, 69, 71, 133, 134, 144
overlapping-generations model 120–1

Patinkin, Don 17
Pareto, Vilfredo 131
partial equilibrium 7–9, 11–12, 131
Pearson, Egon 147
Pearson, Karl 138
perfect foresight 10, 66, 83–4, 89, 90, 104, 117
'perfectly possible' hypothesis 87
Perlman, Mark xii, 132, 147

Printed in the United States
by Baker & Taylor Publisher Services